SNAPSHOT PAGAN, BURMA

A Photographic Exploration

SCOTT SHAW

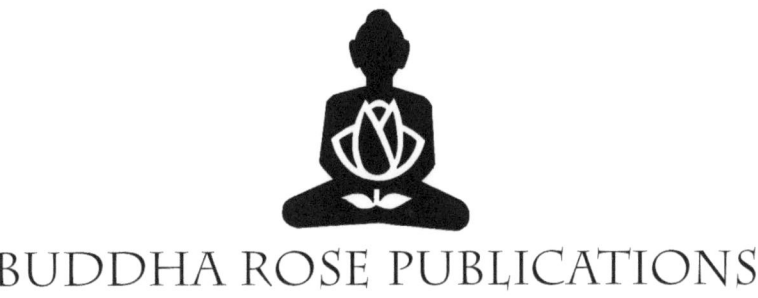

BUDDHA ROSE PUBLICATIONS

Snapshot Pagan, Burma
A Photographic Exploration
Copyright © 1984 By Scott Shaw
www.scottshaw.com
All Rights Reserved

No part of this book may be reproduced in any manner without the expressed permission of the author or the publishing company.

ISBN 10: 1-949251-33-0
ISBN 13: 978-1-949251-33-3

Photographed with a vintage Leica camera.

Printed in the United States of America
10 9 8 7 6 5 4 3 2 1

SNAPSHOT PAGAN, BURMA

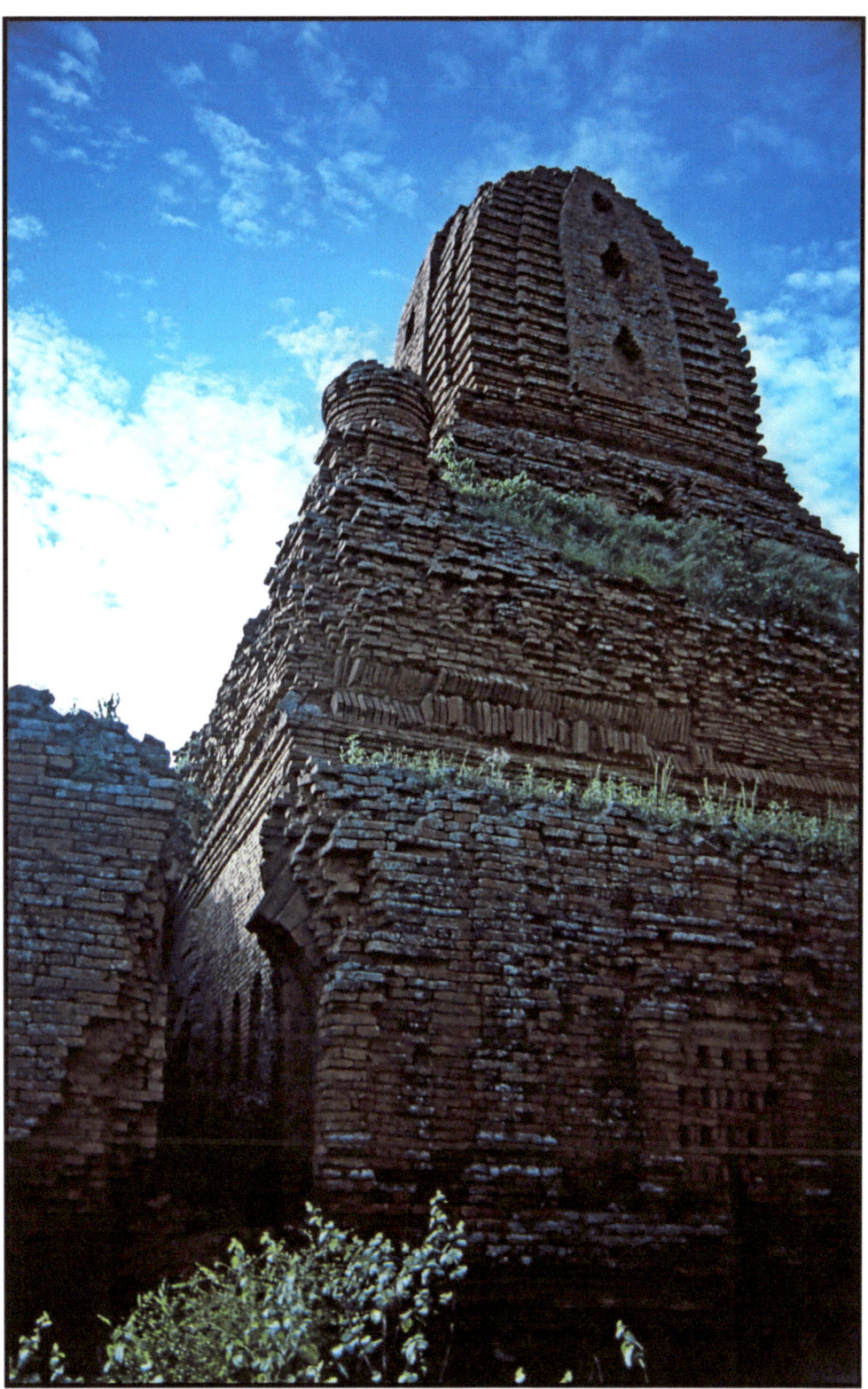

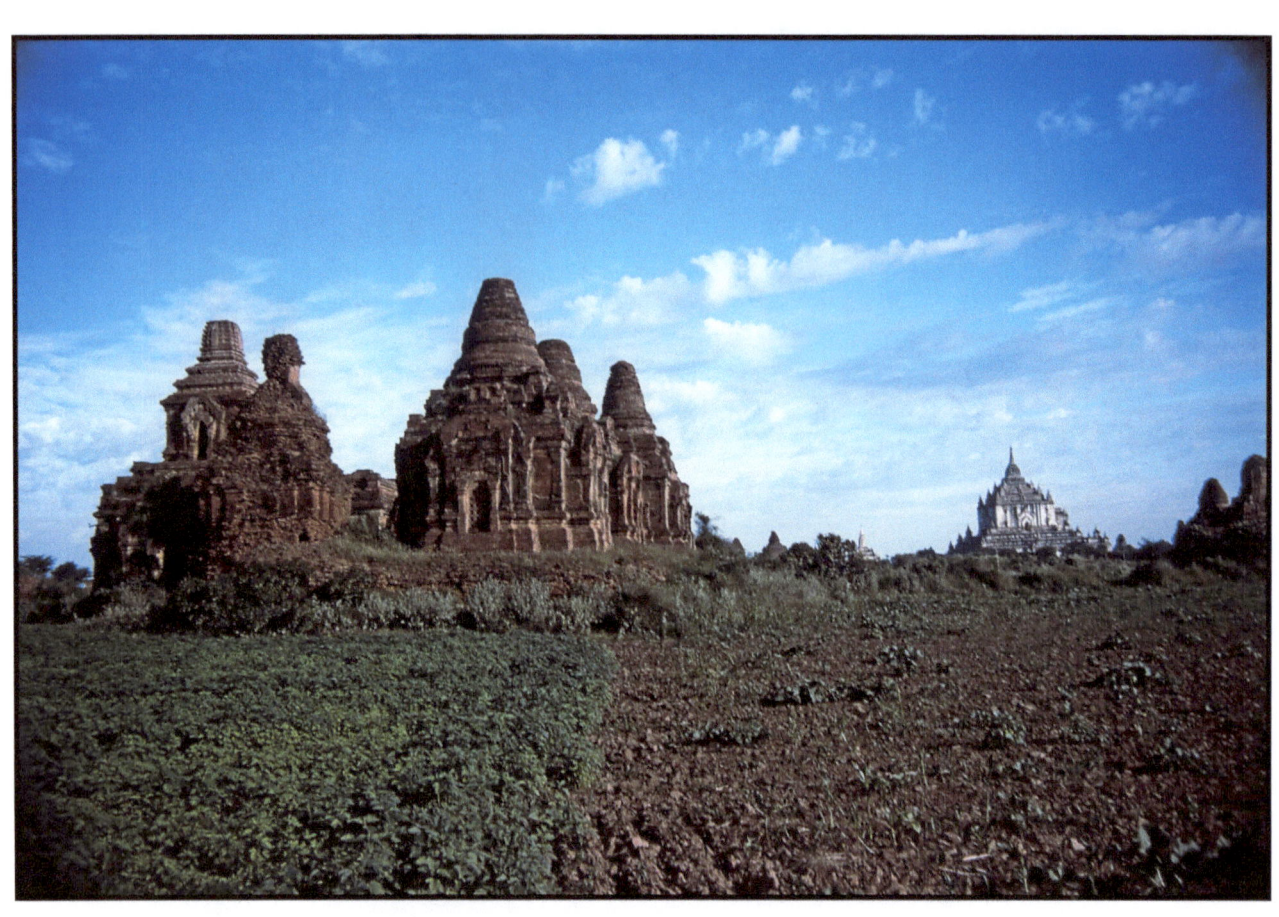

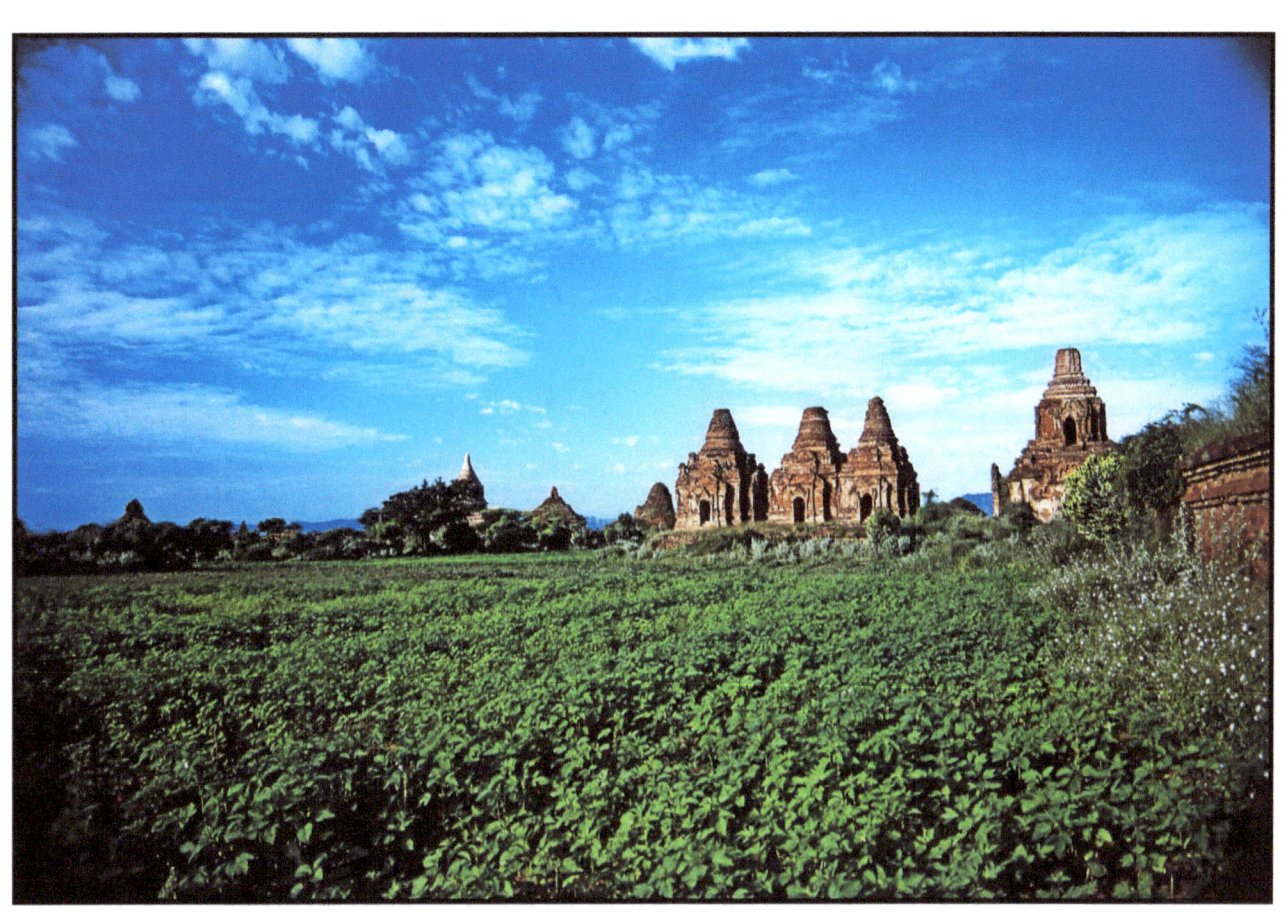

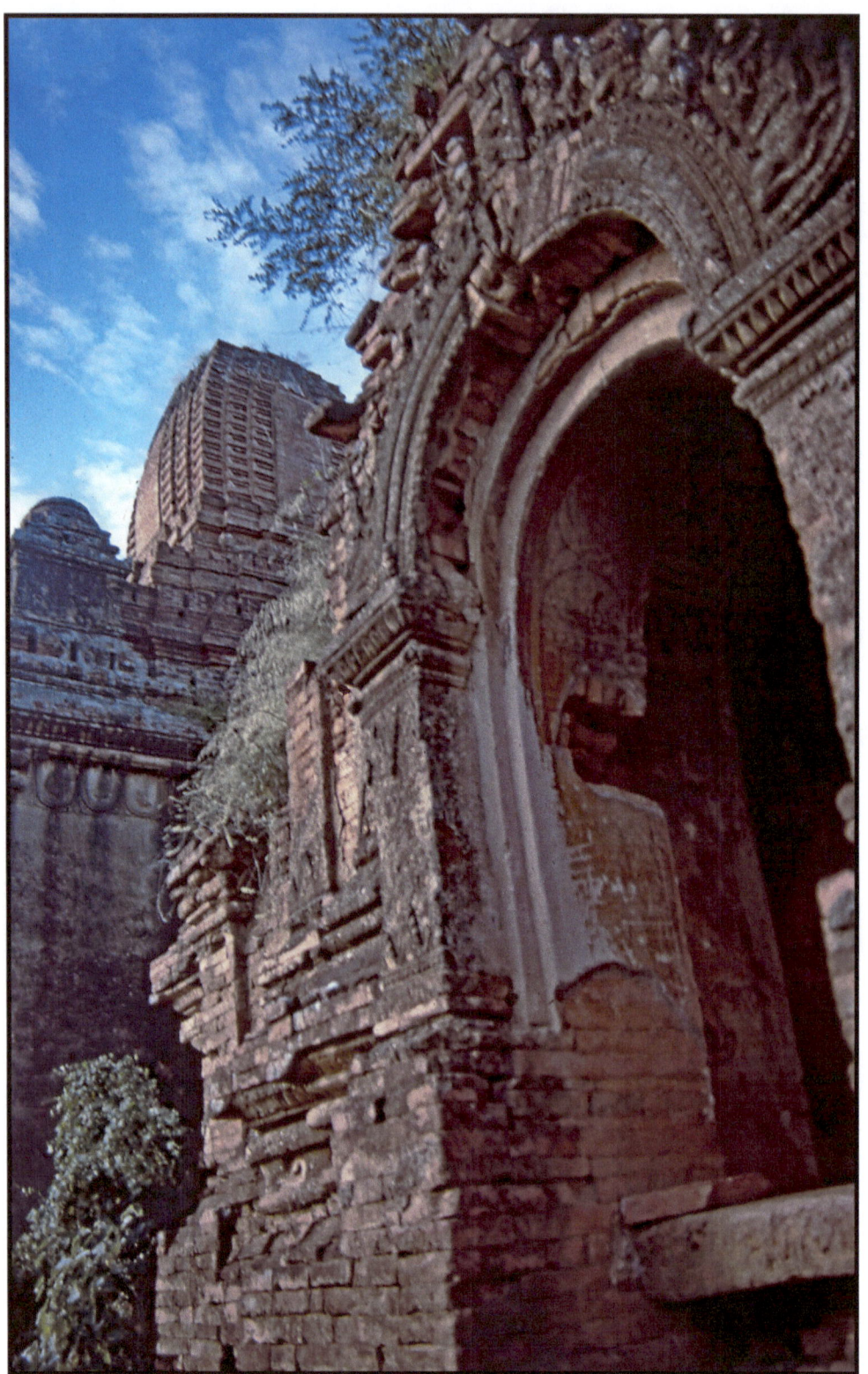

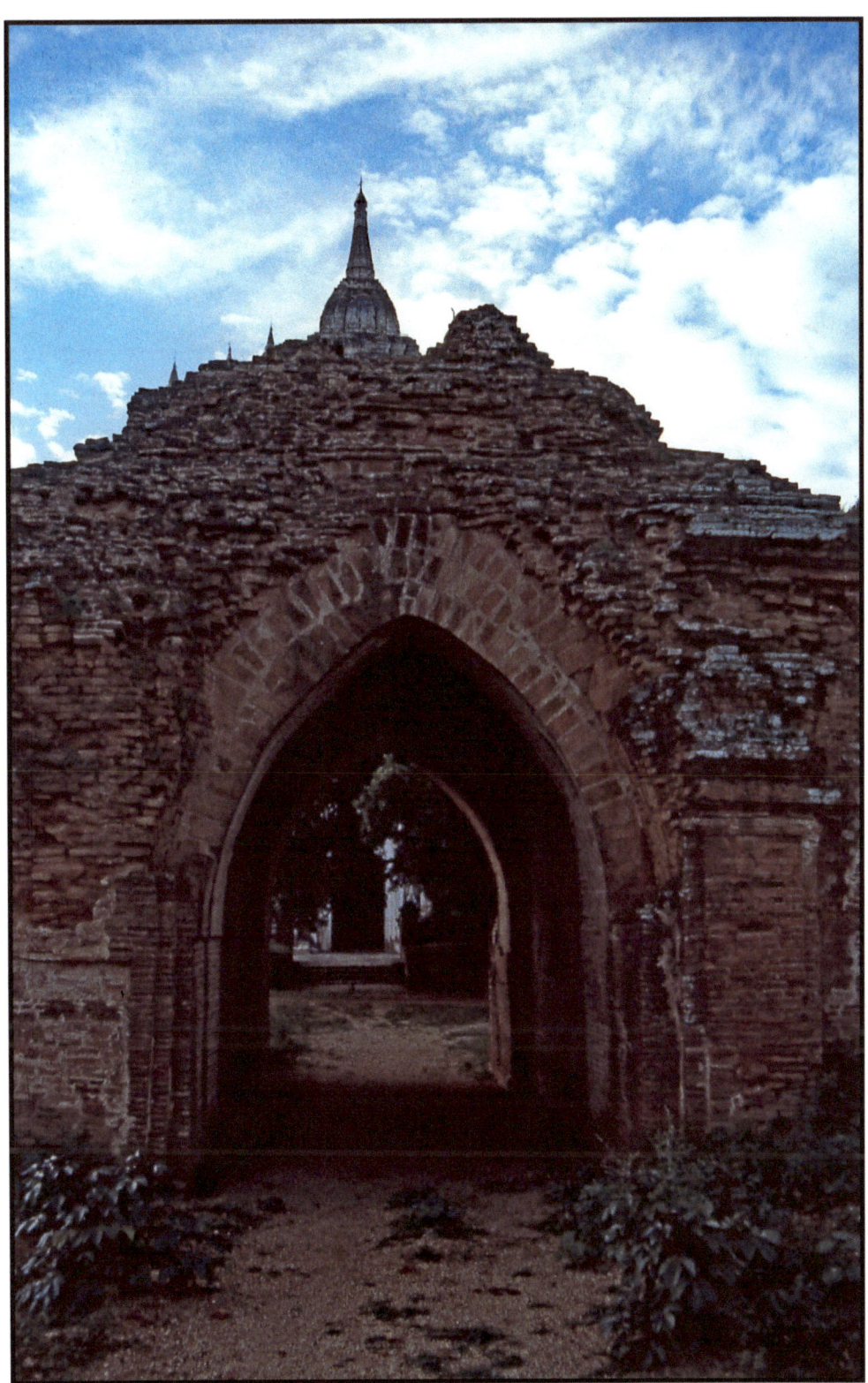

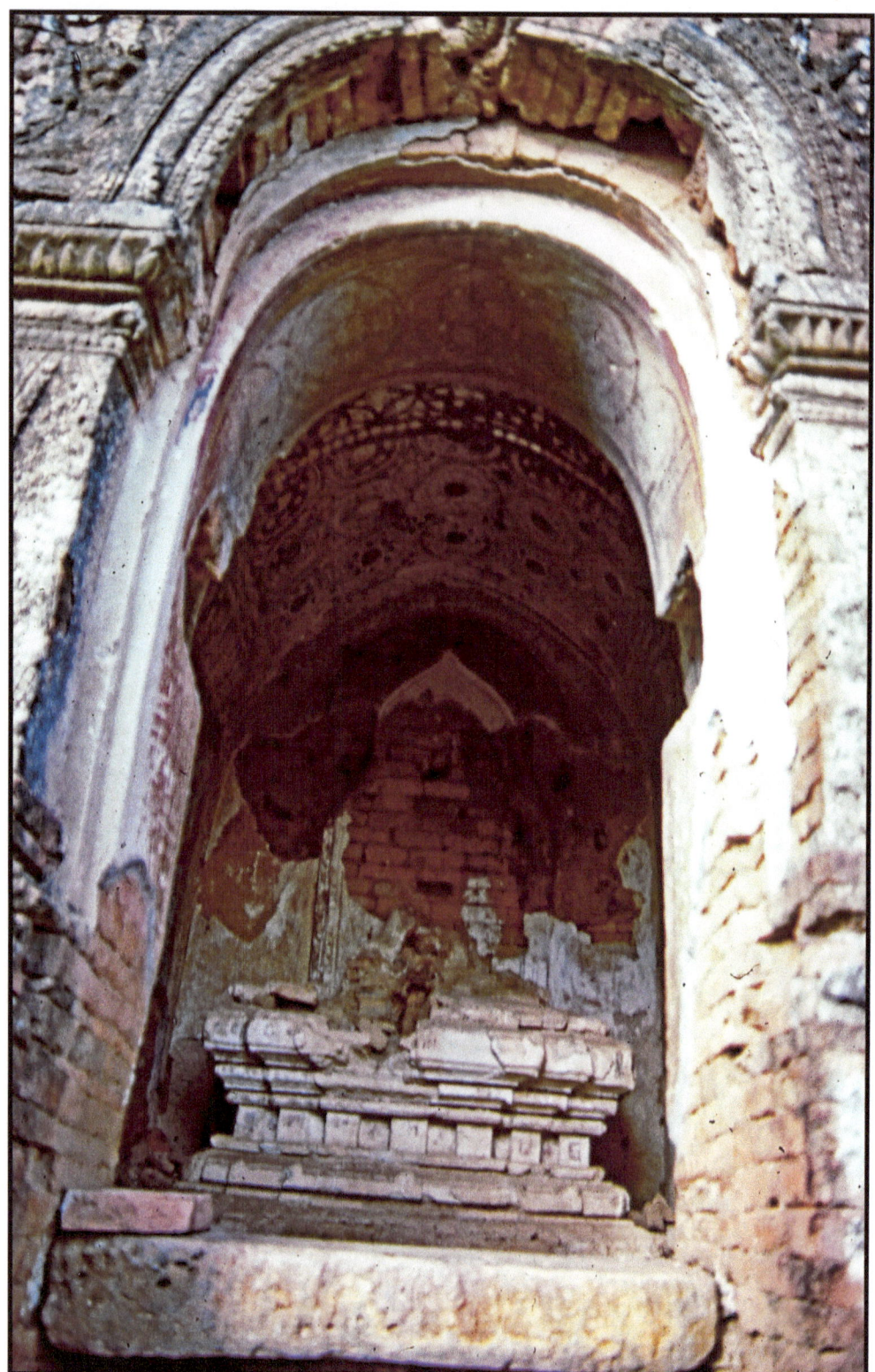

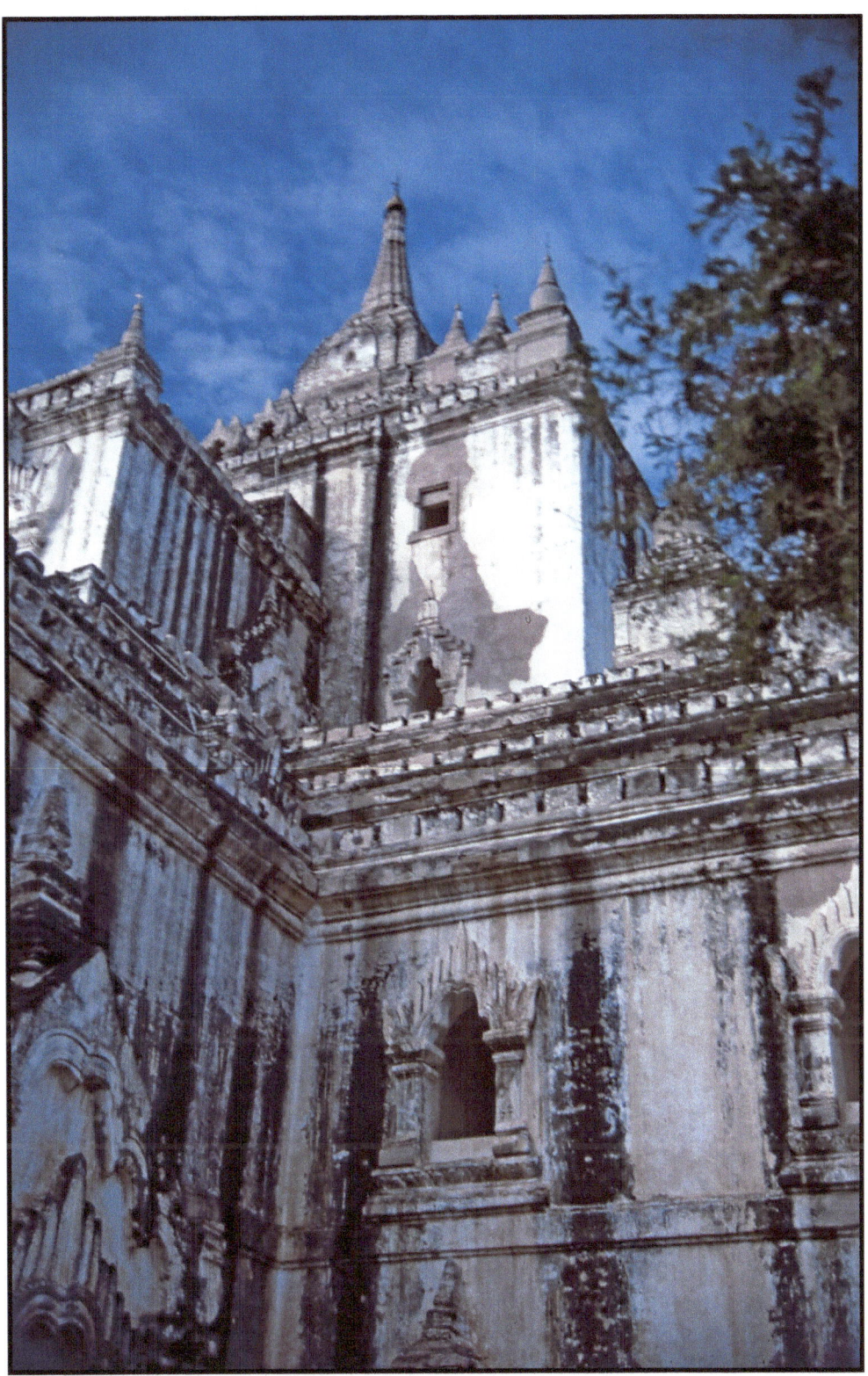

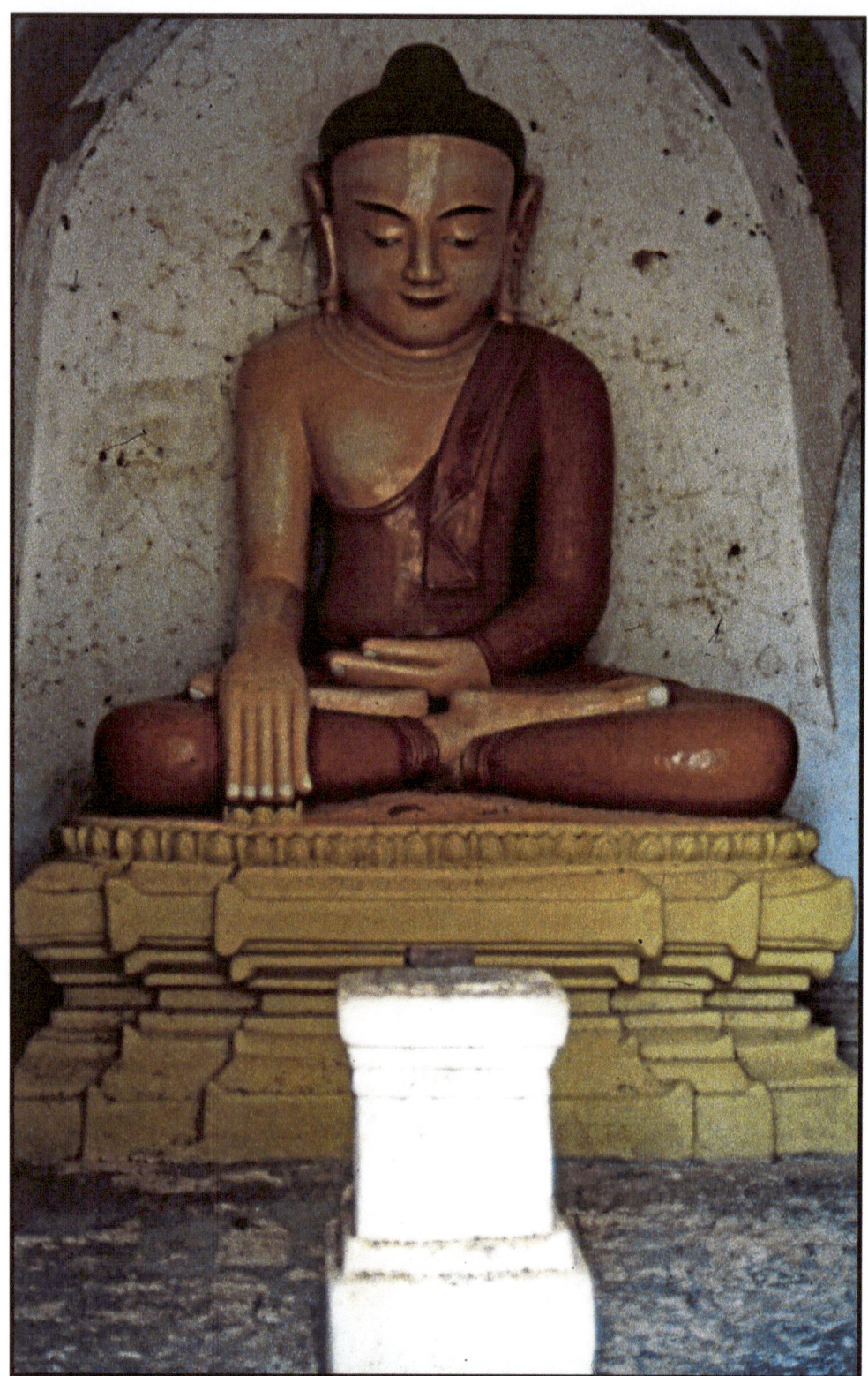

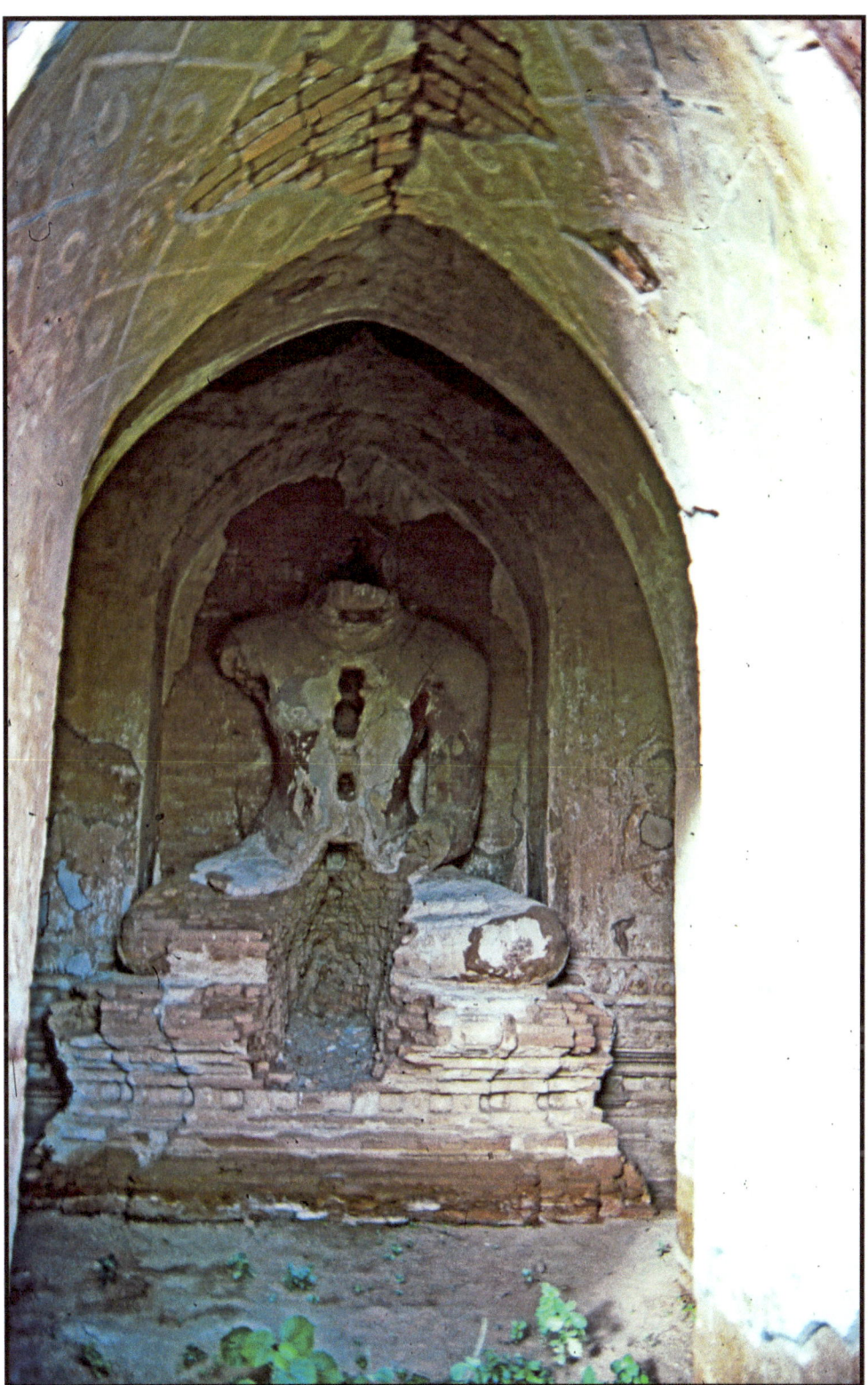

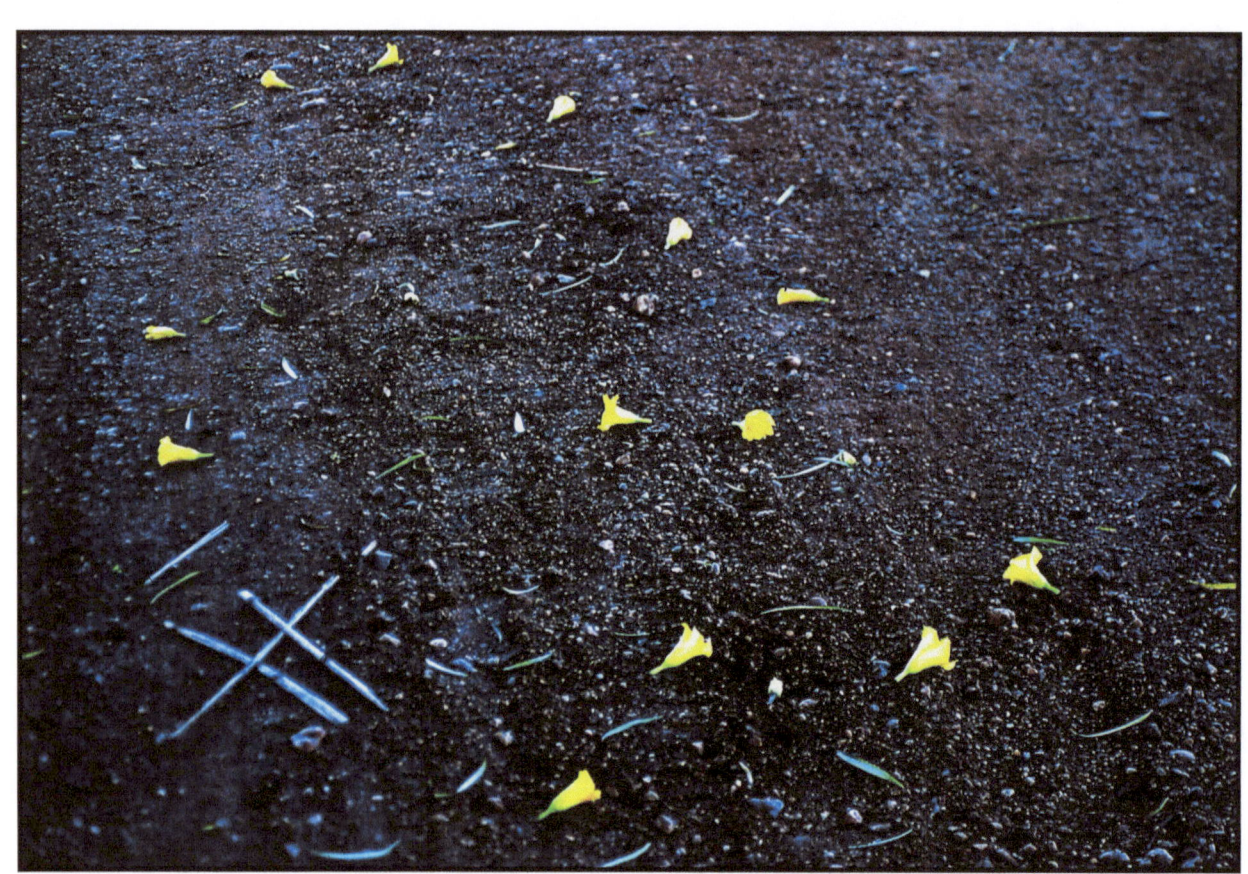

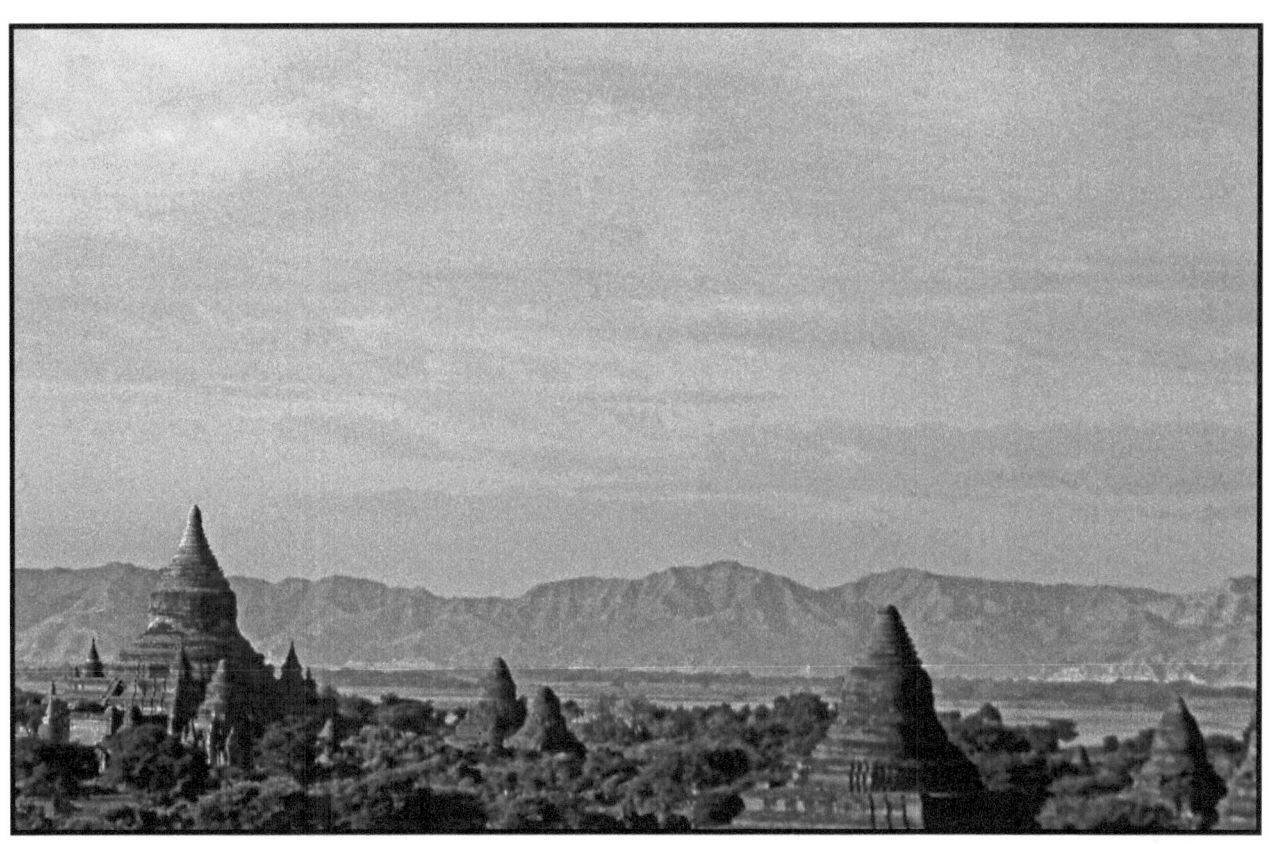

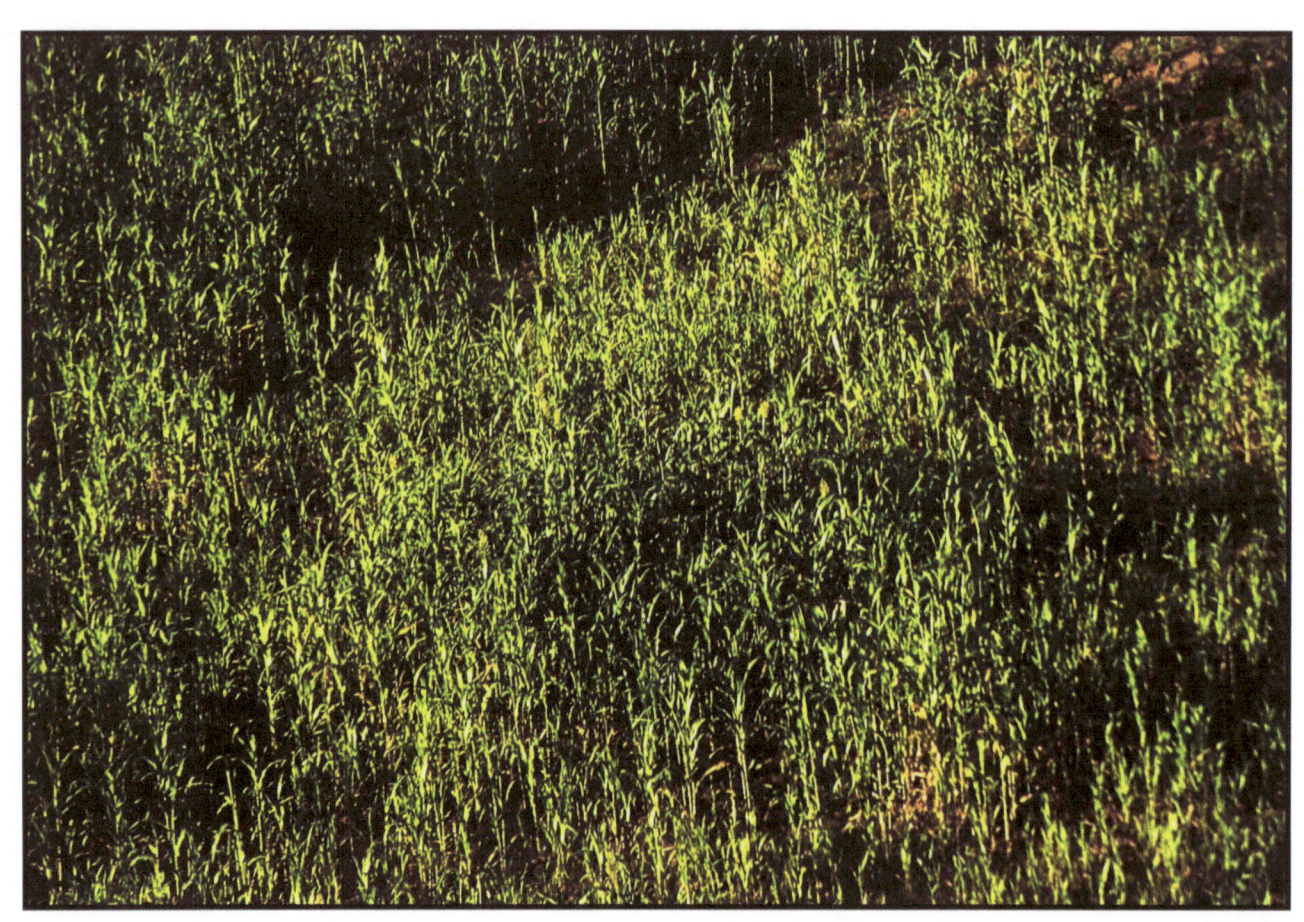

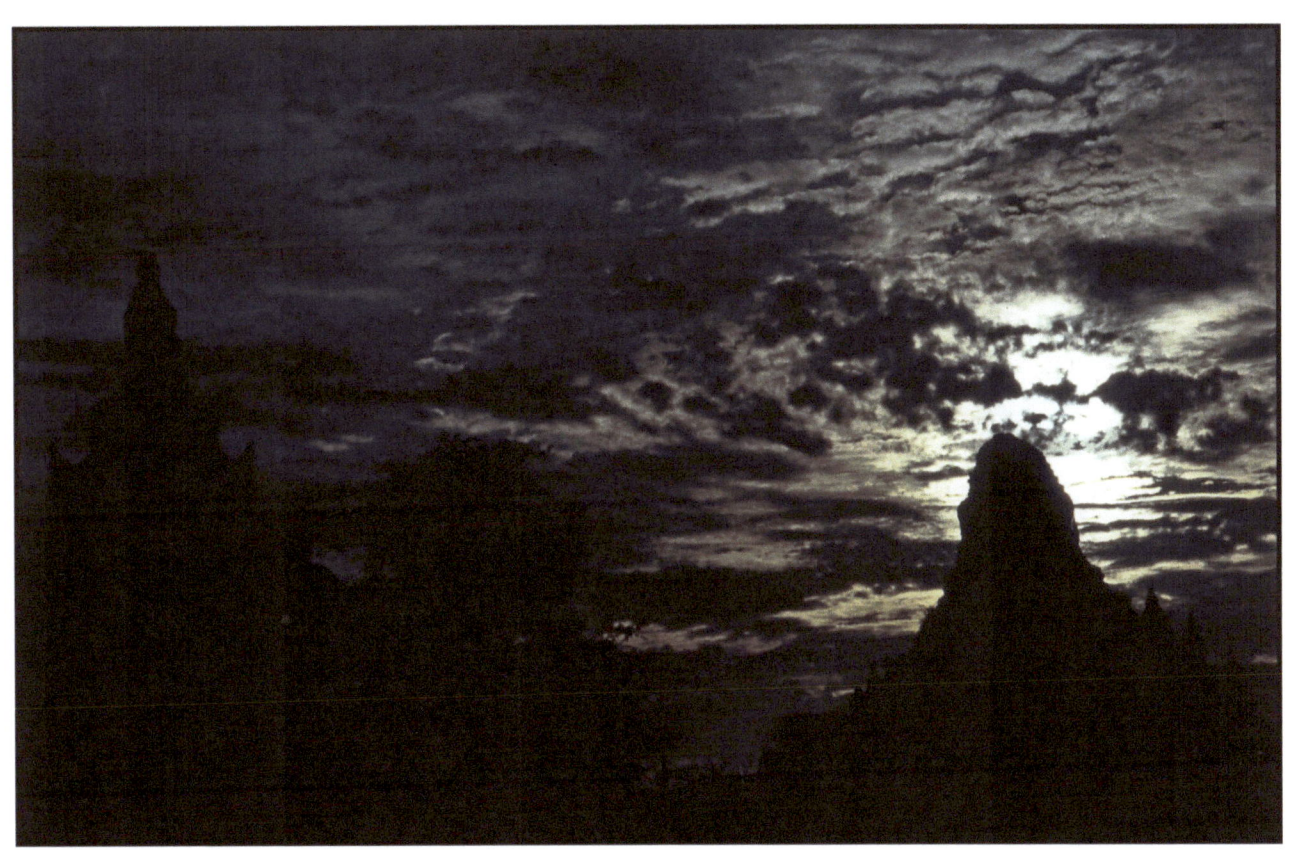

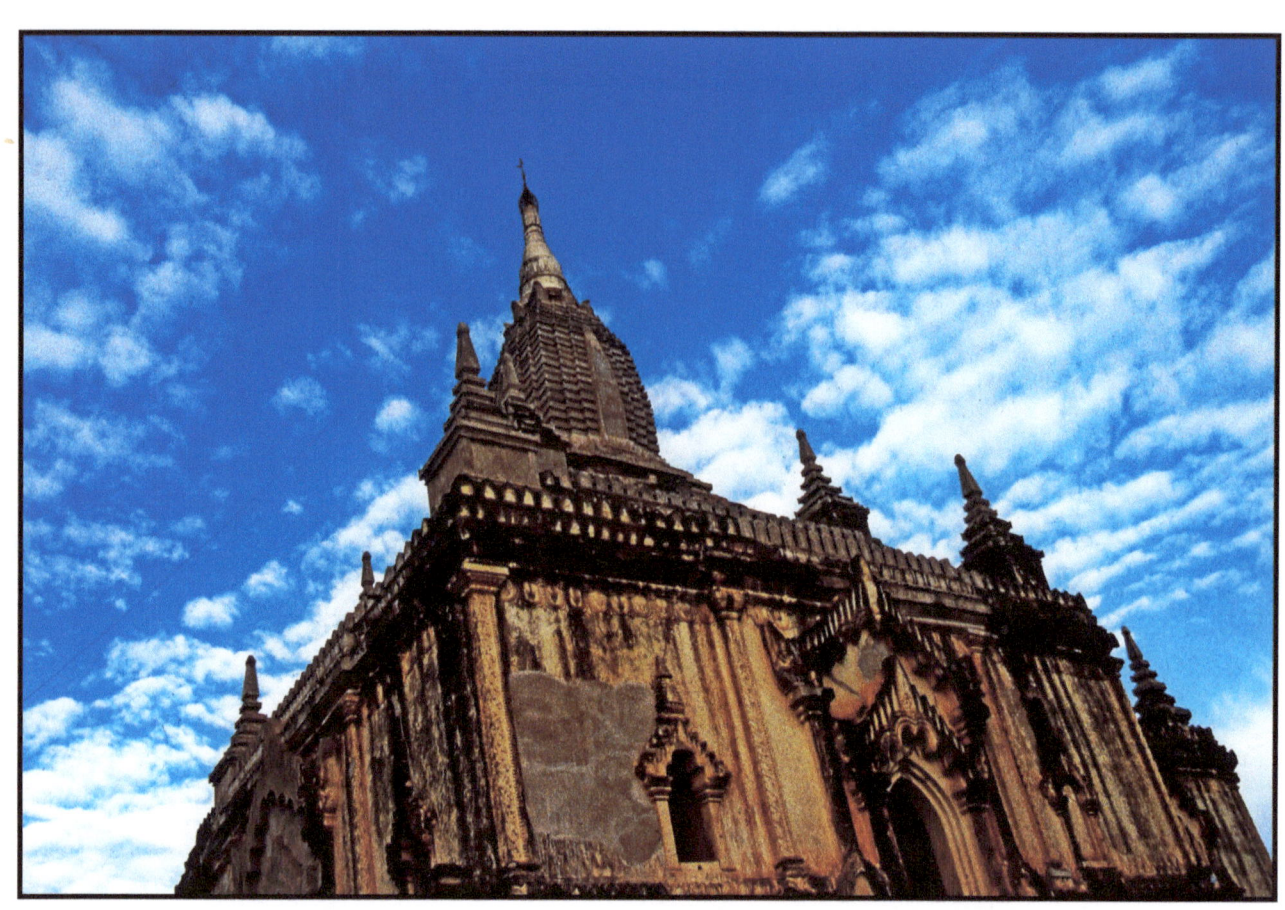

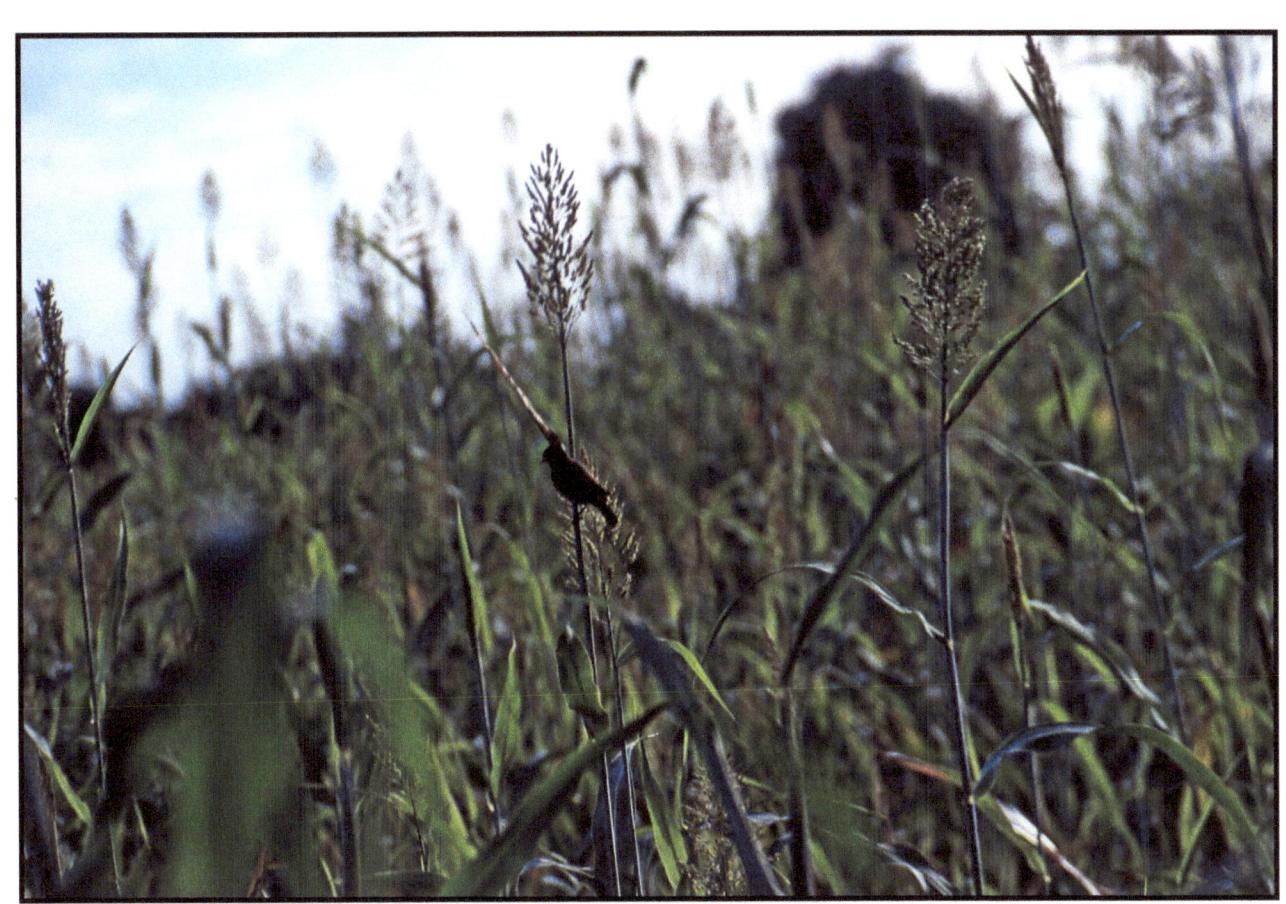

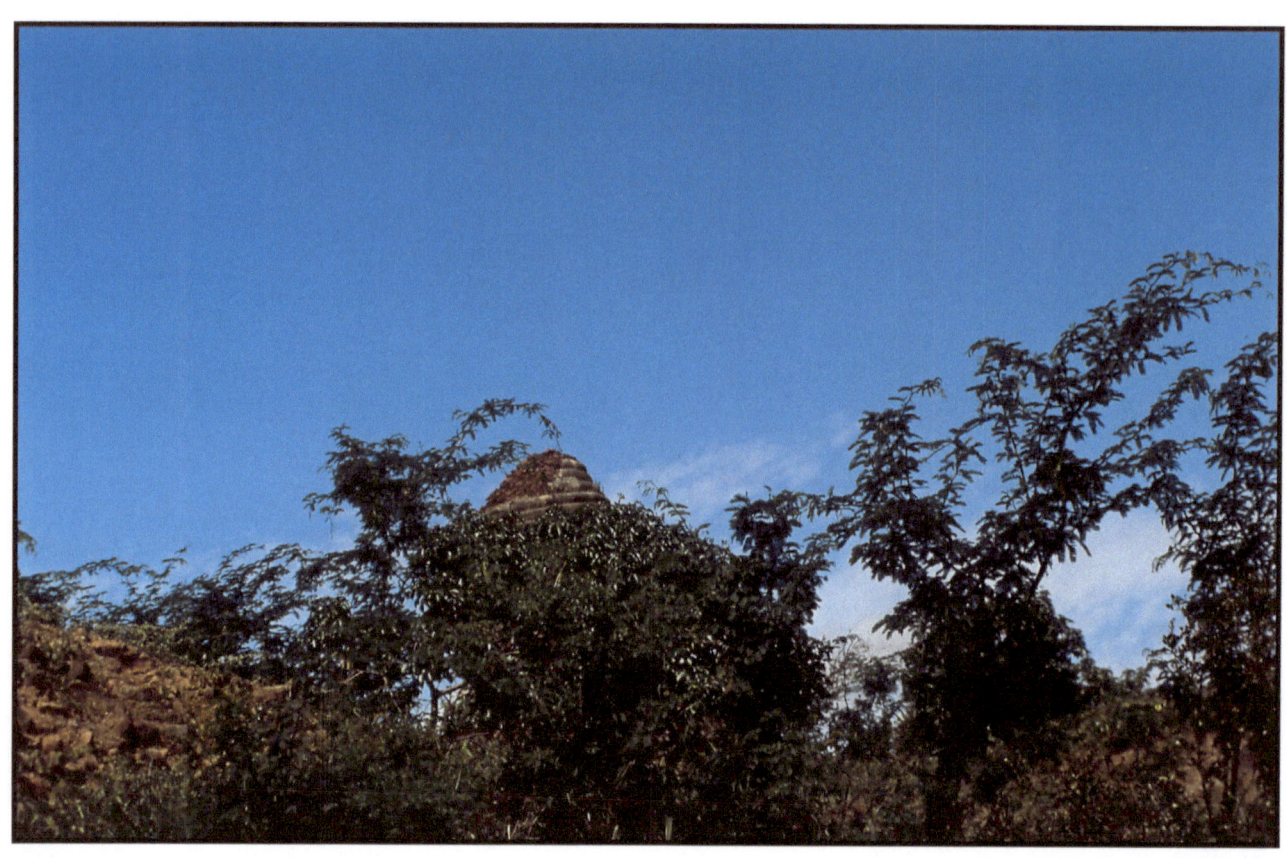

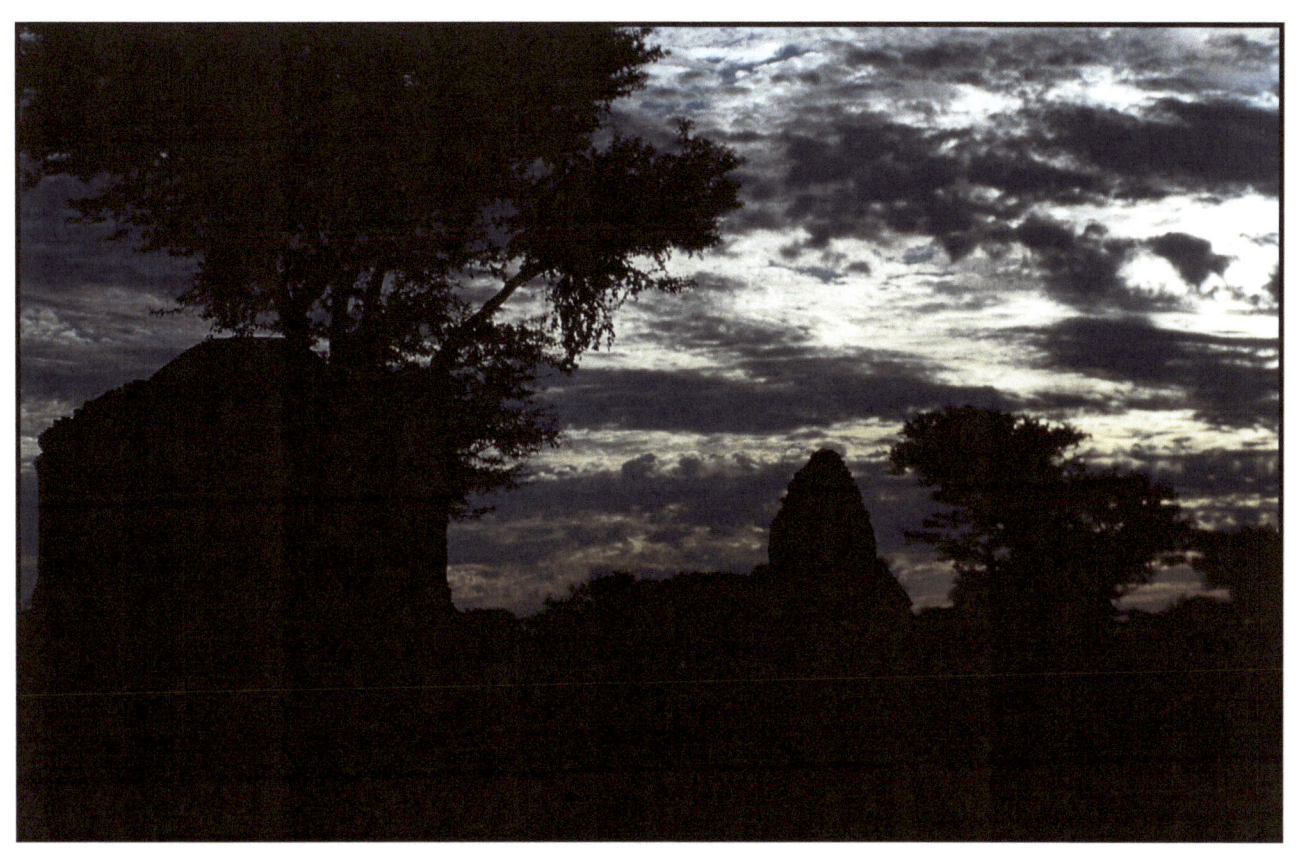

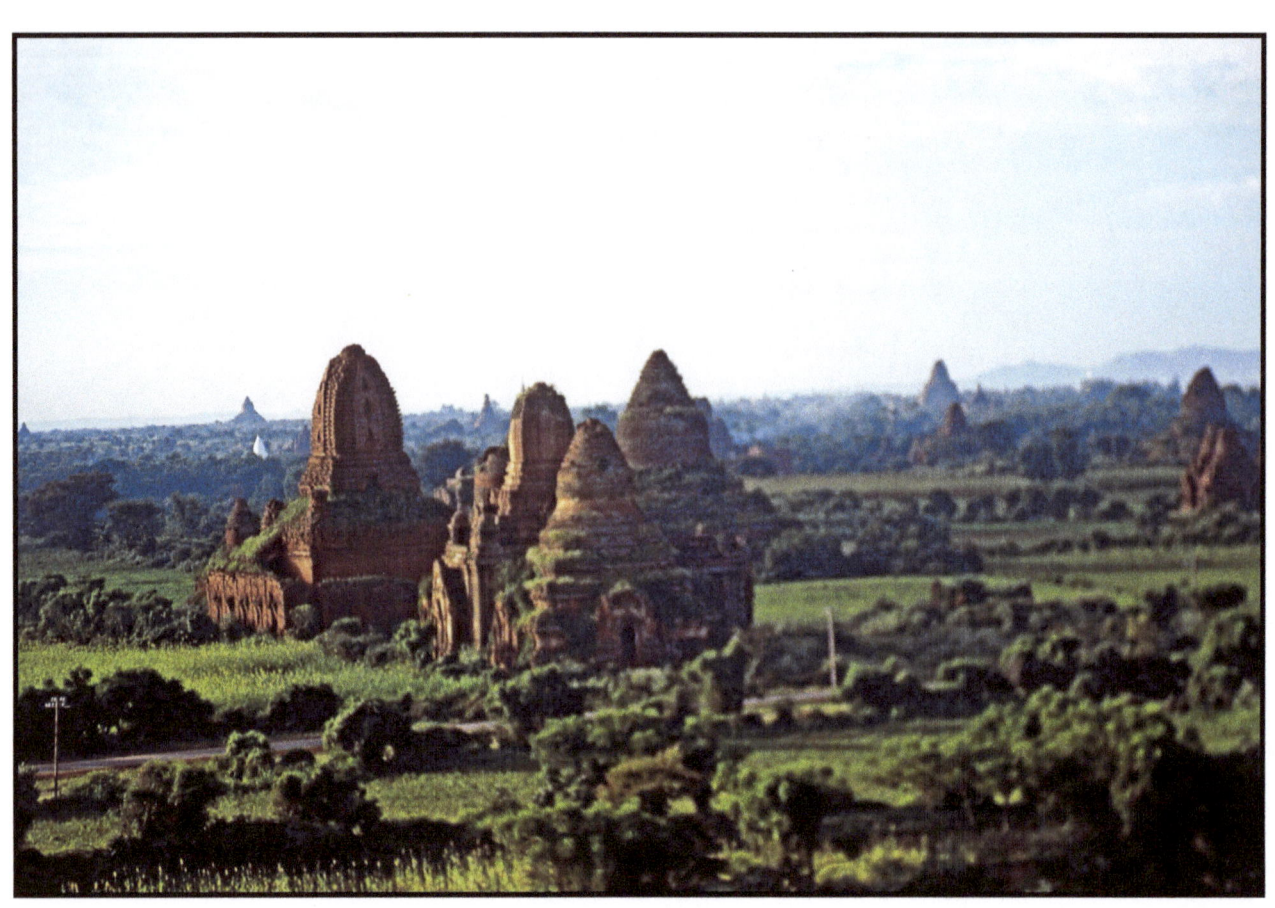

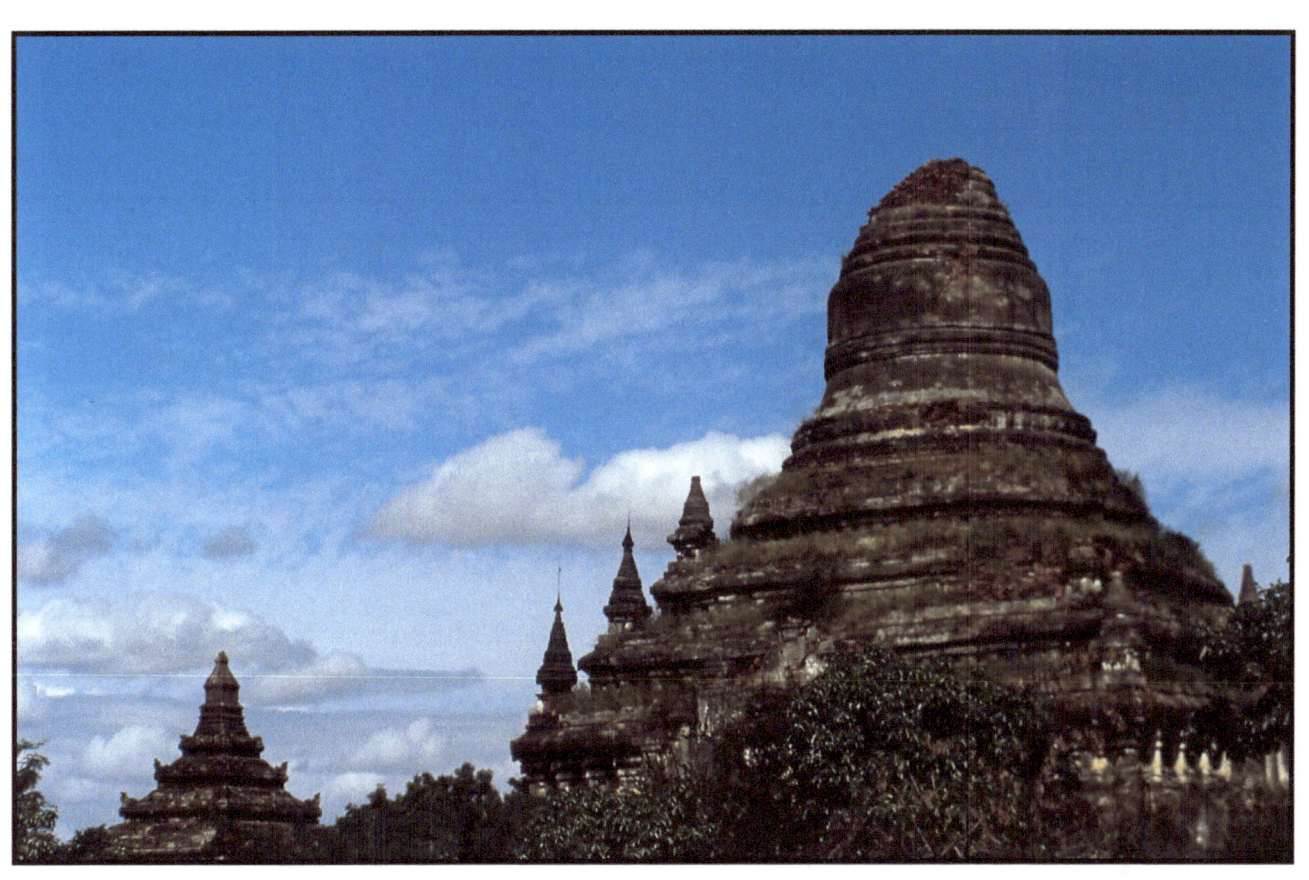

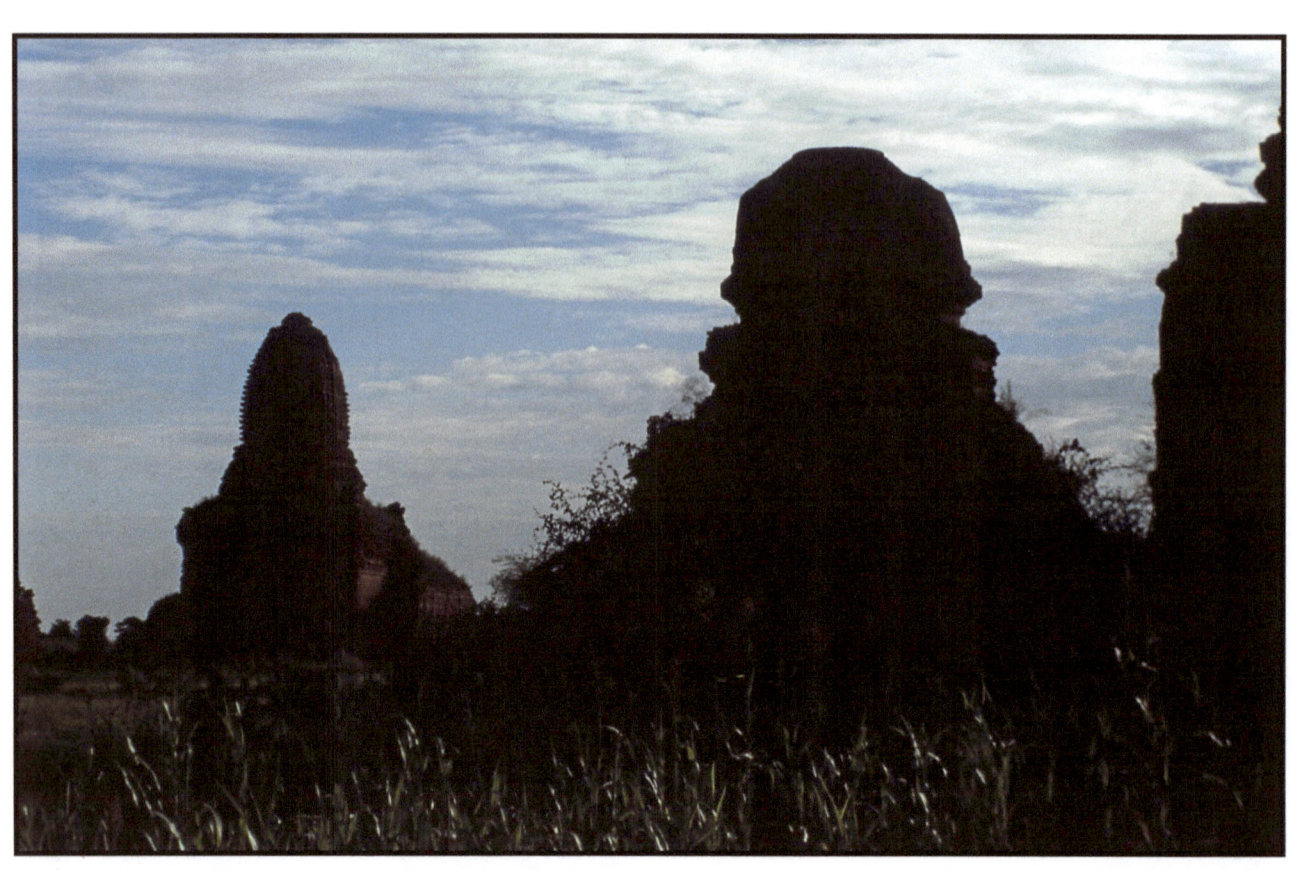

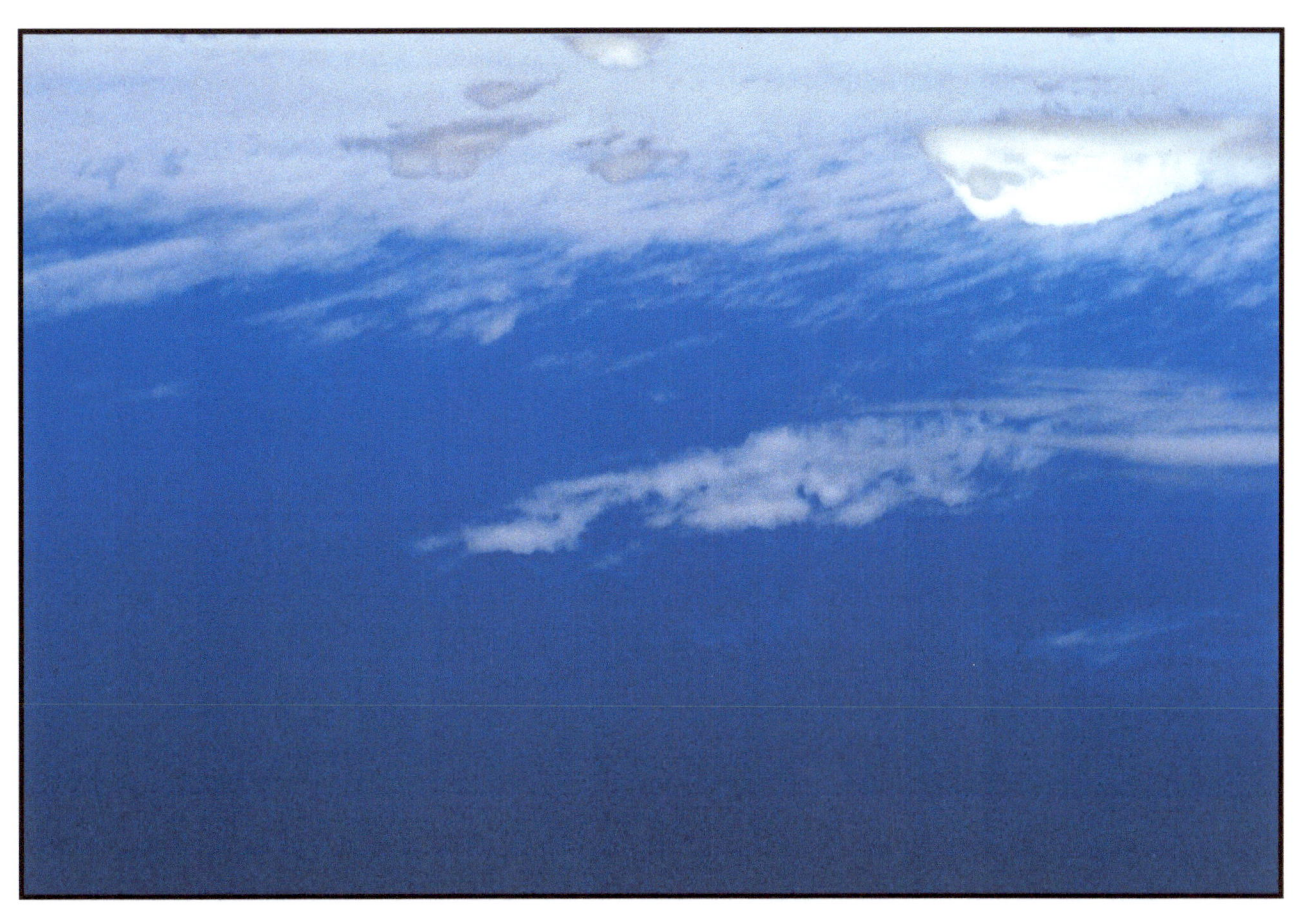

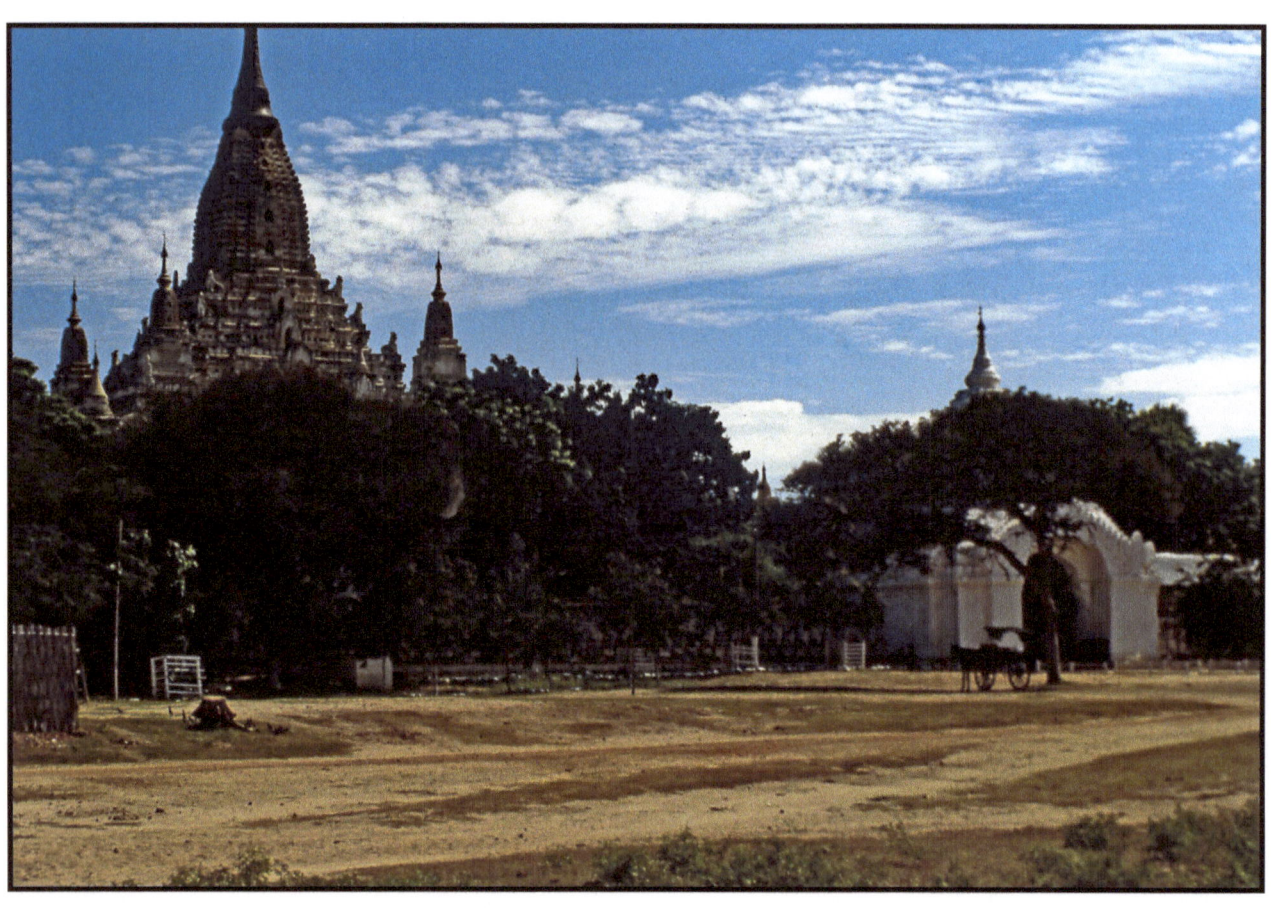

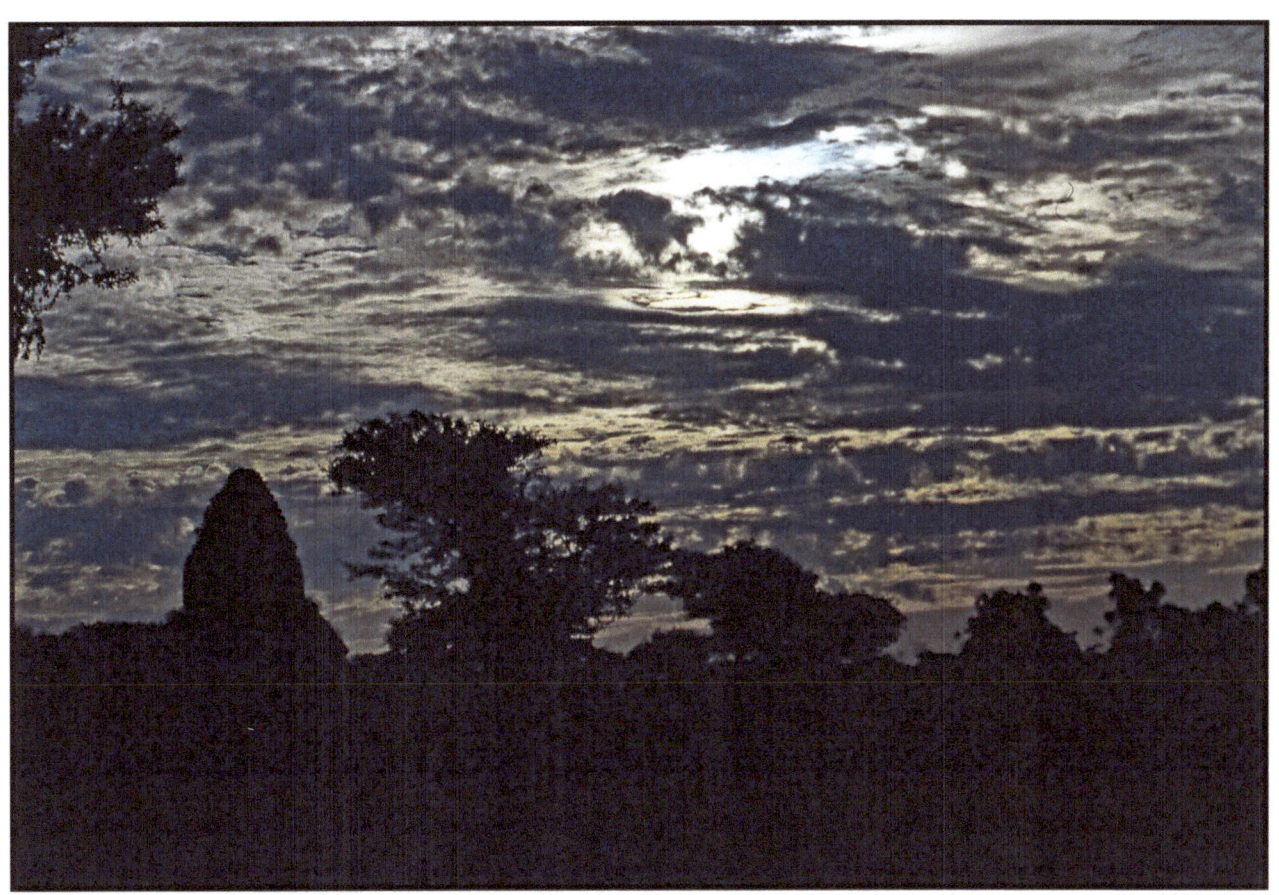

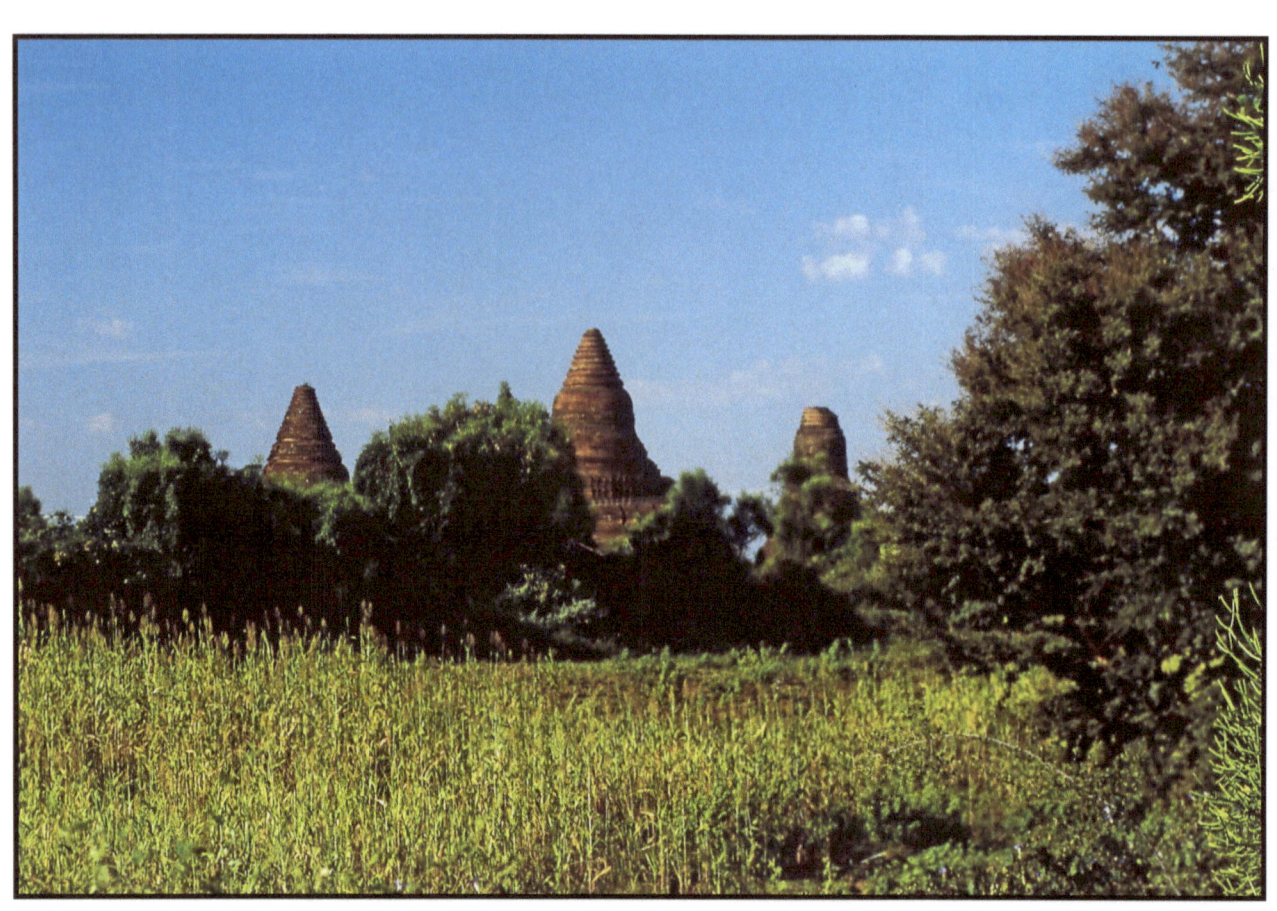

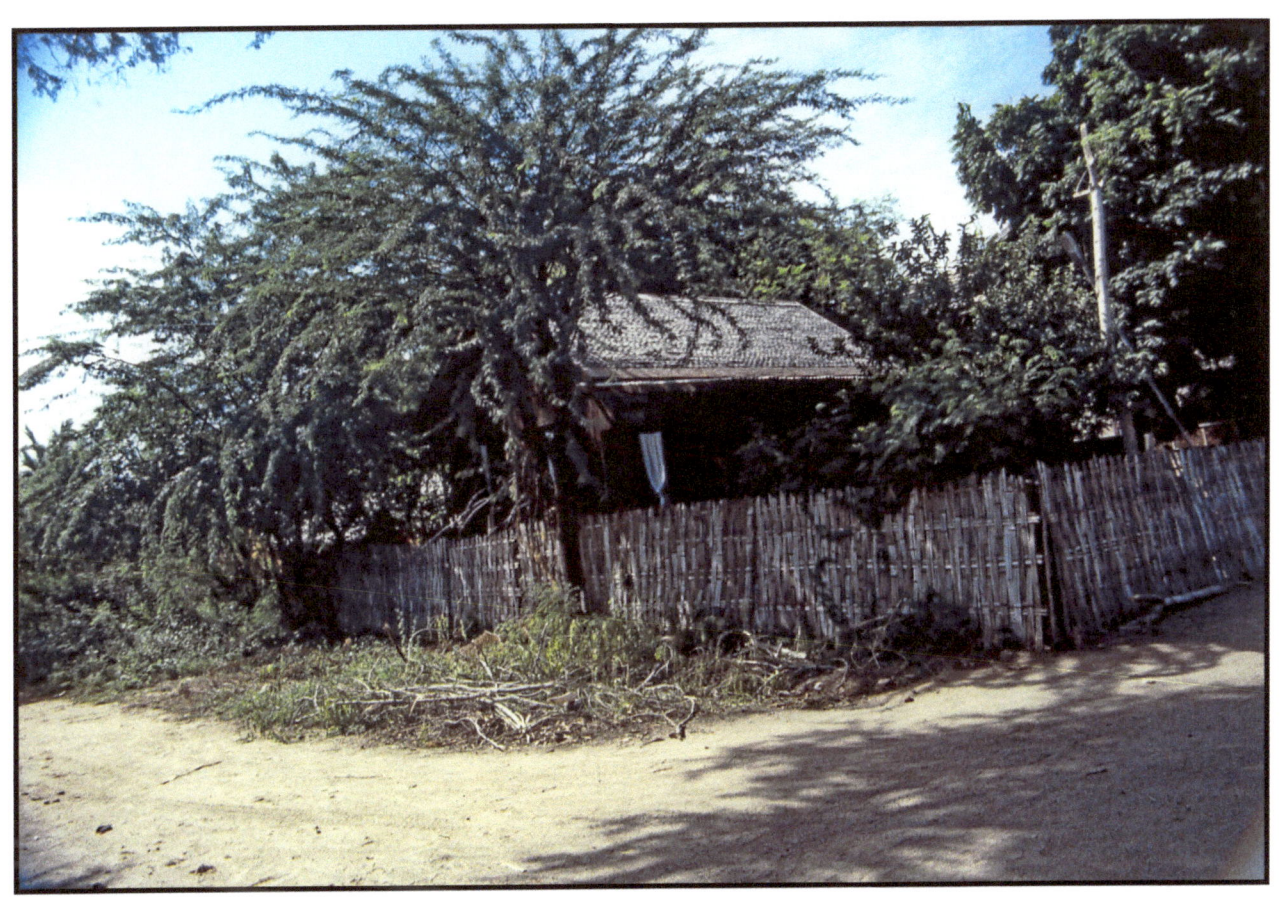

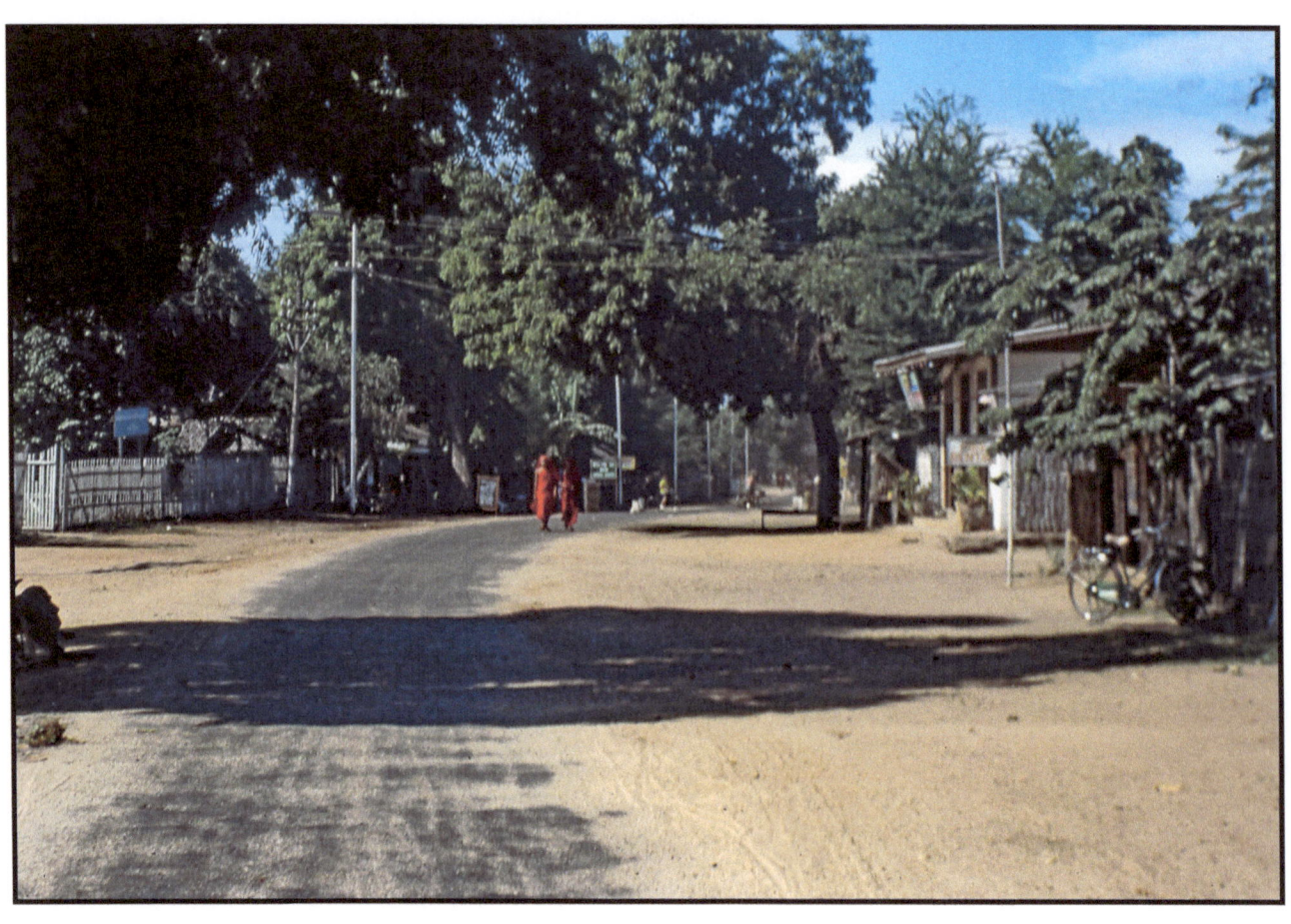

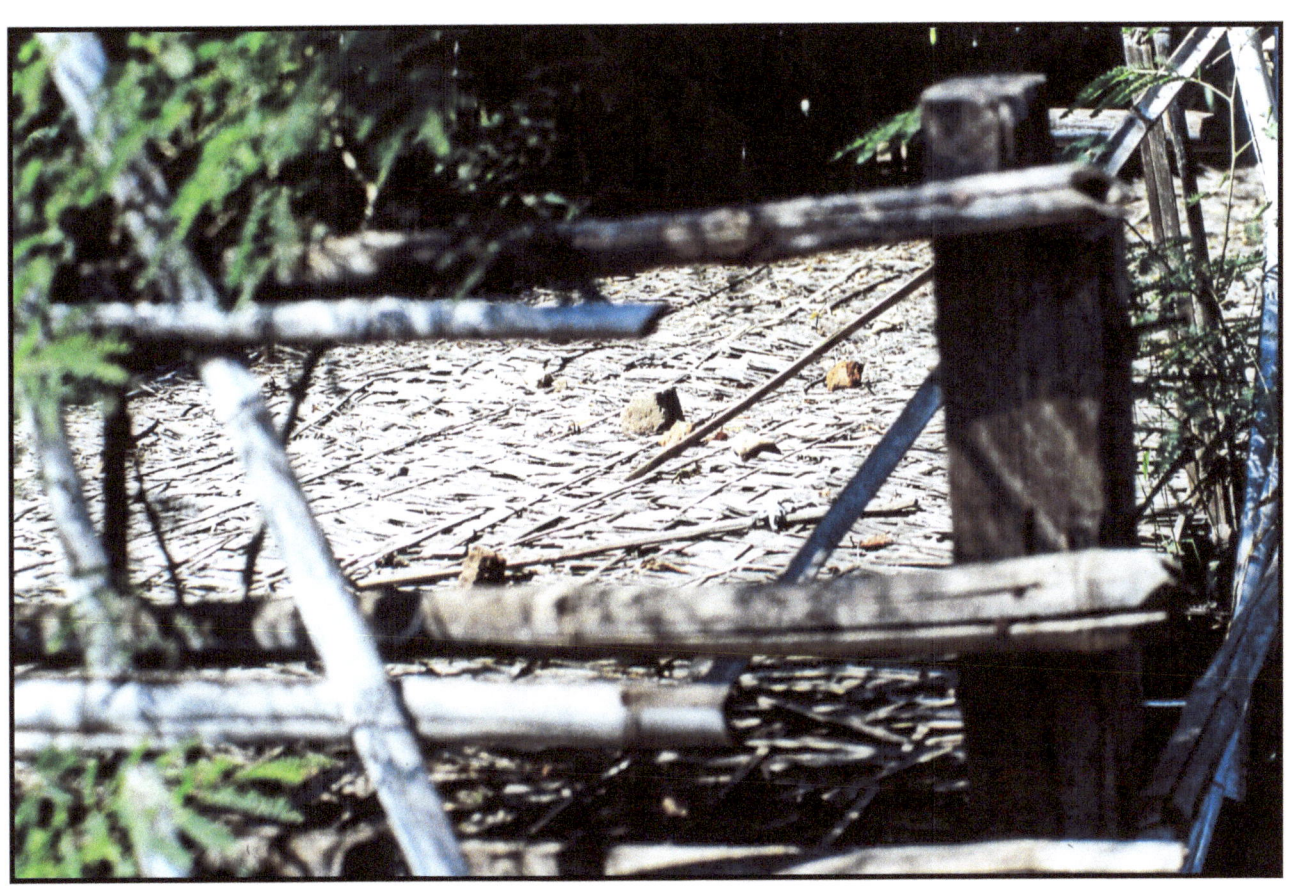

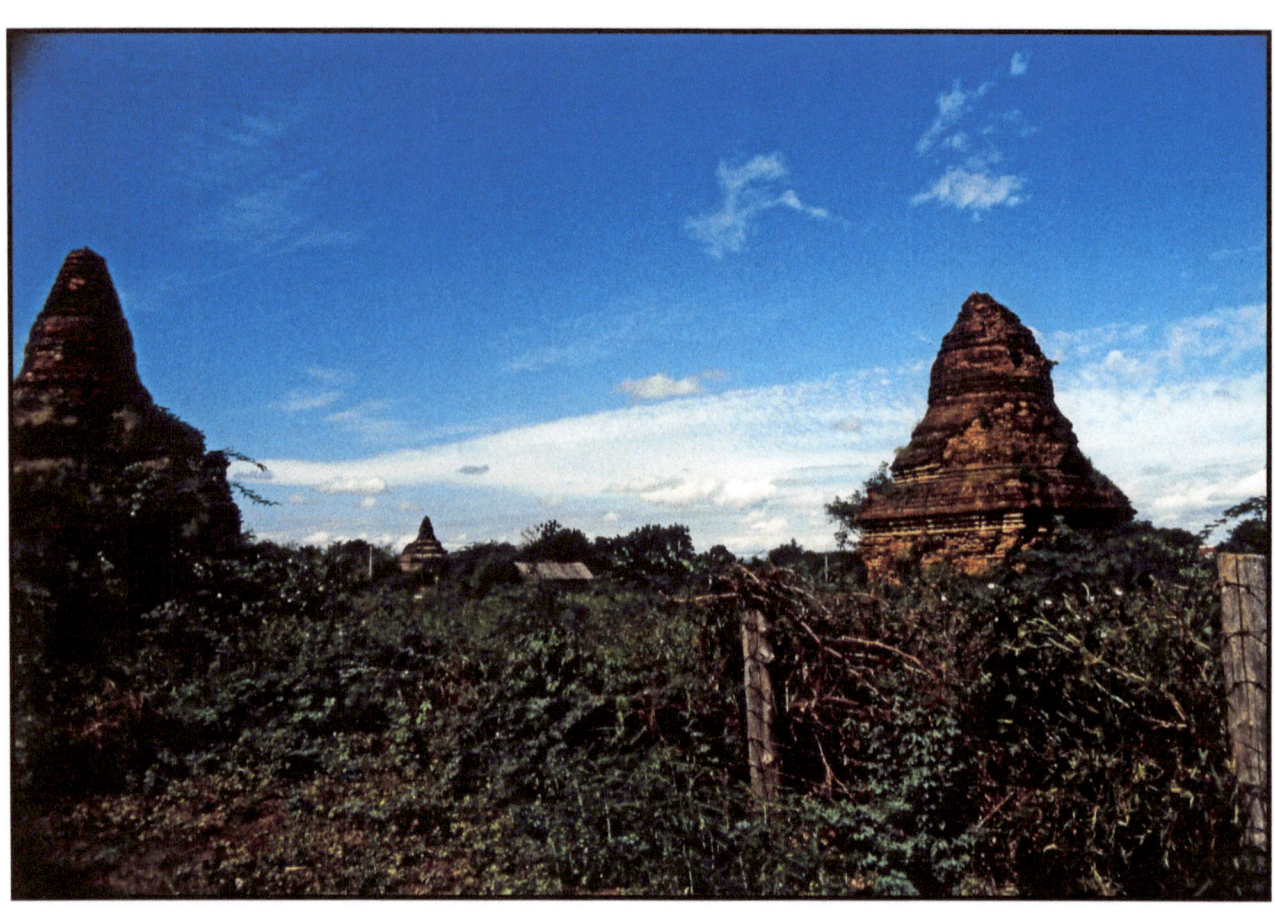

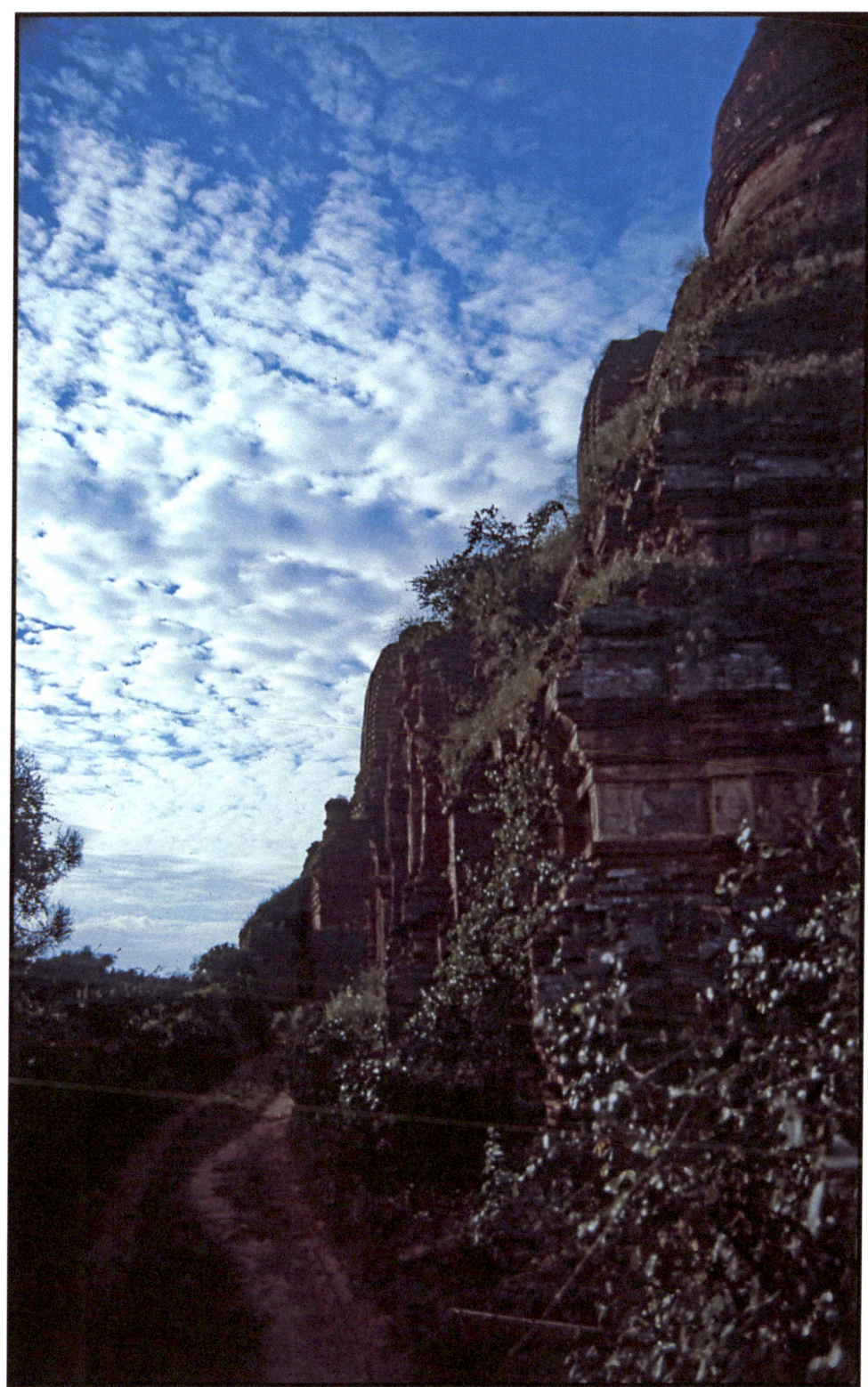

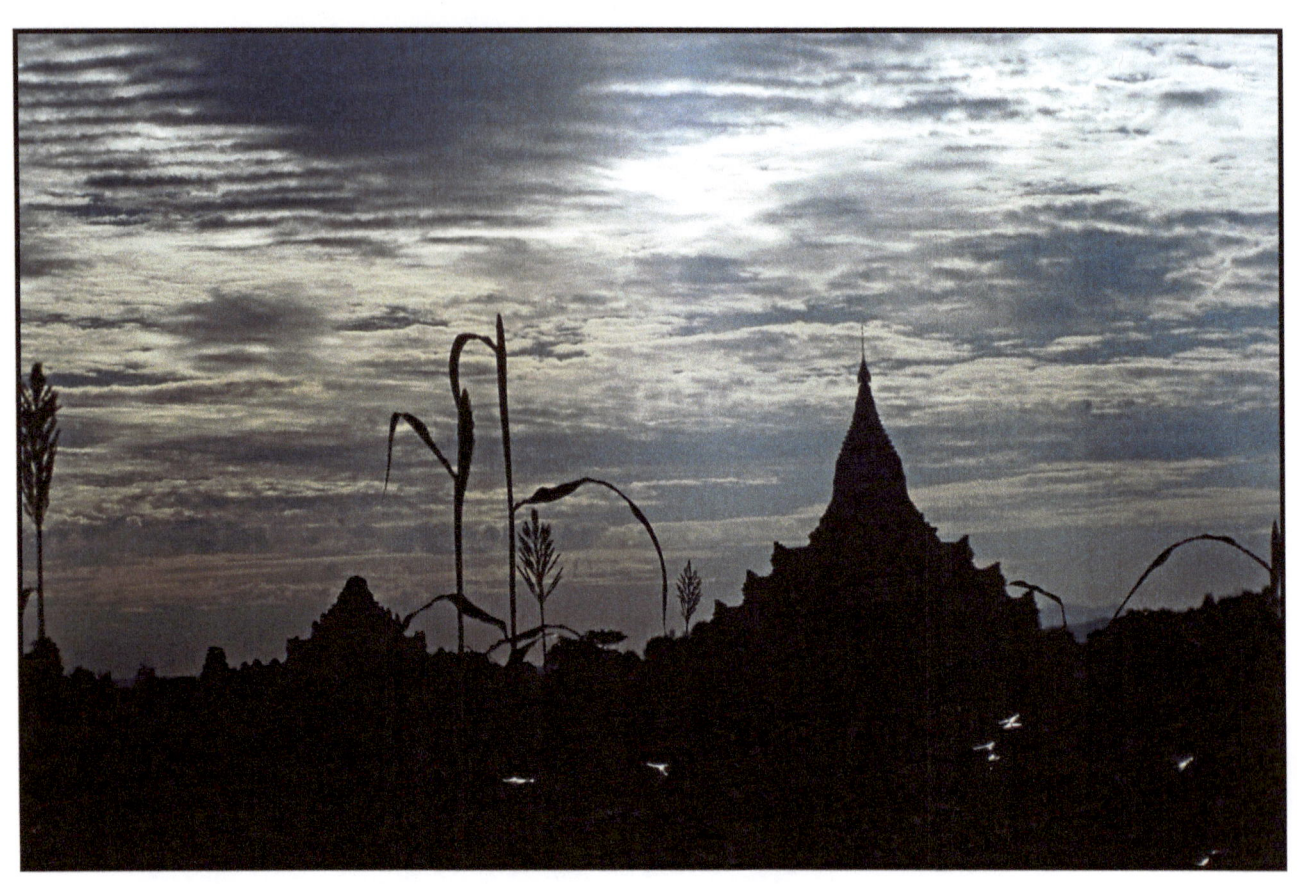

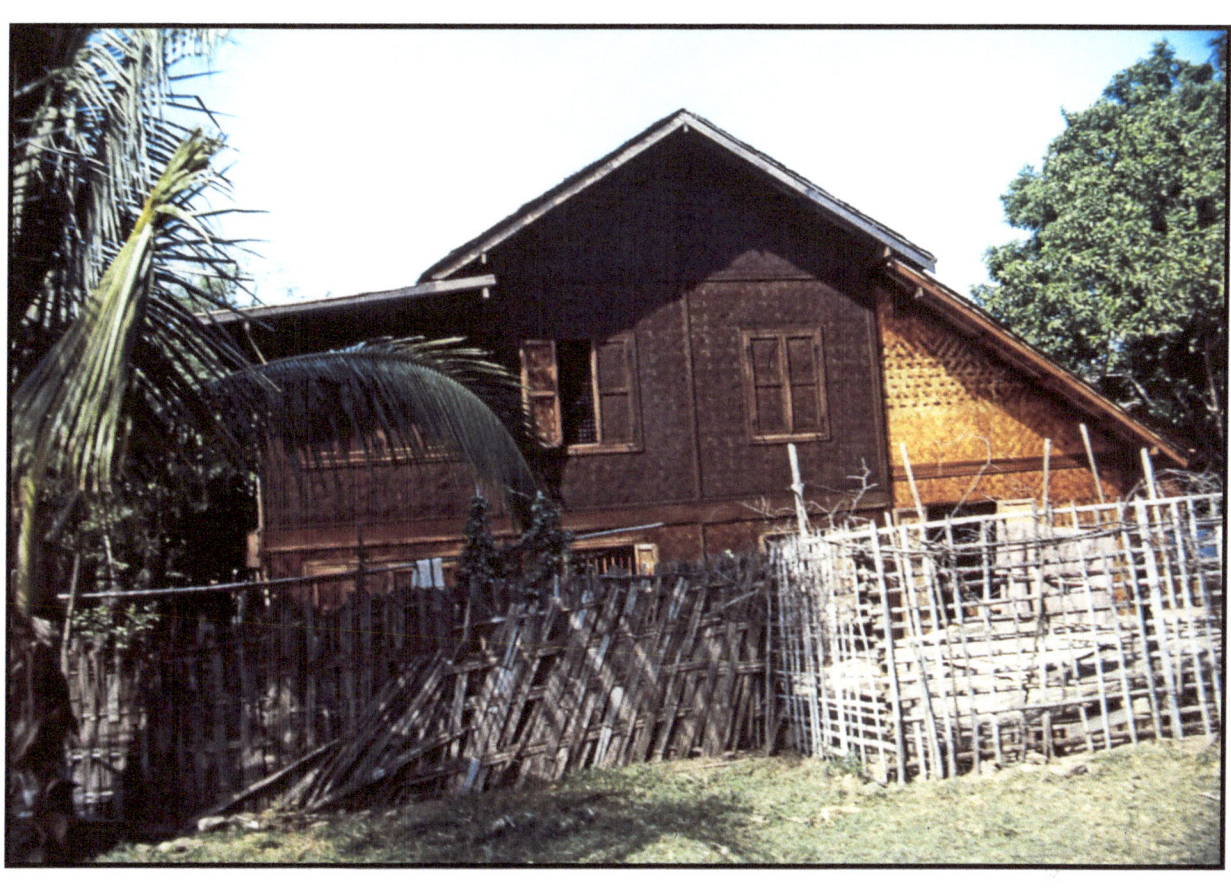

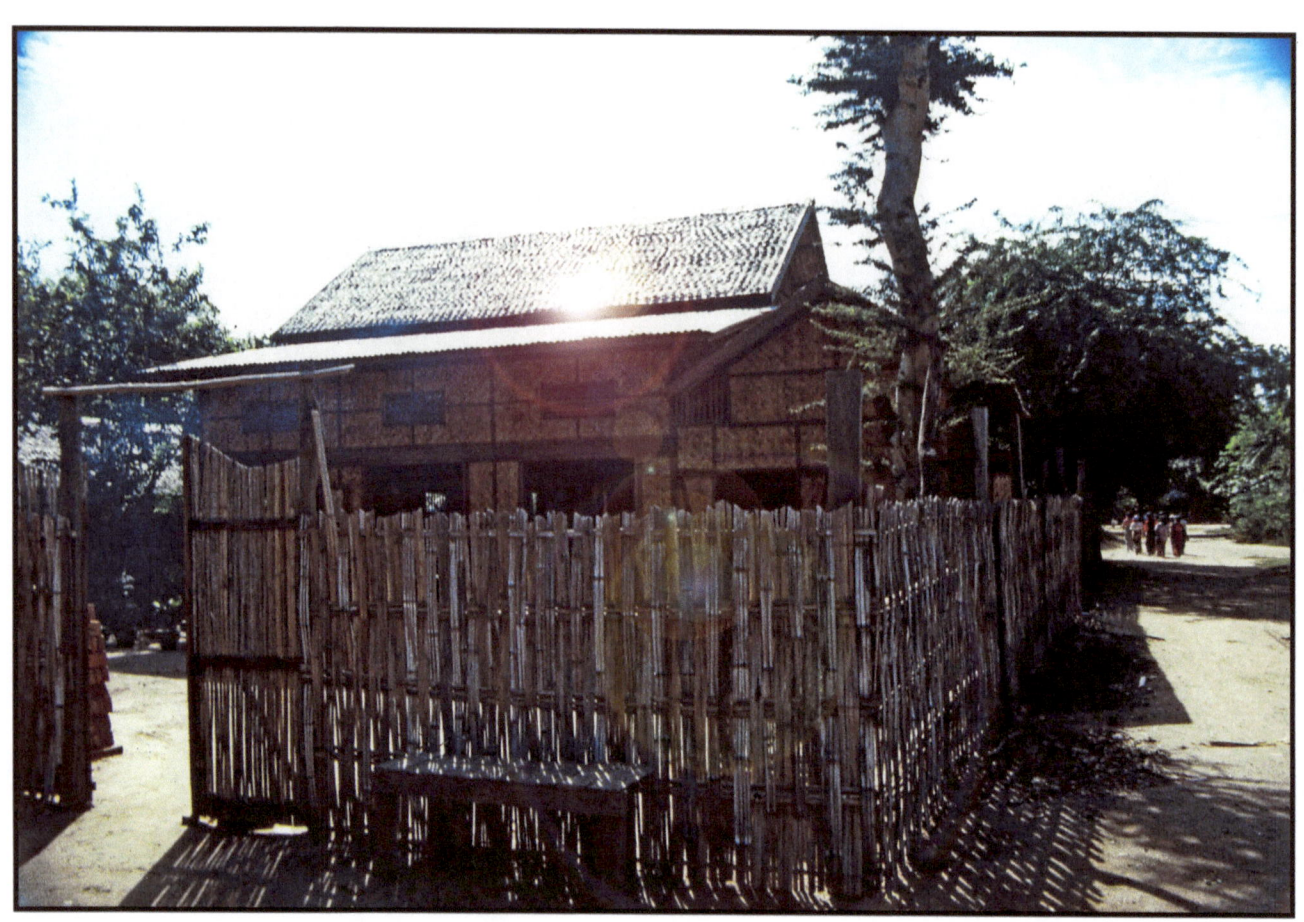

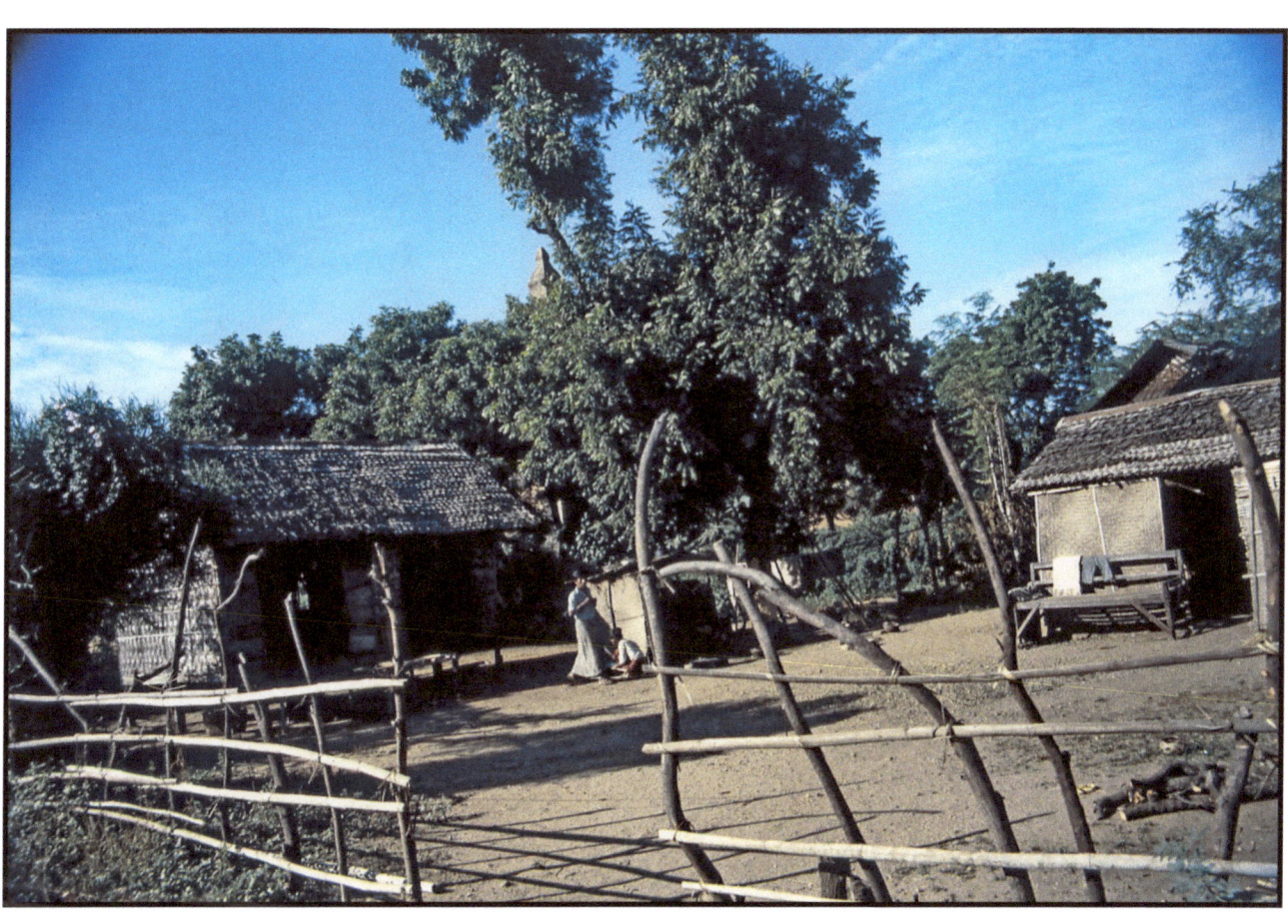

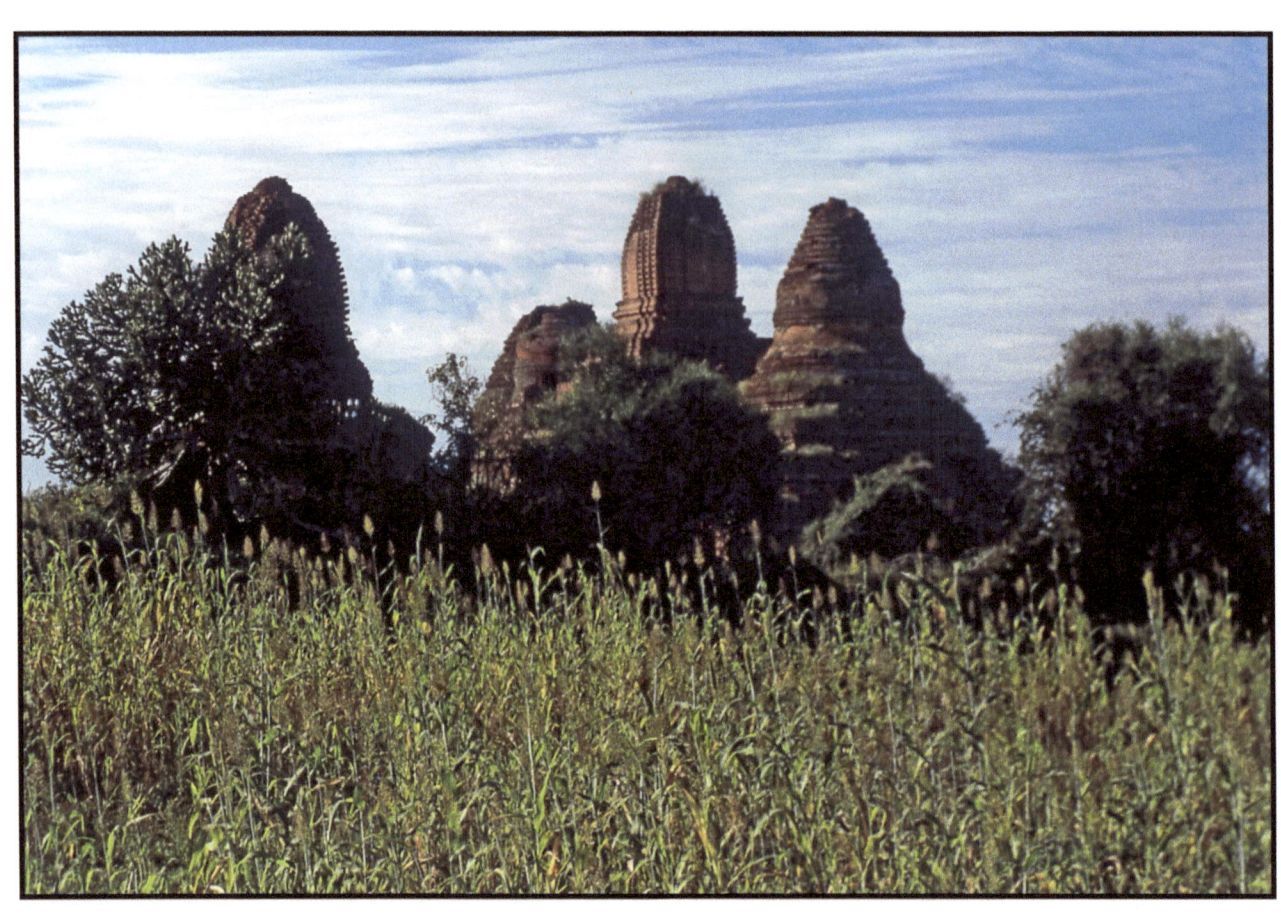

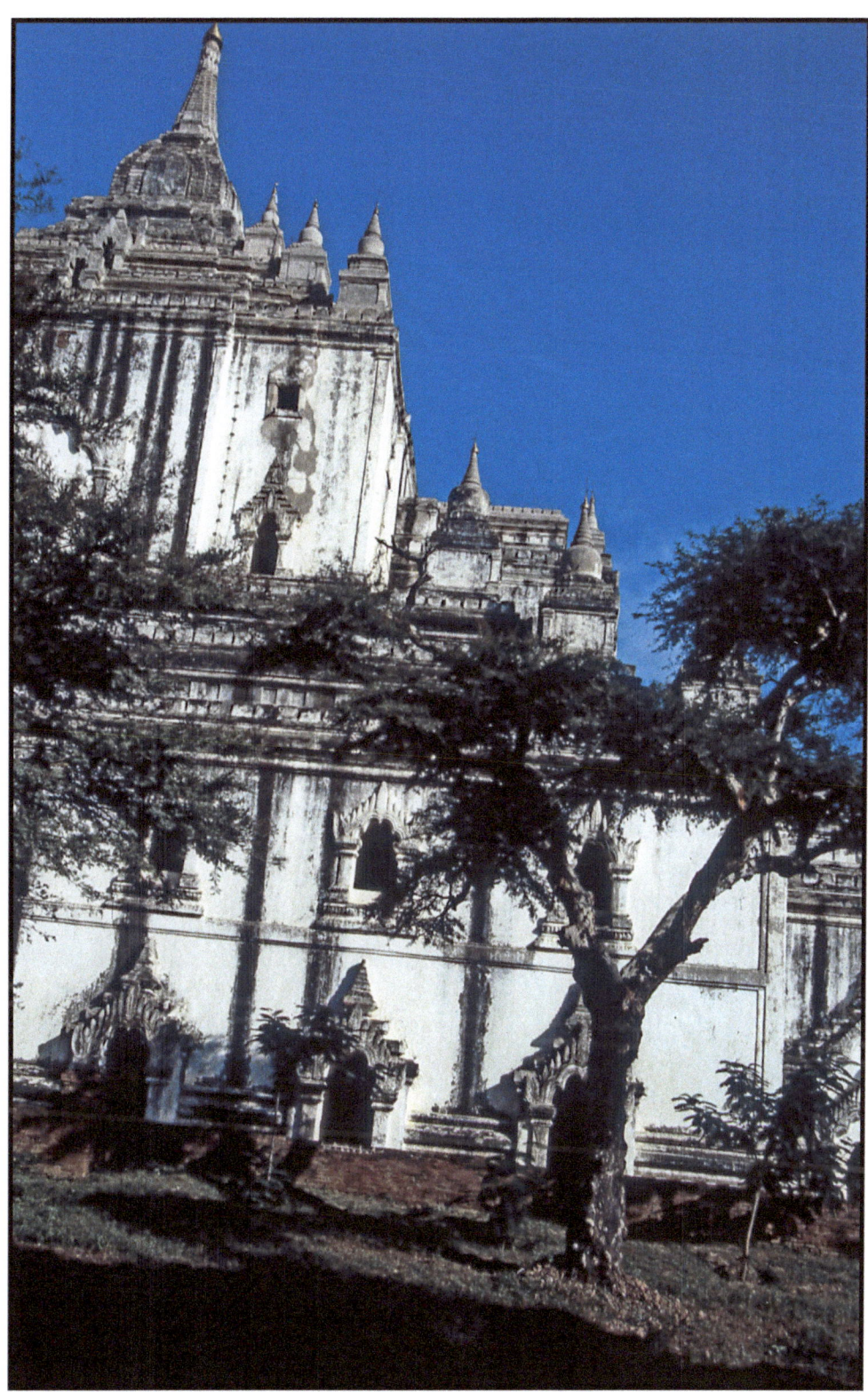

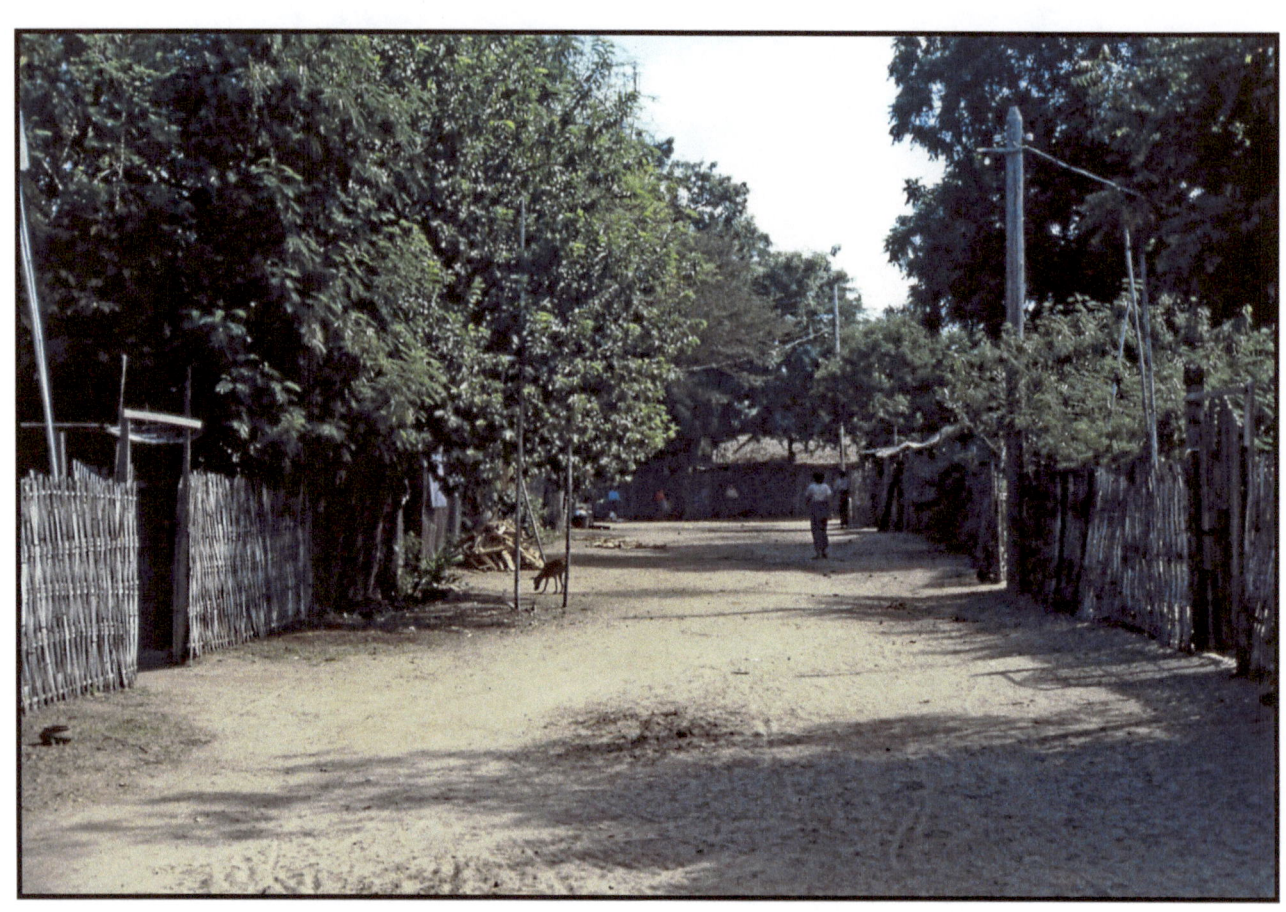

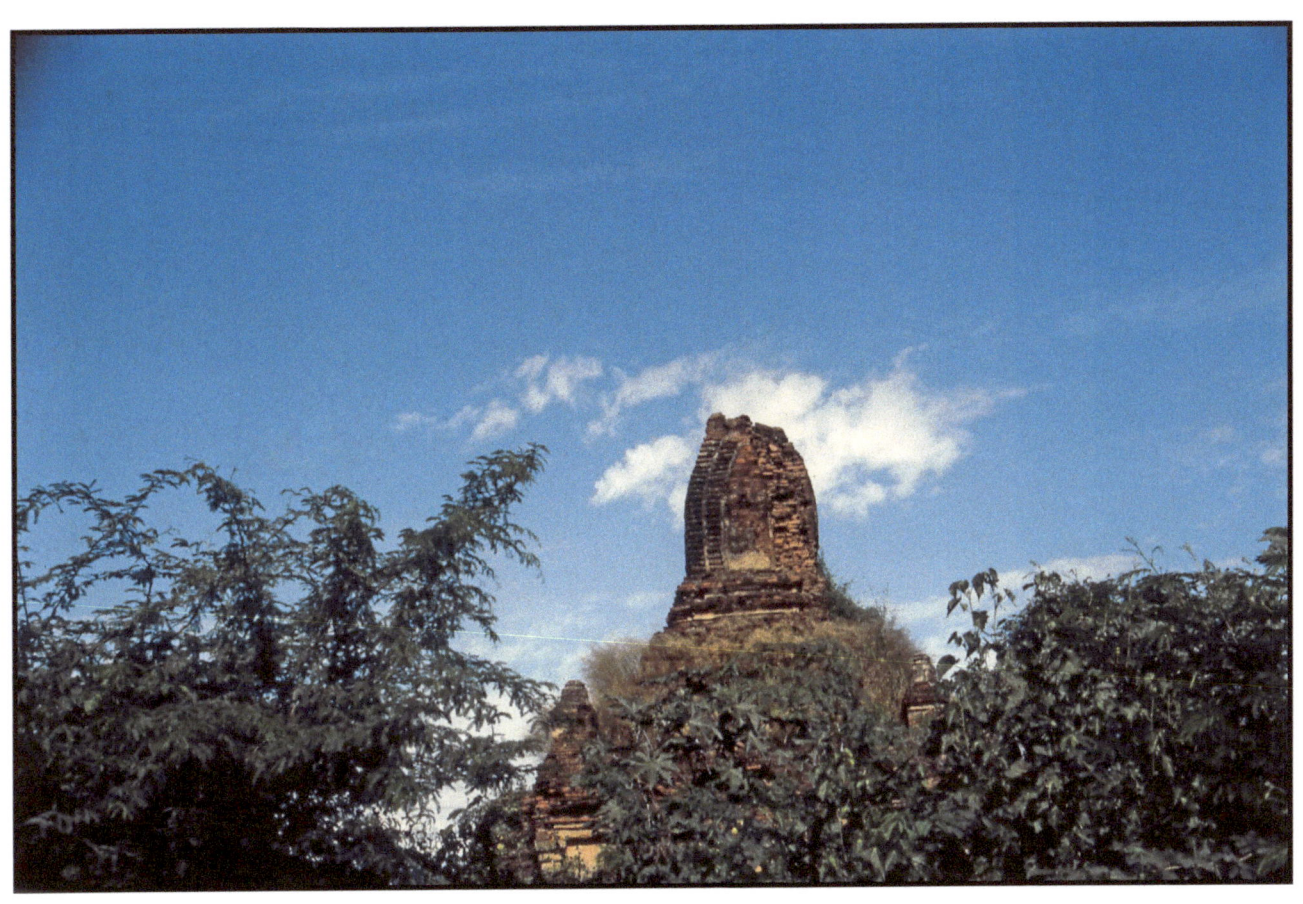

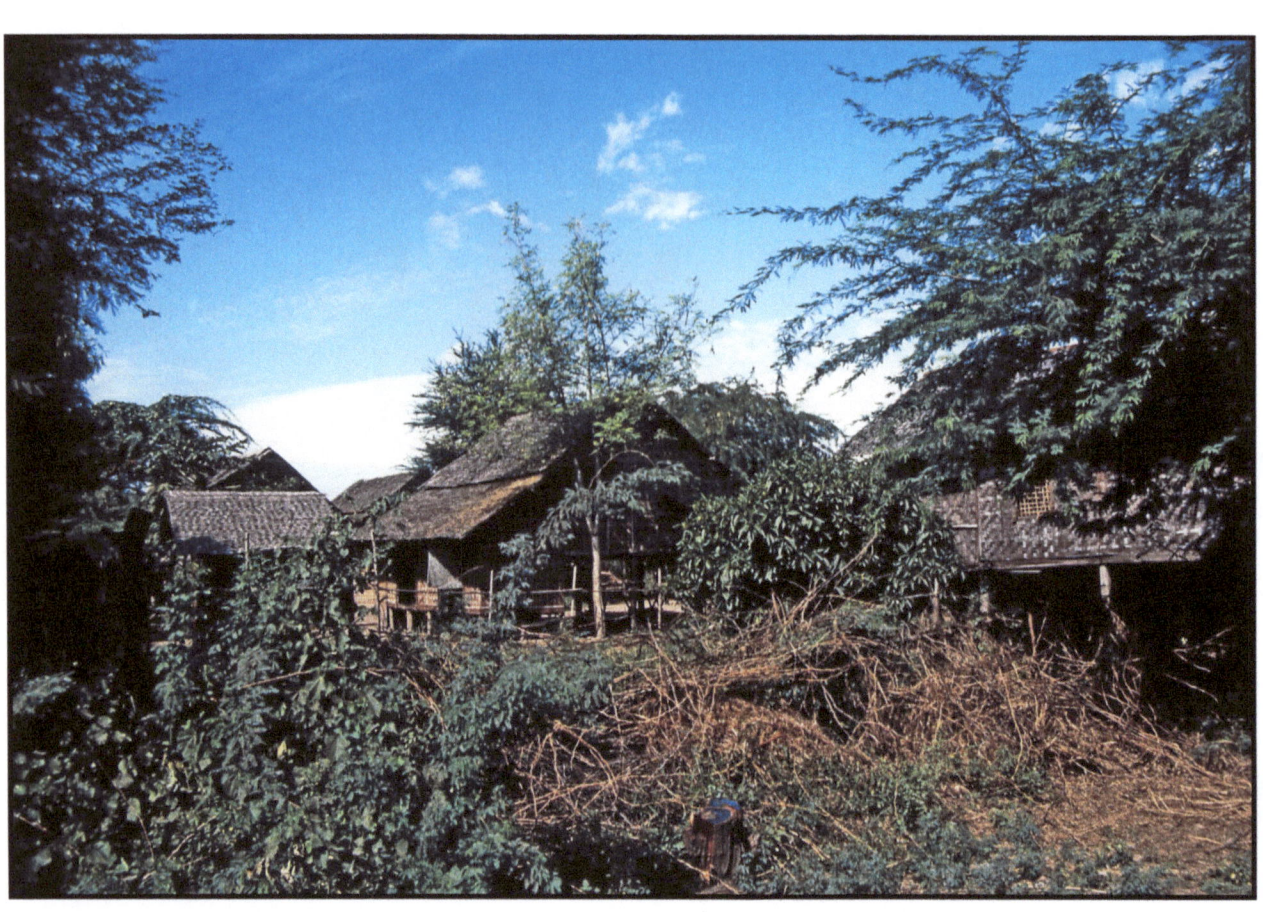

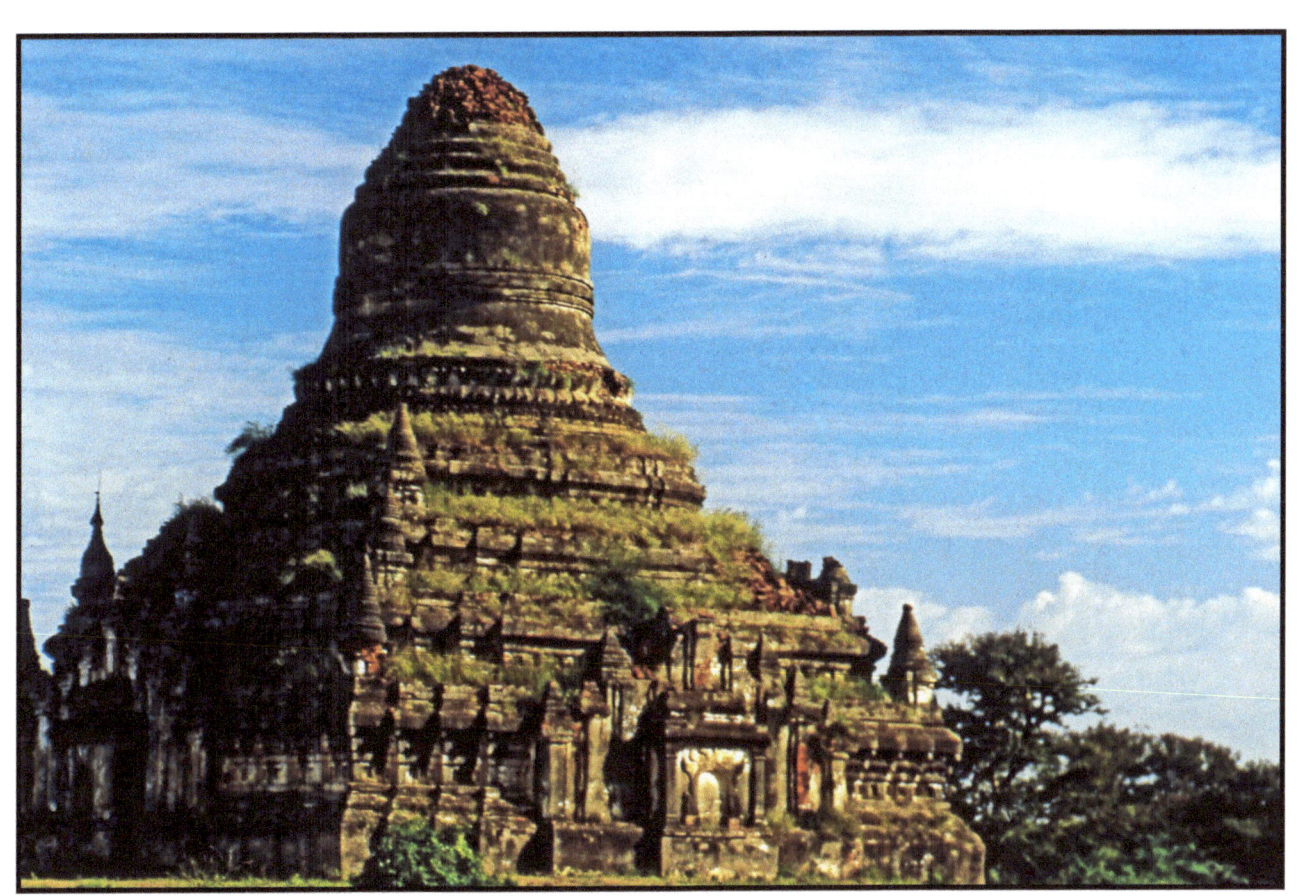

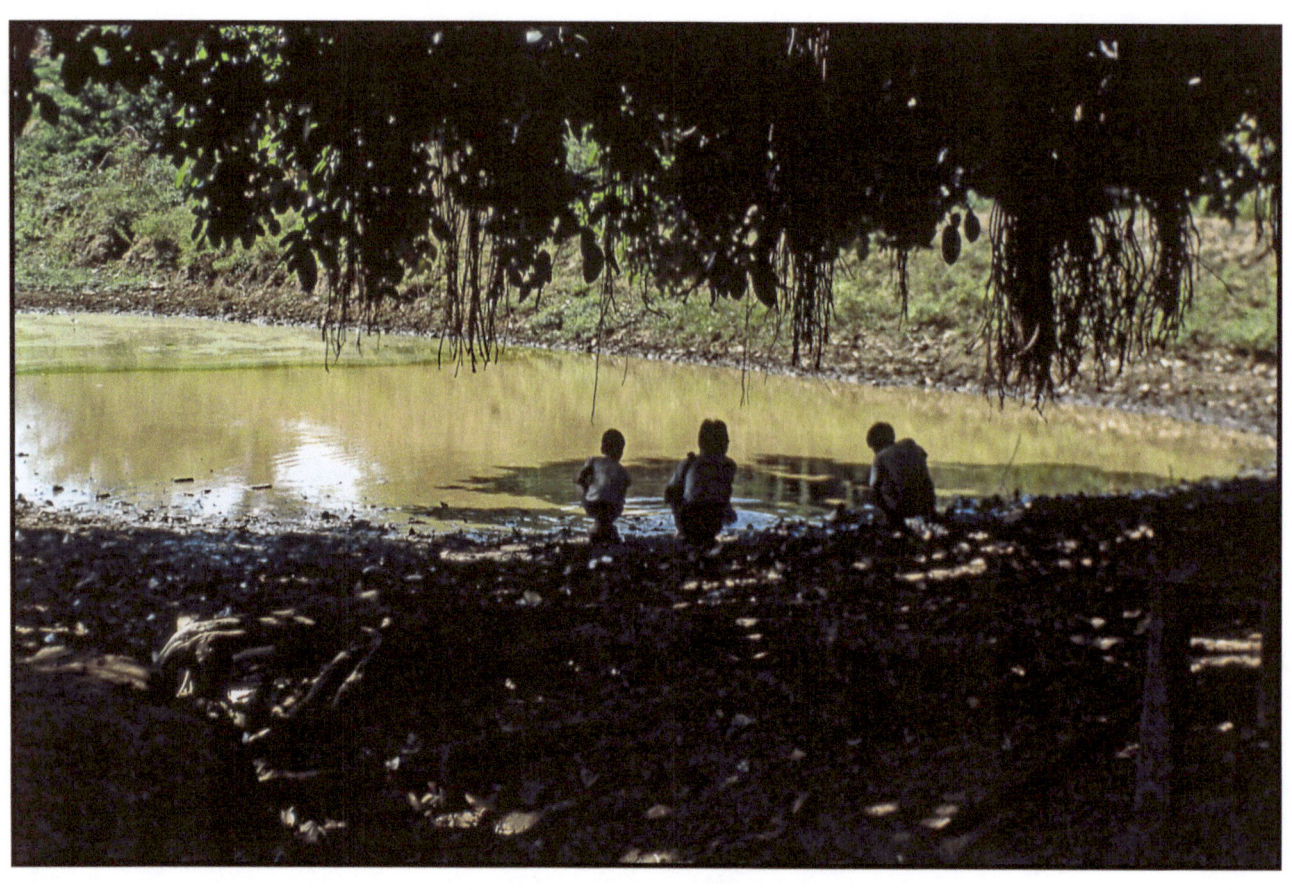

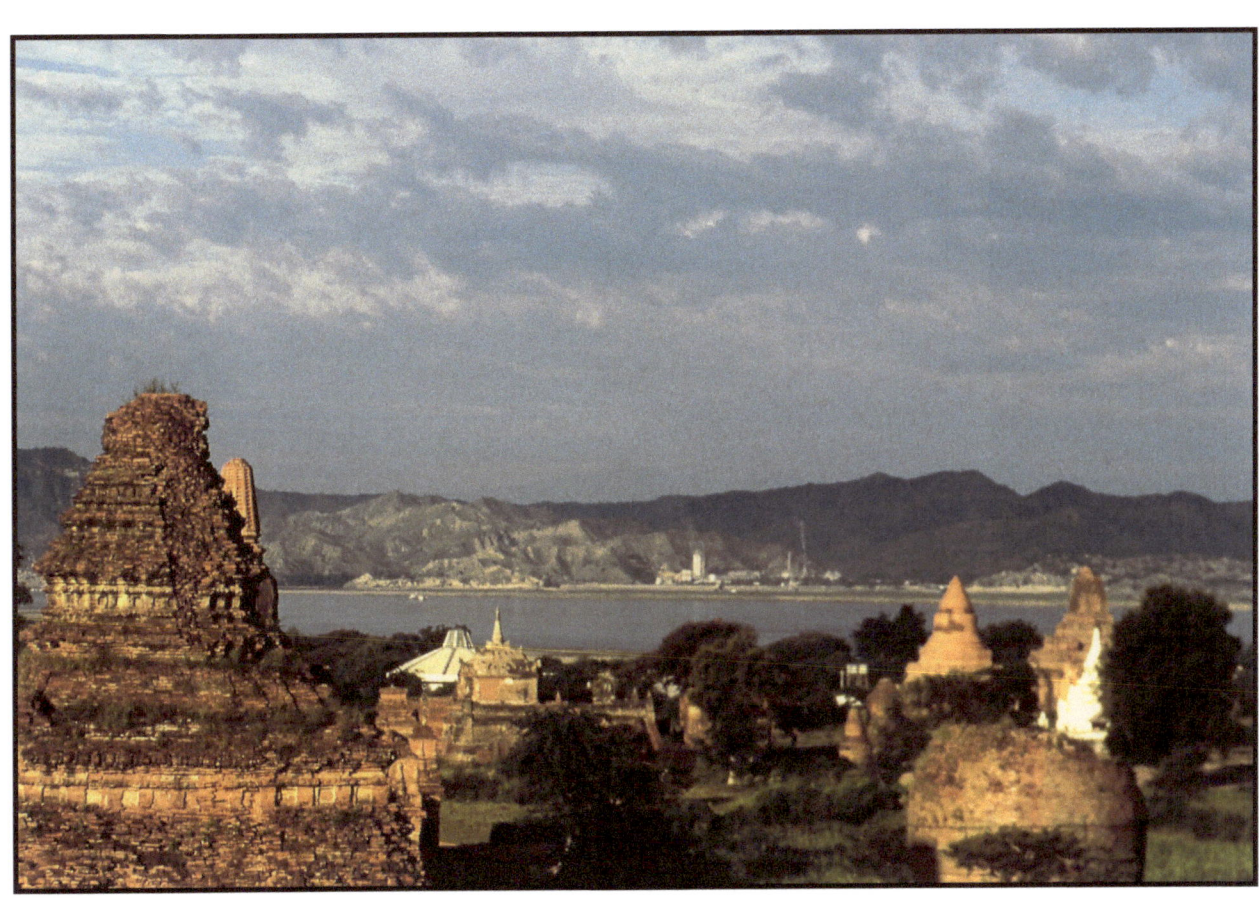

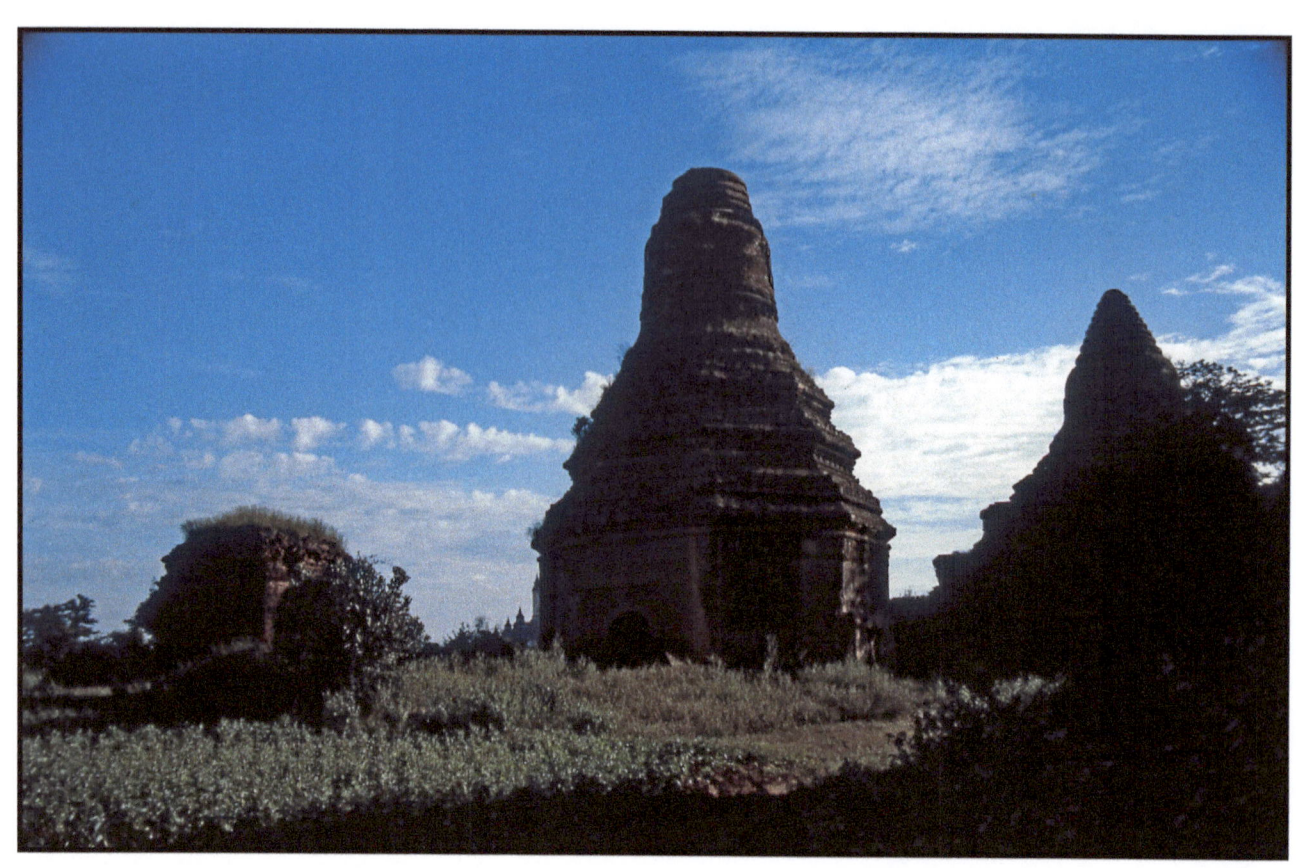

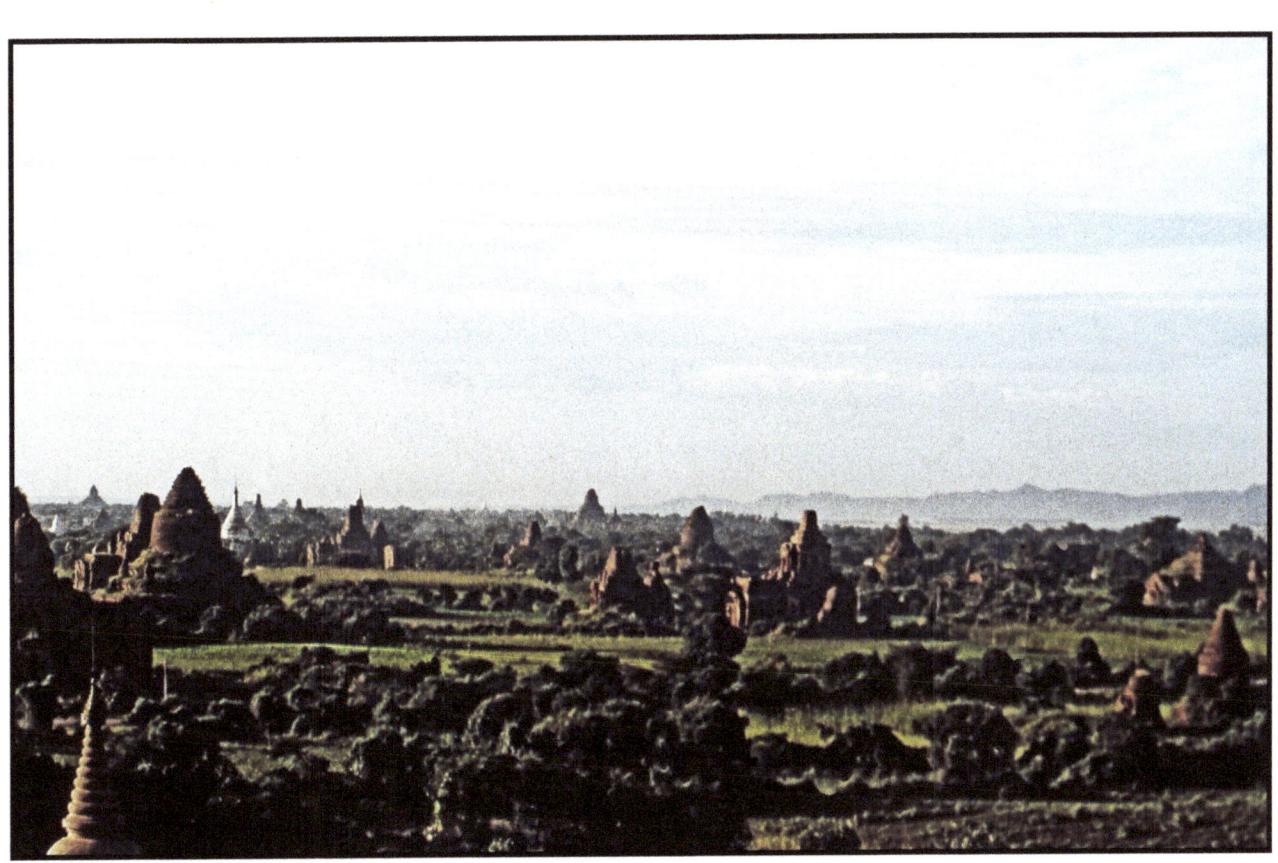

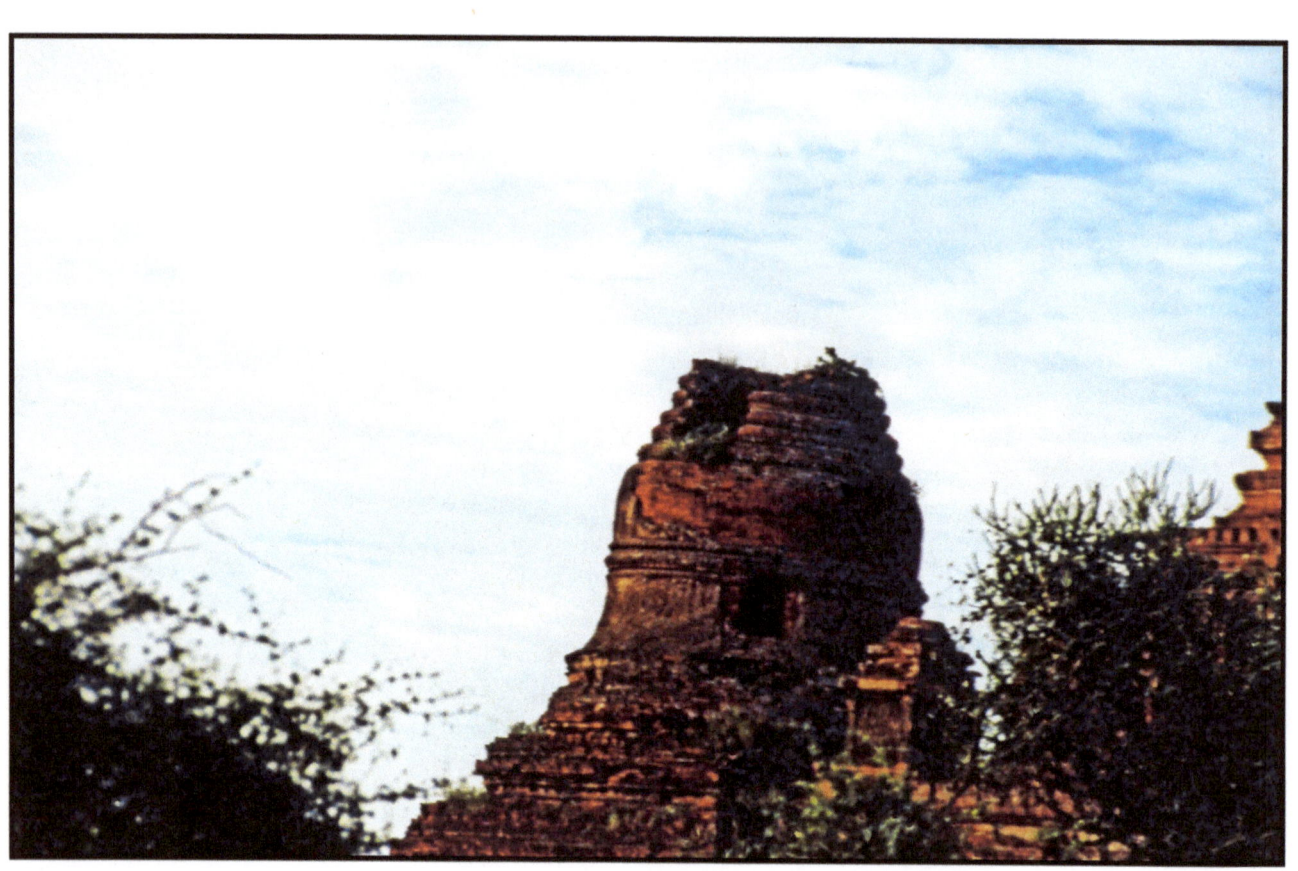

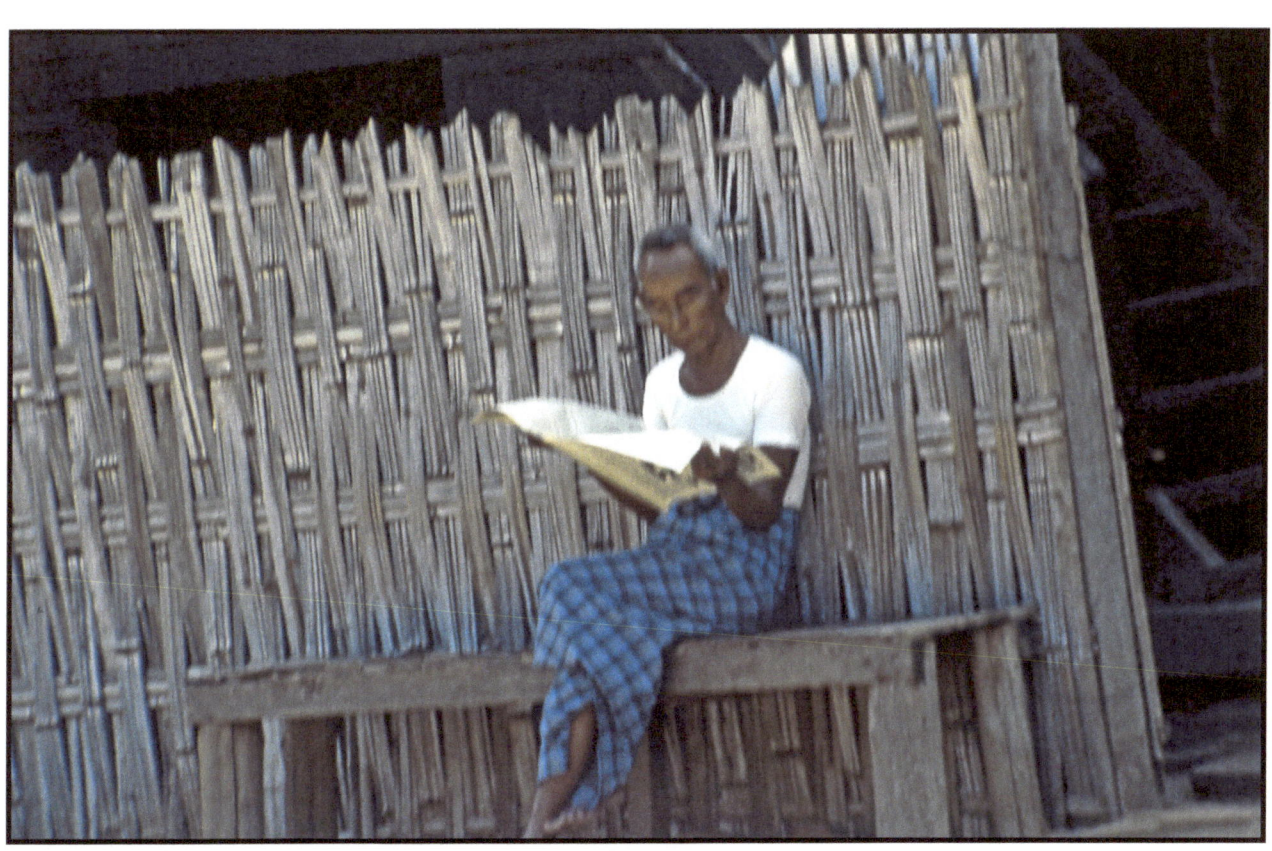

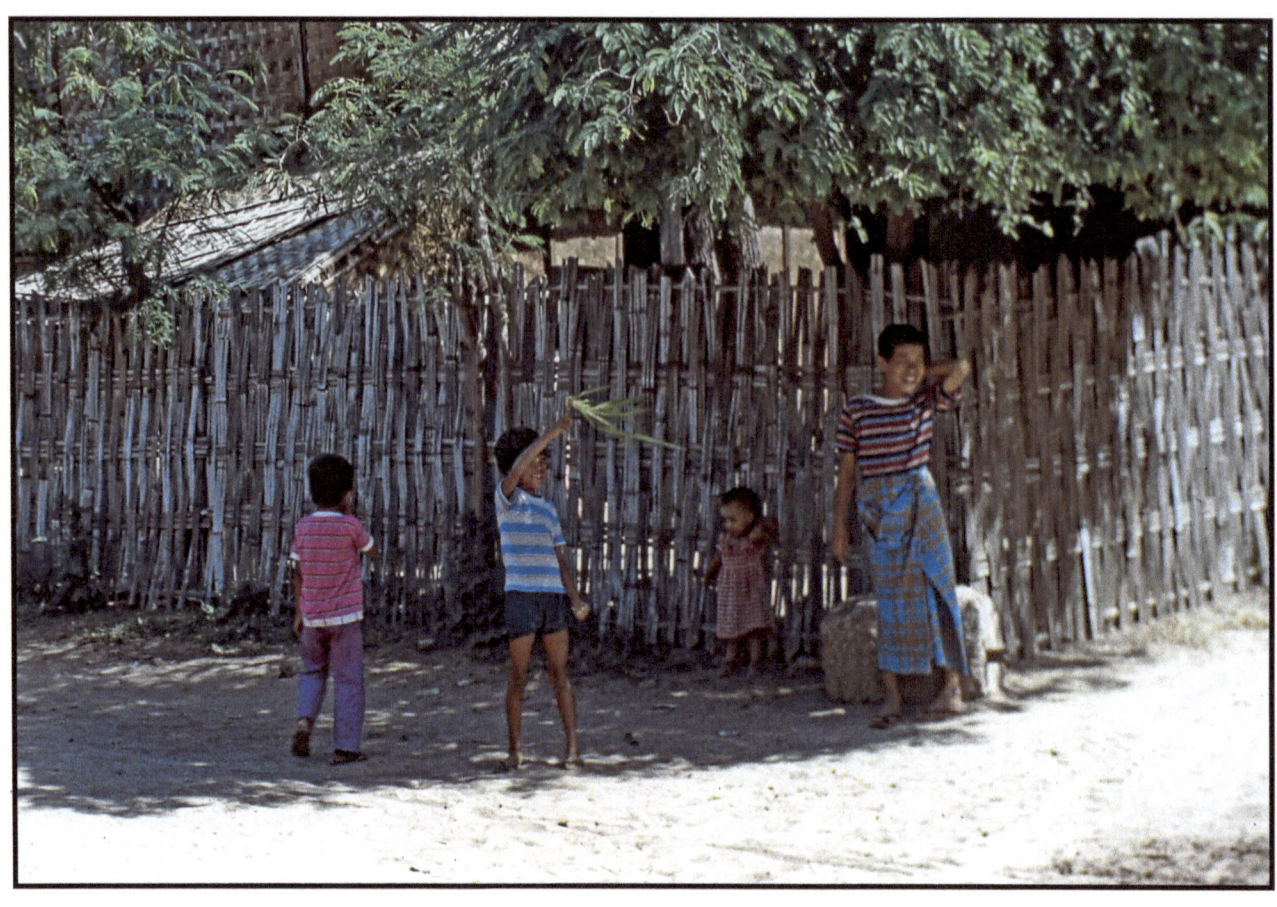

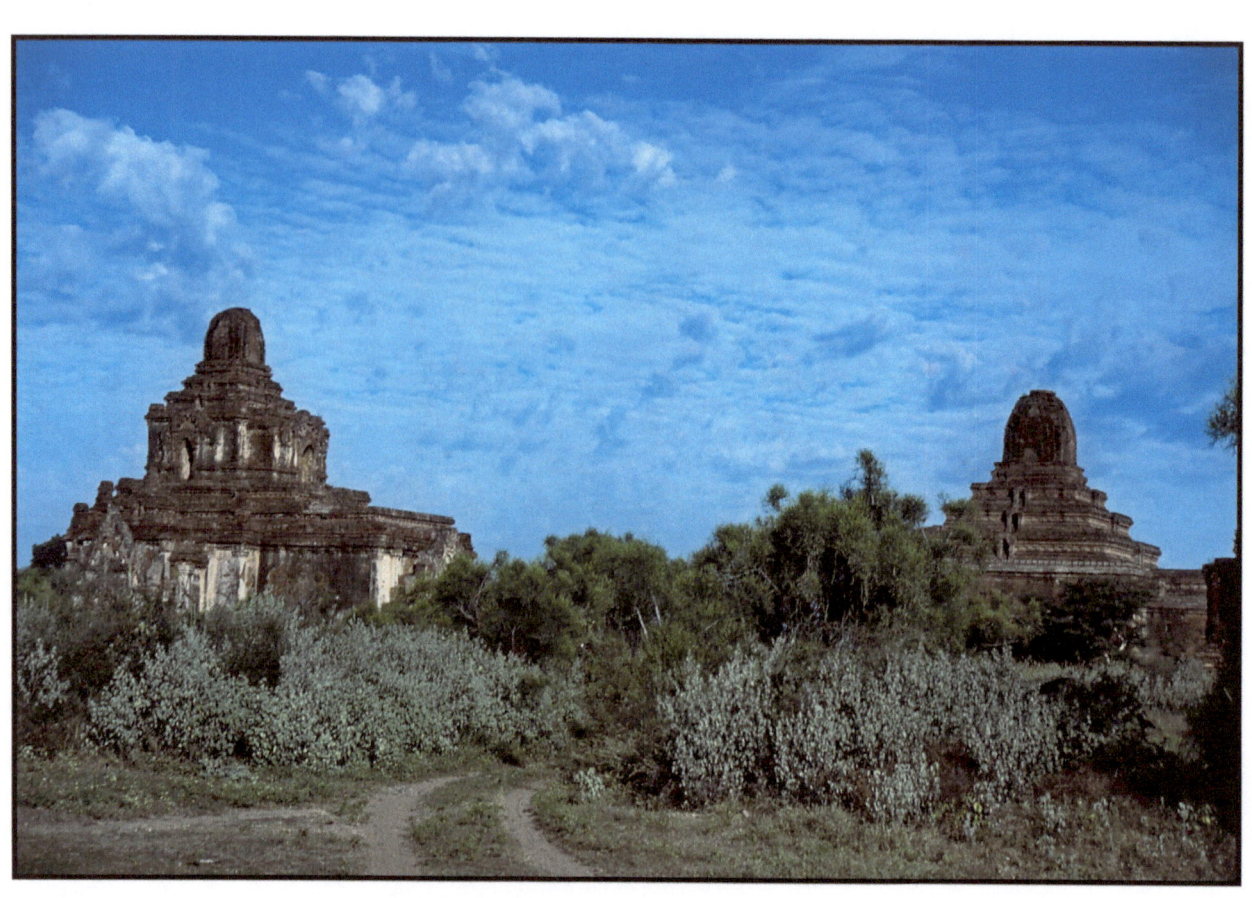

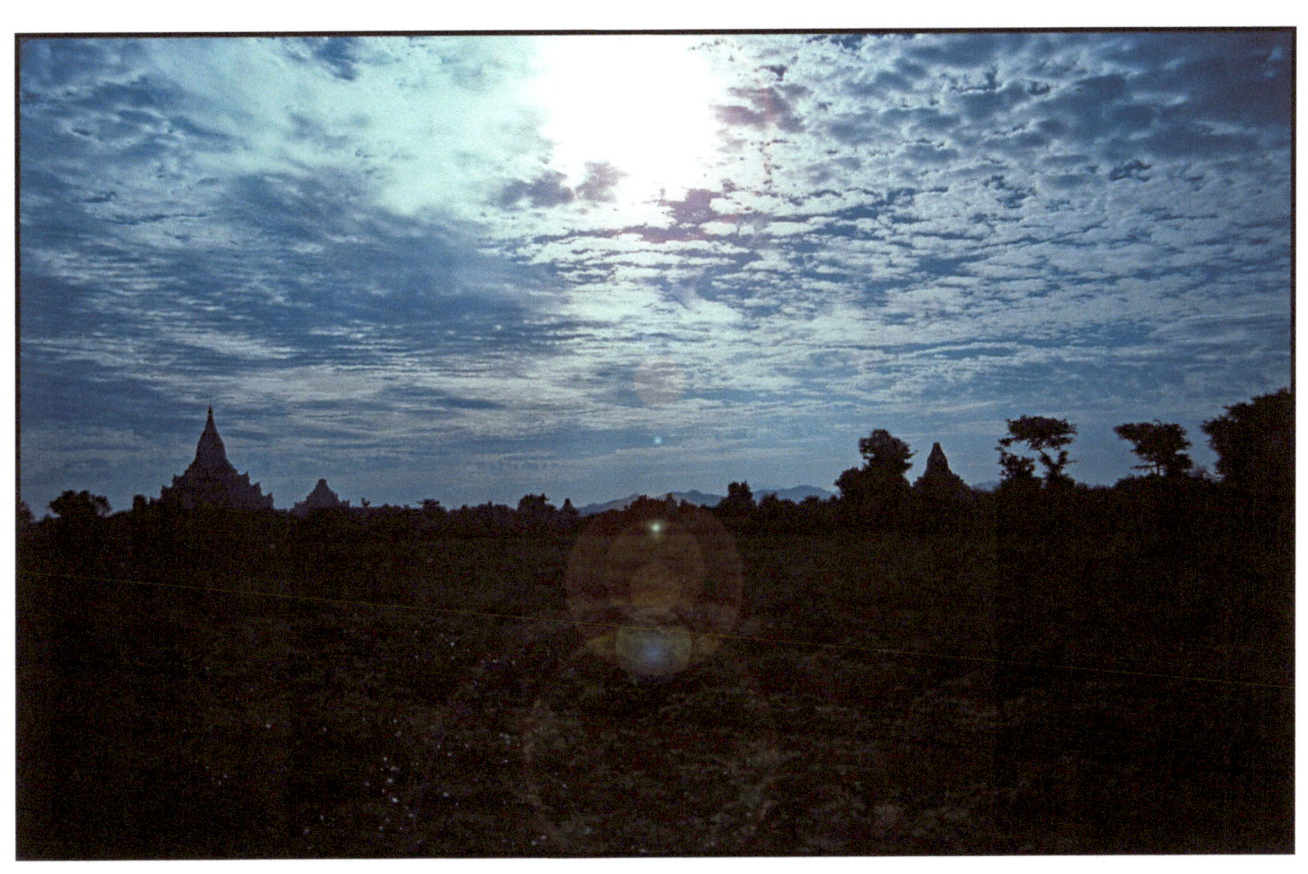

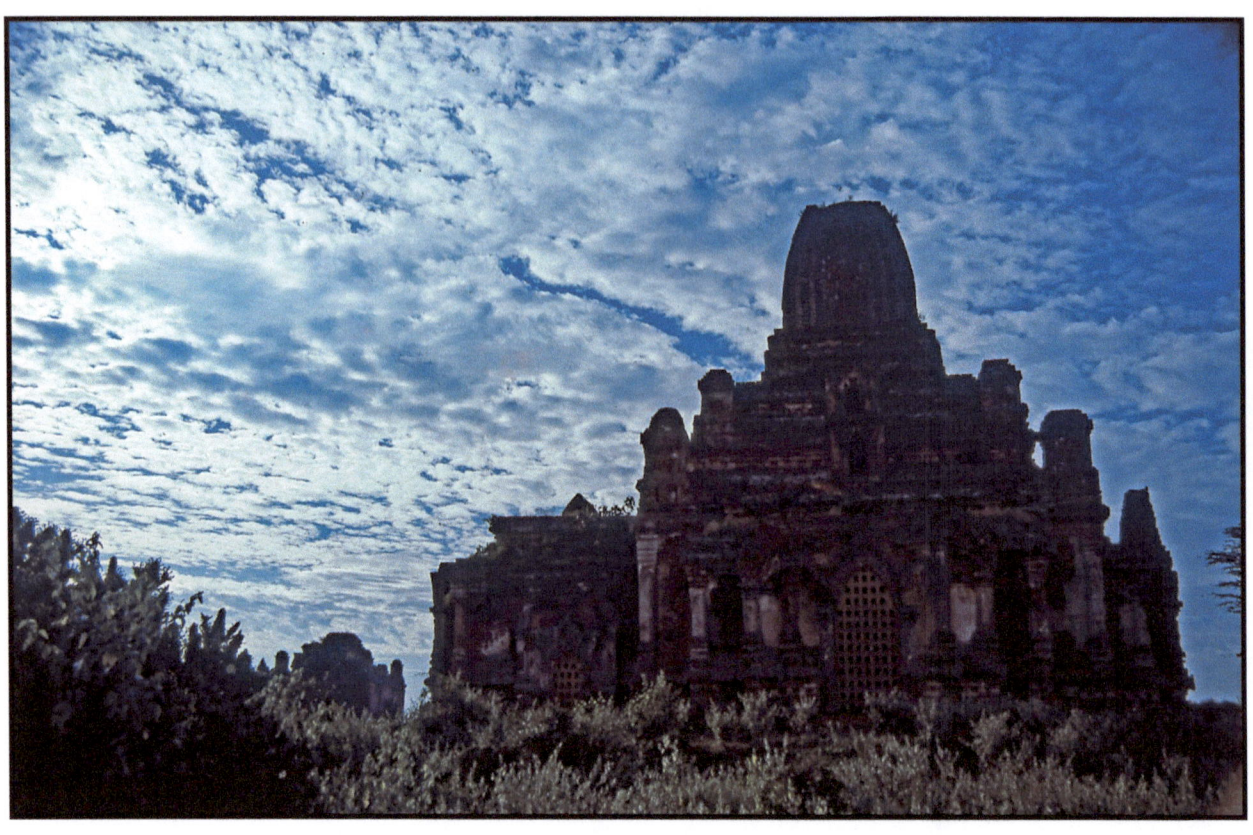

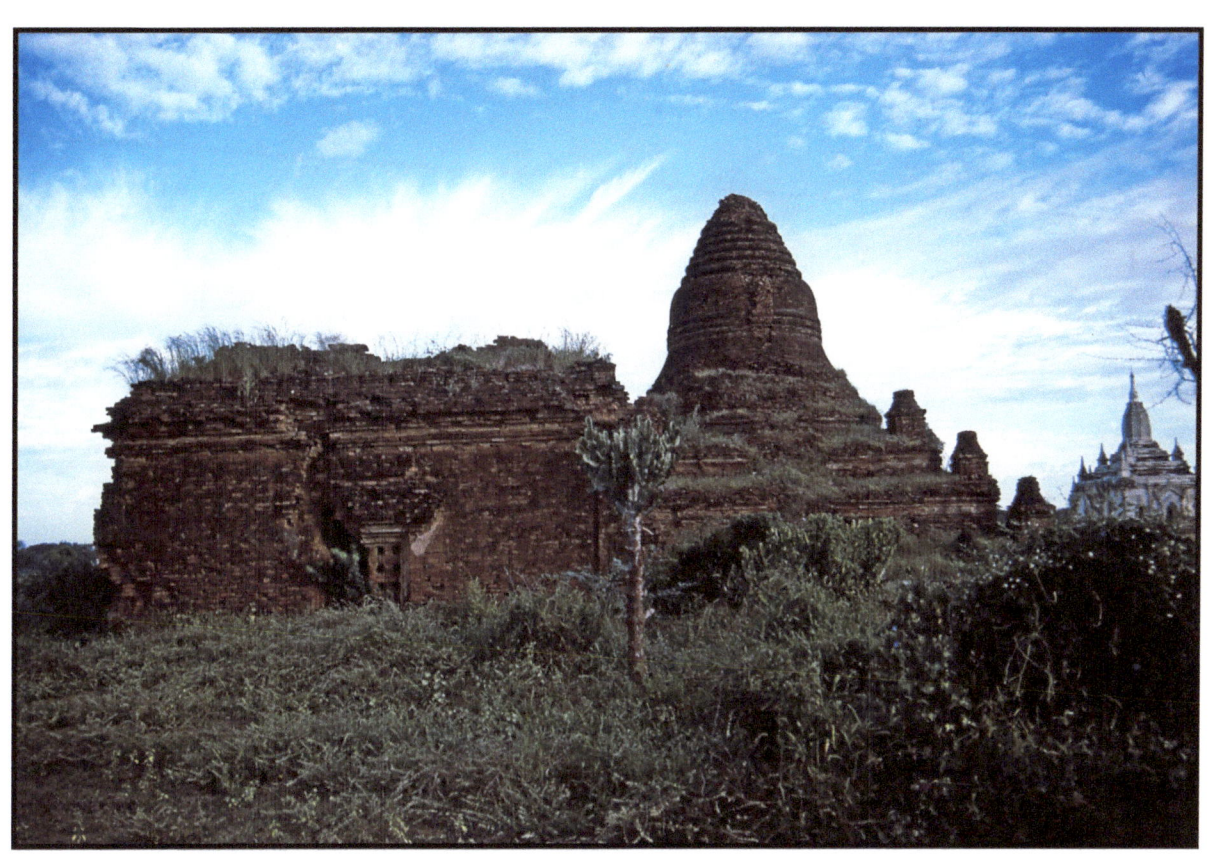

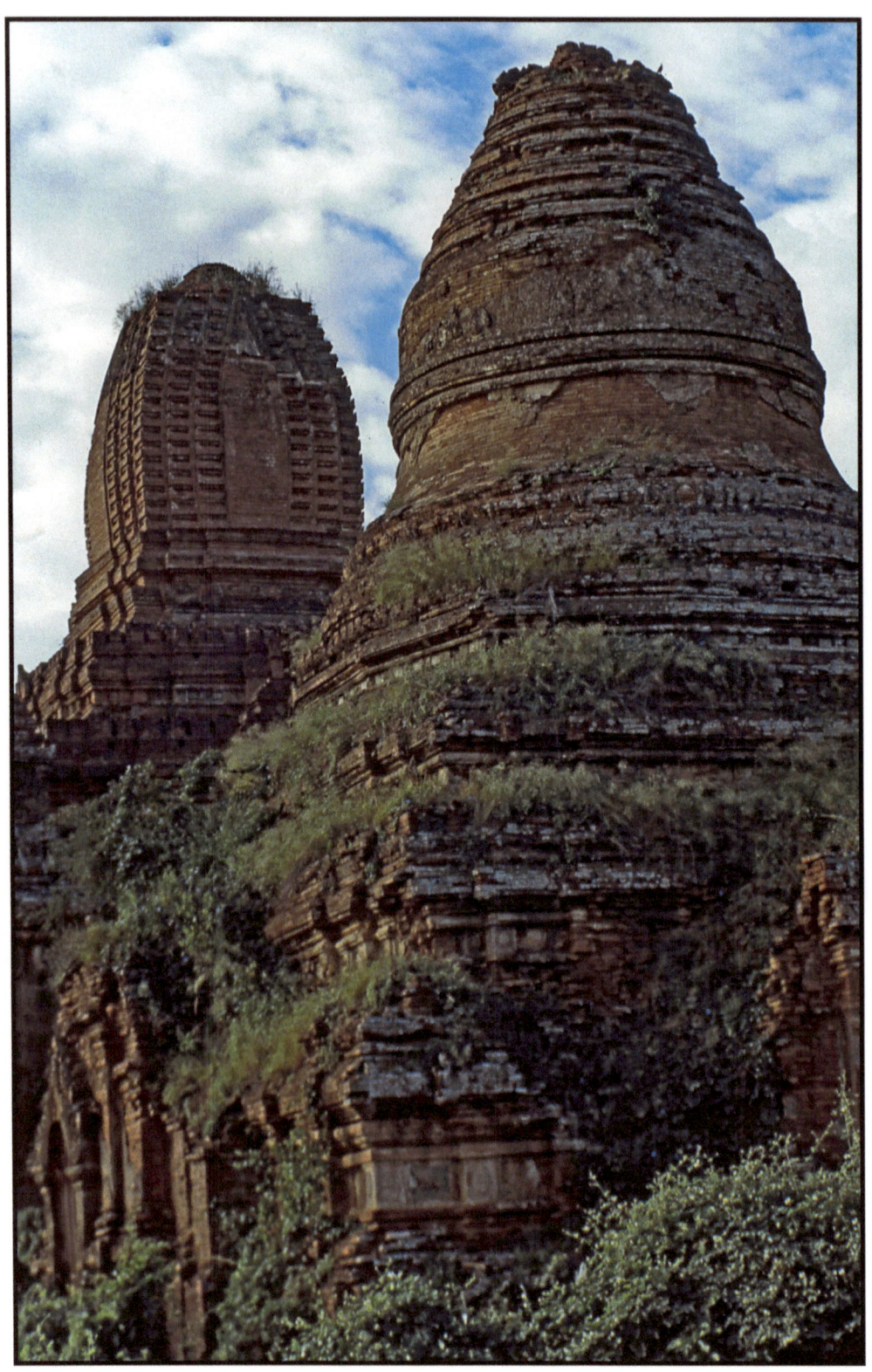

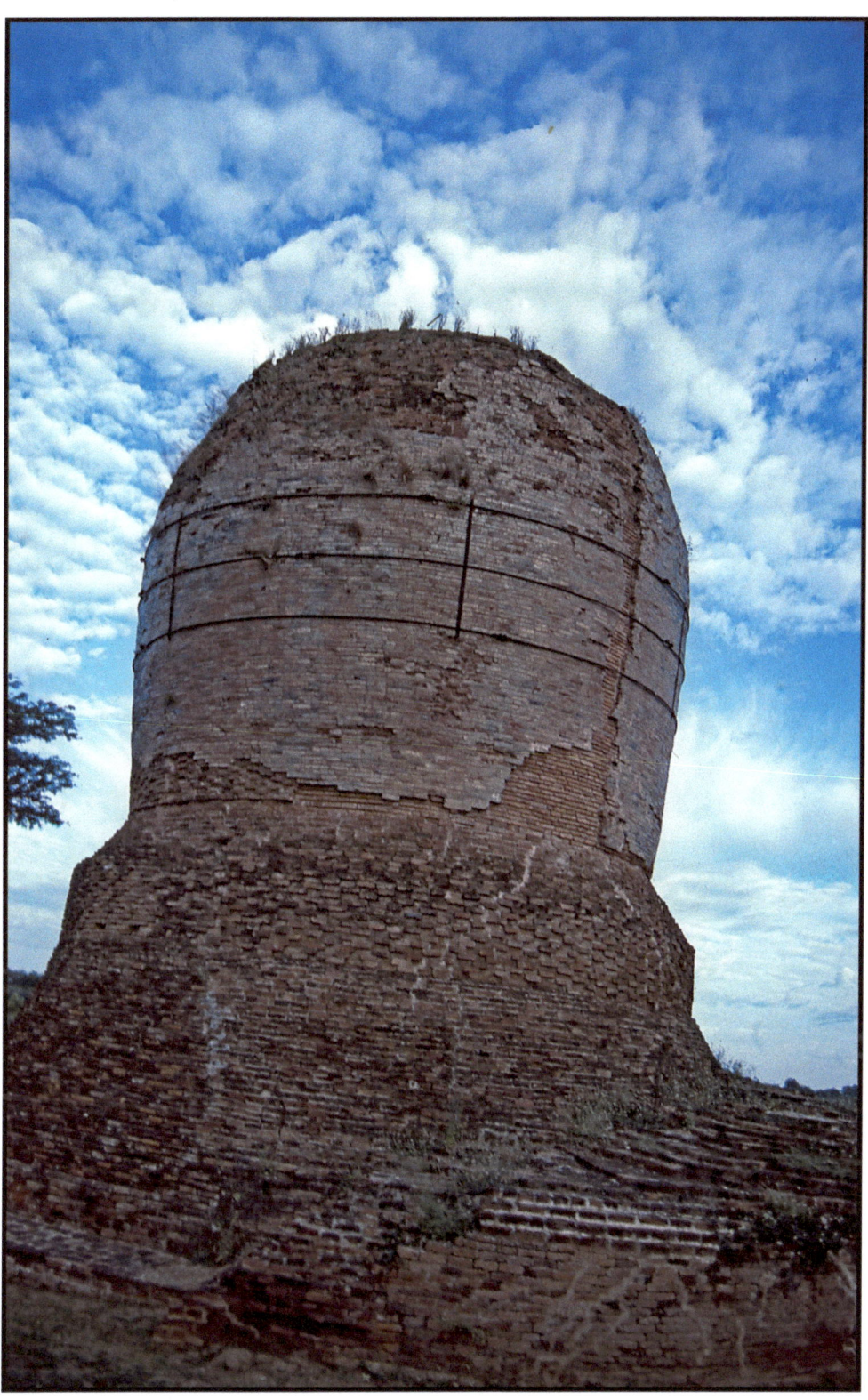

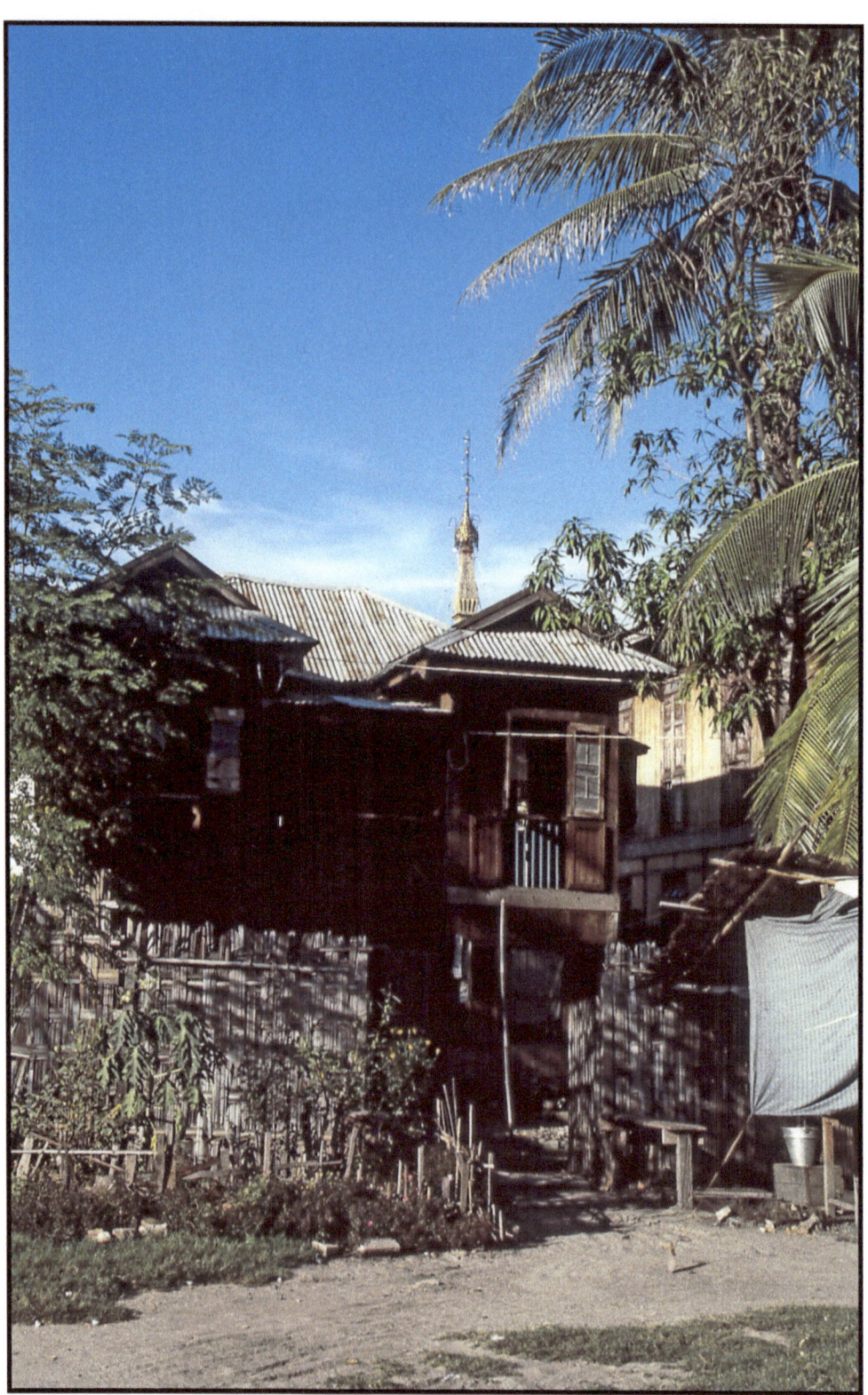

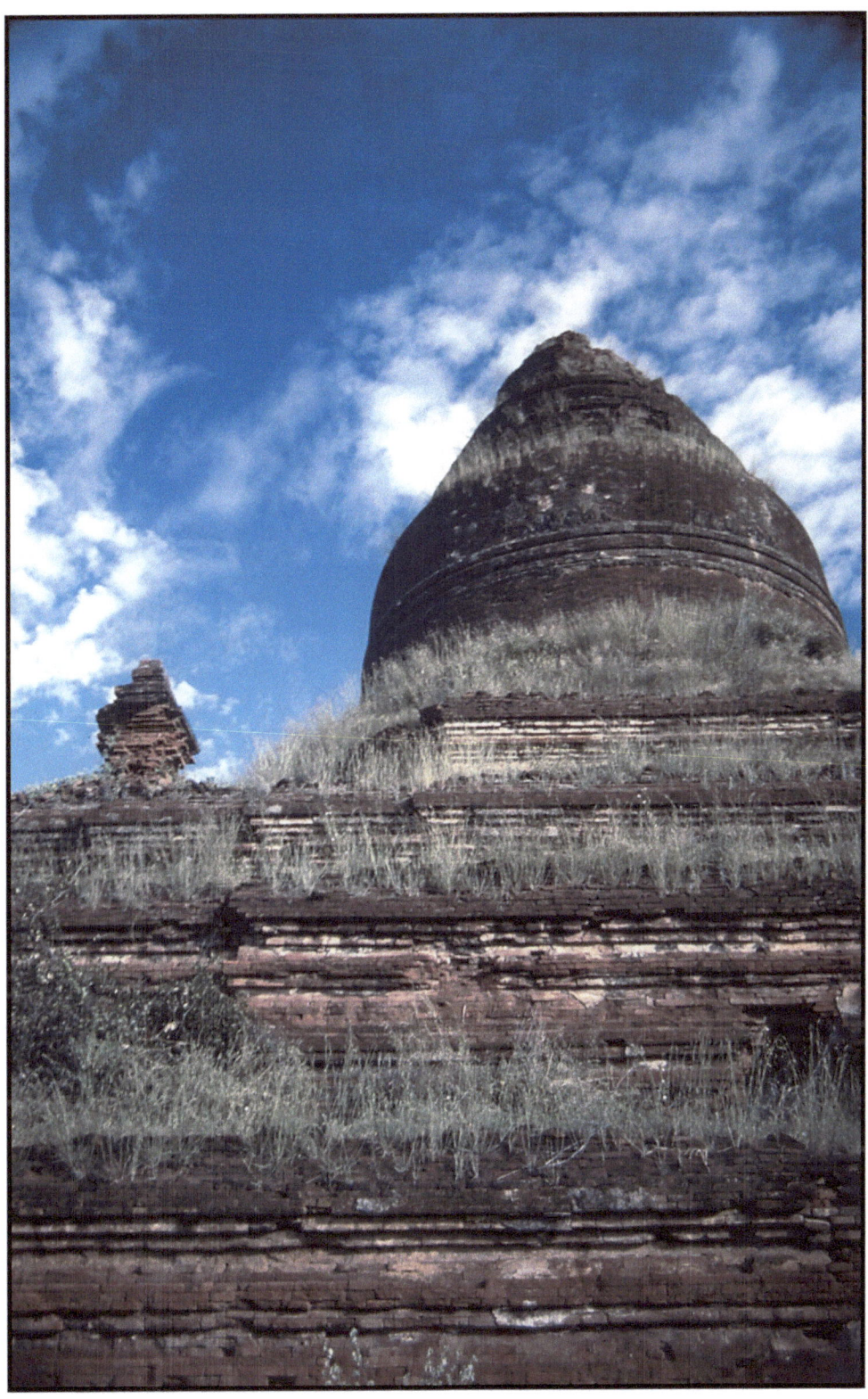

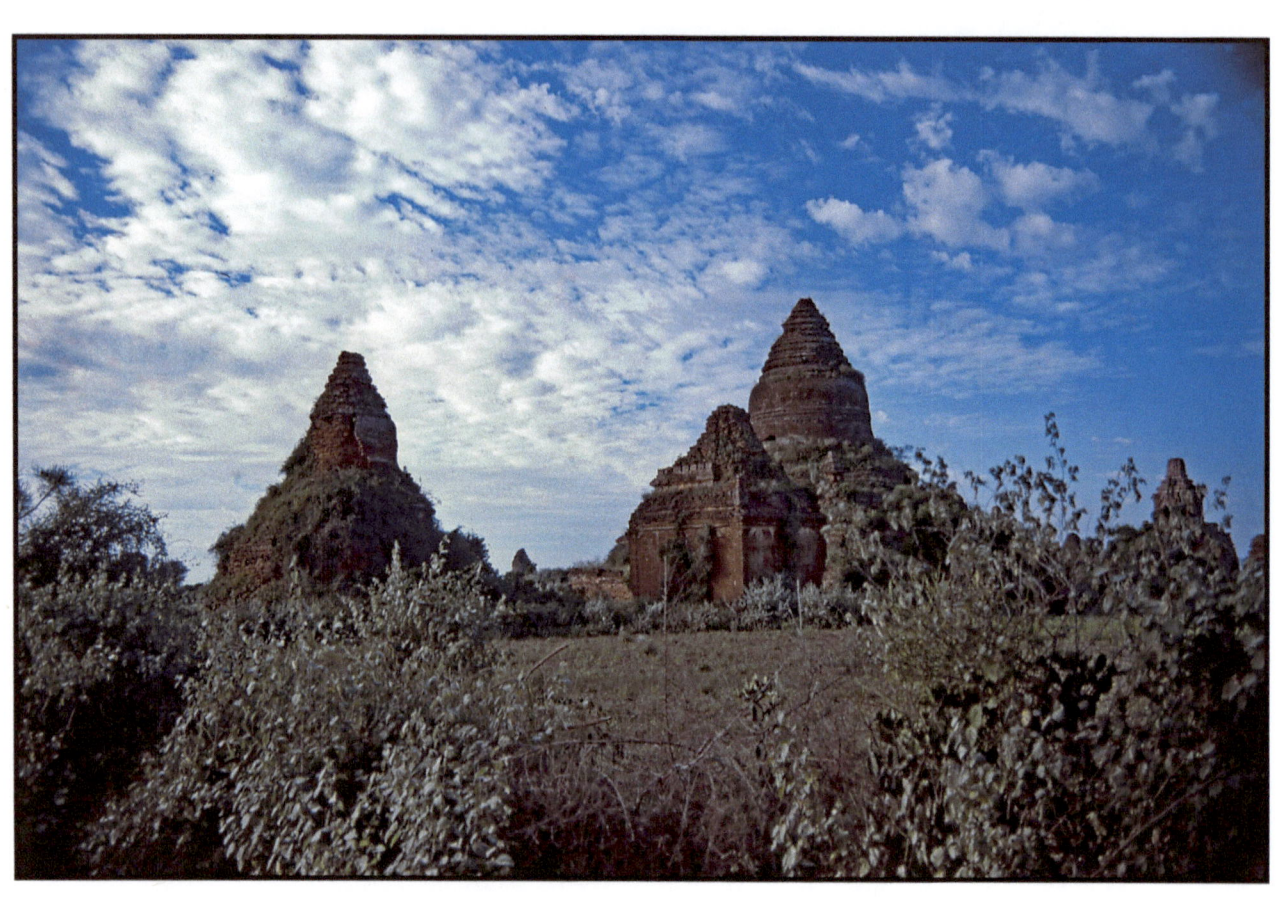

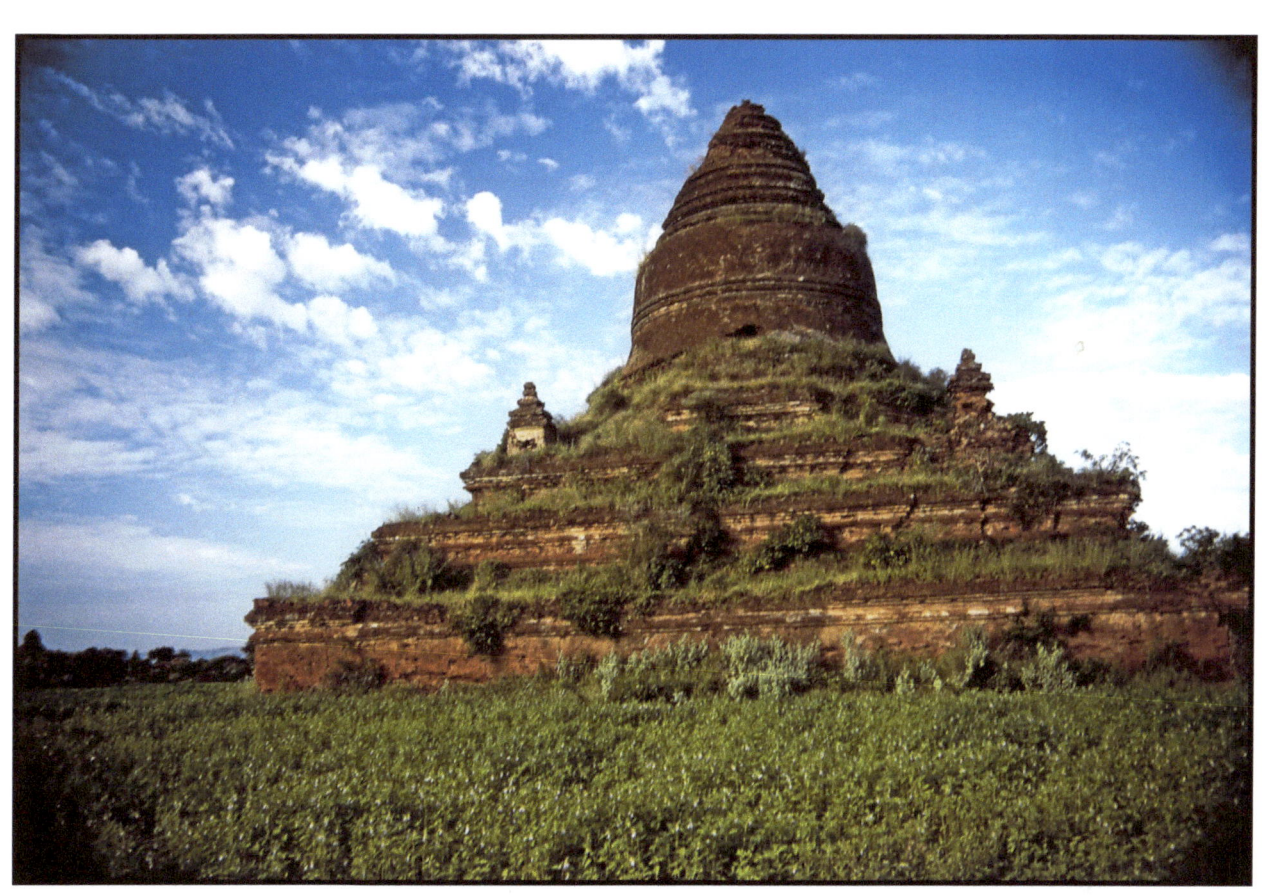

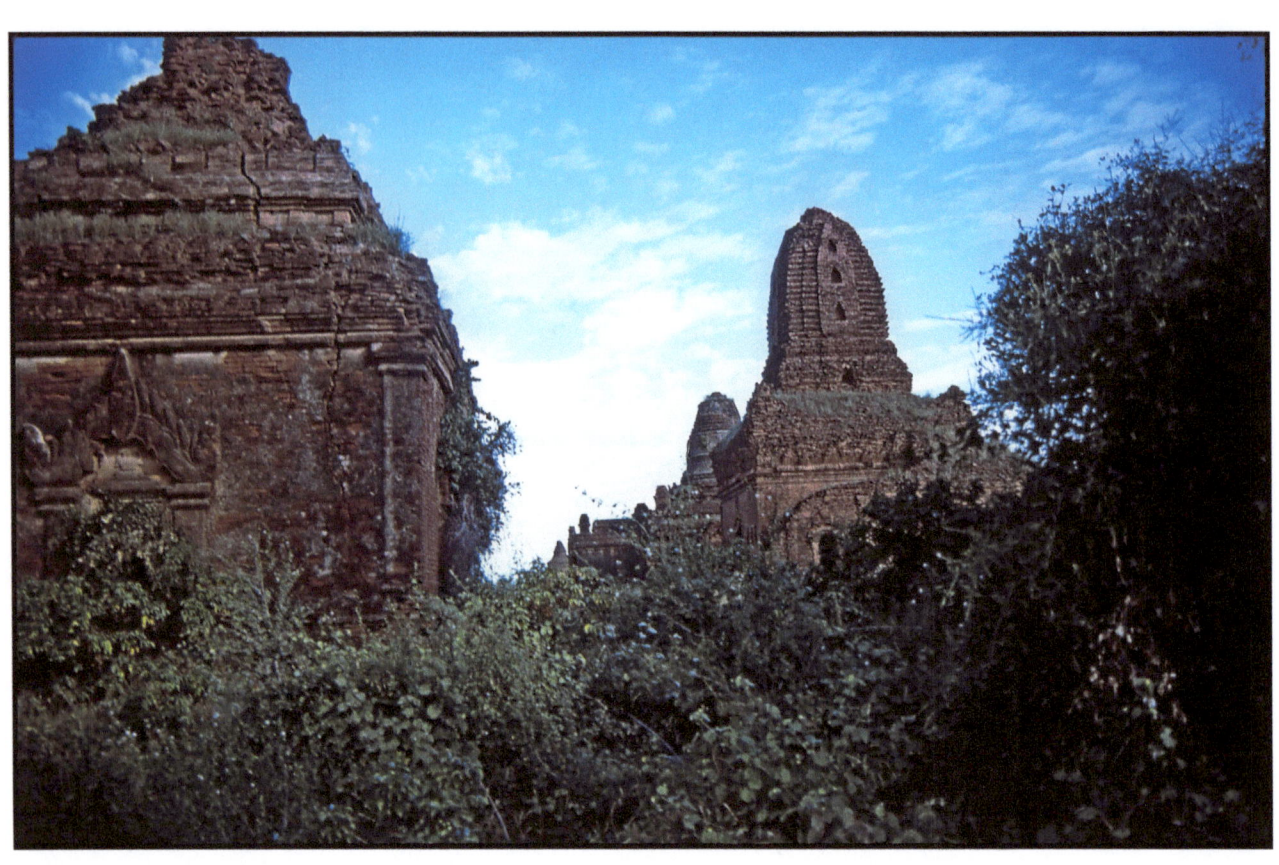

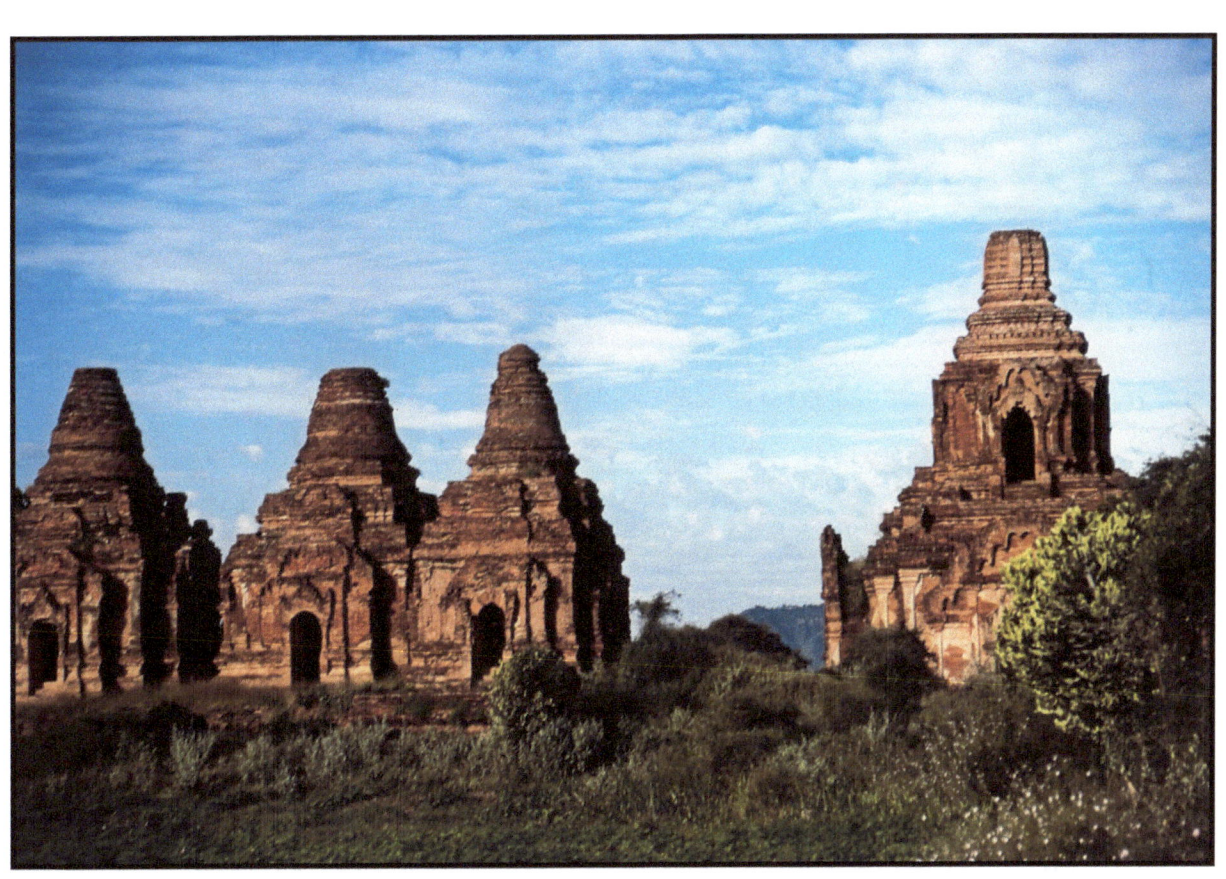

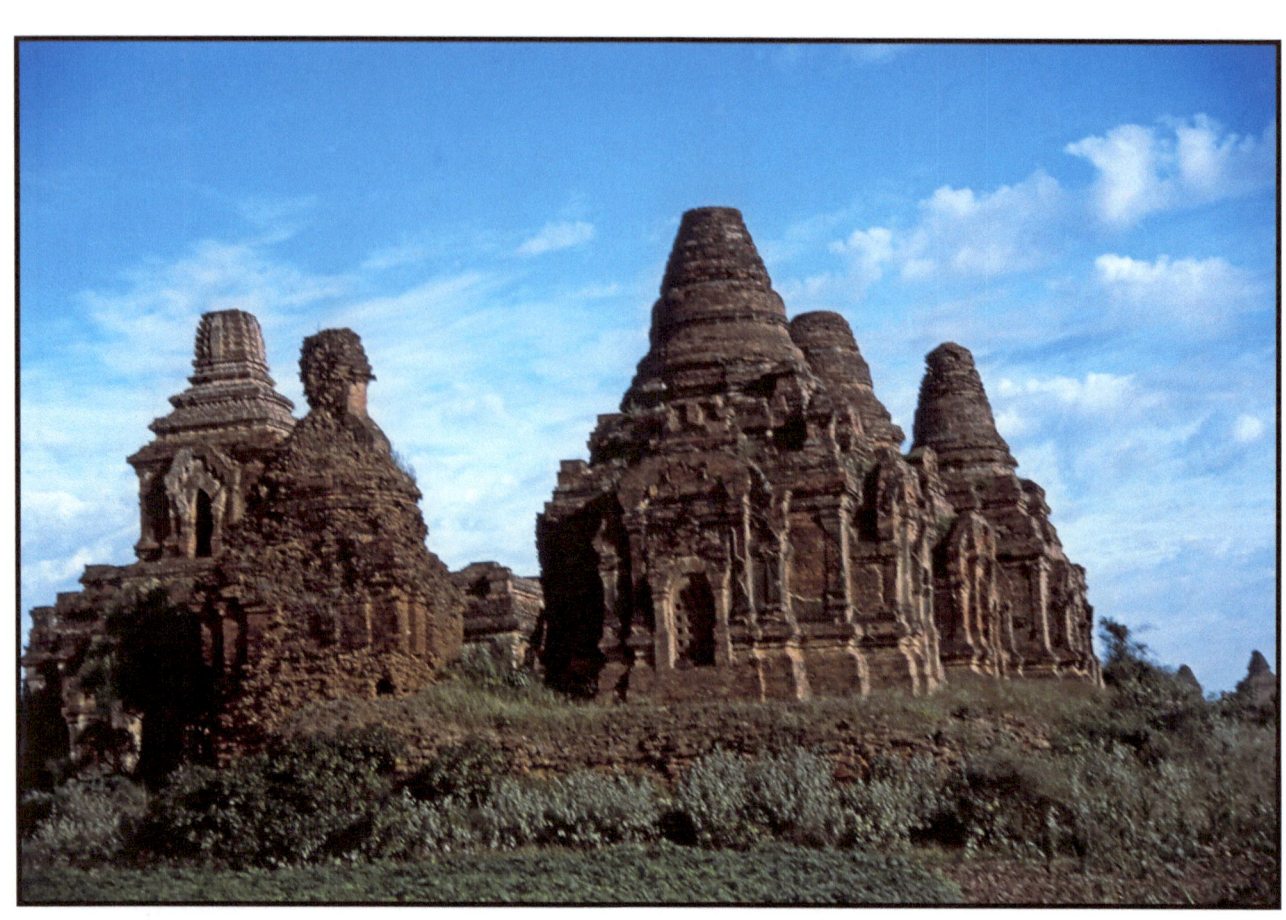

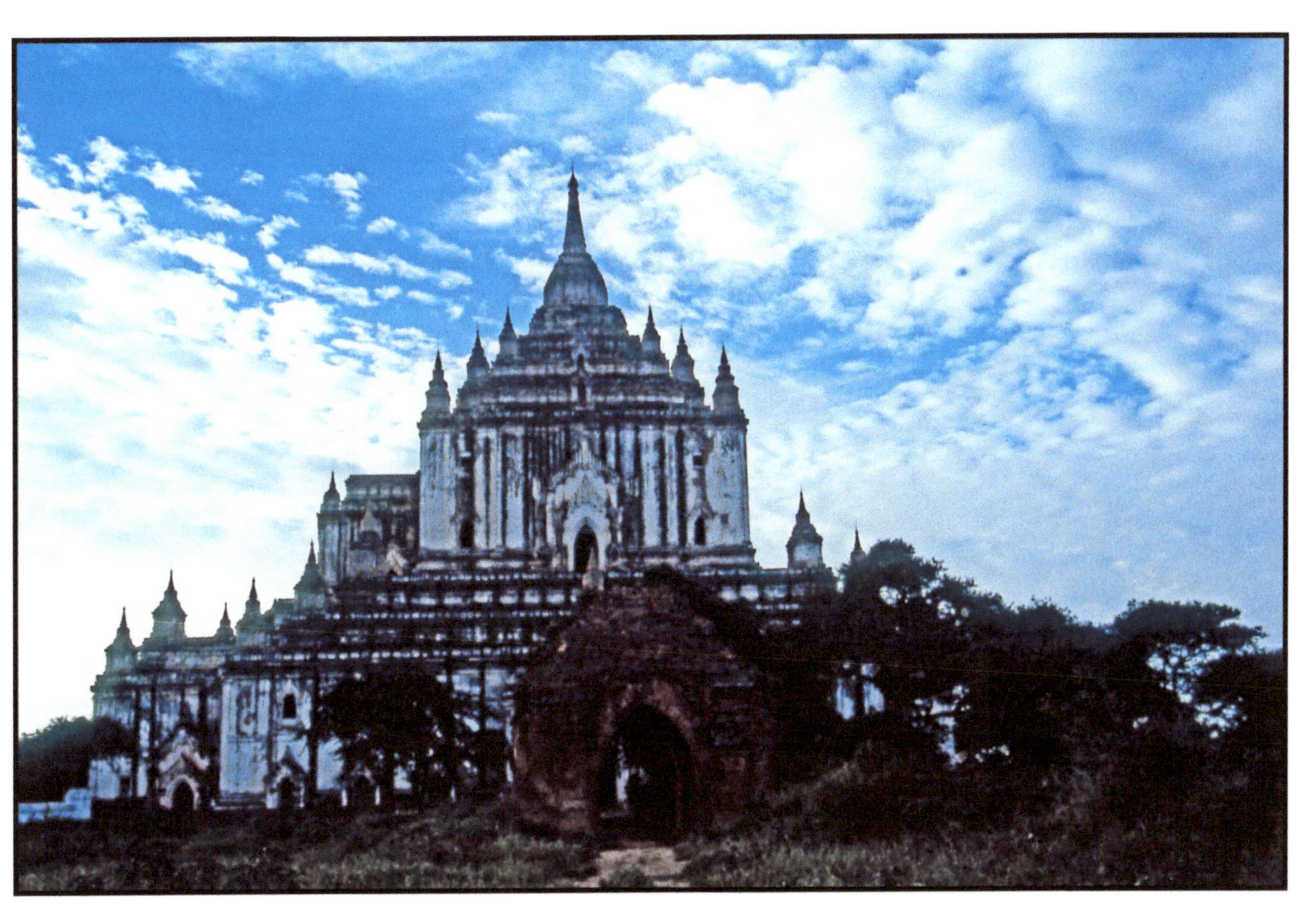

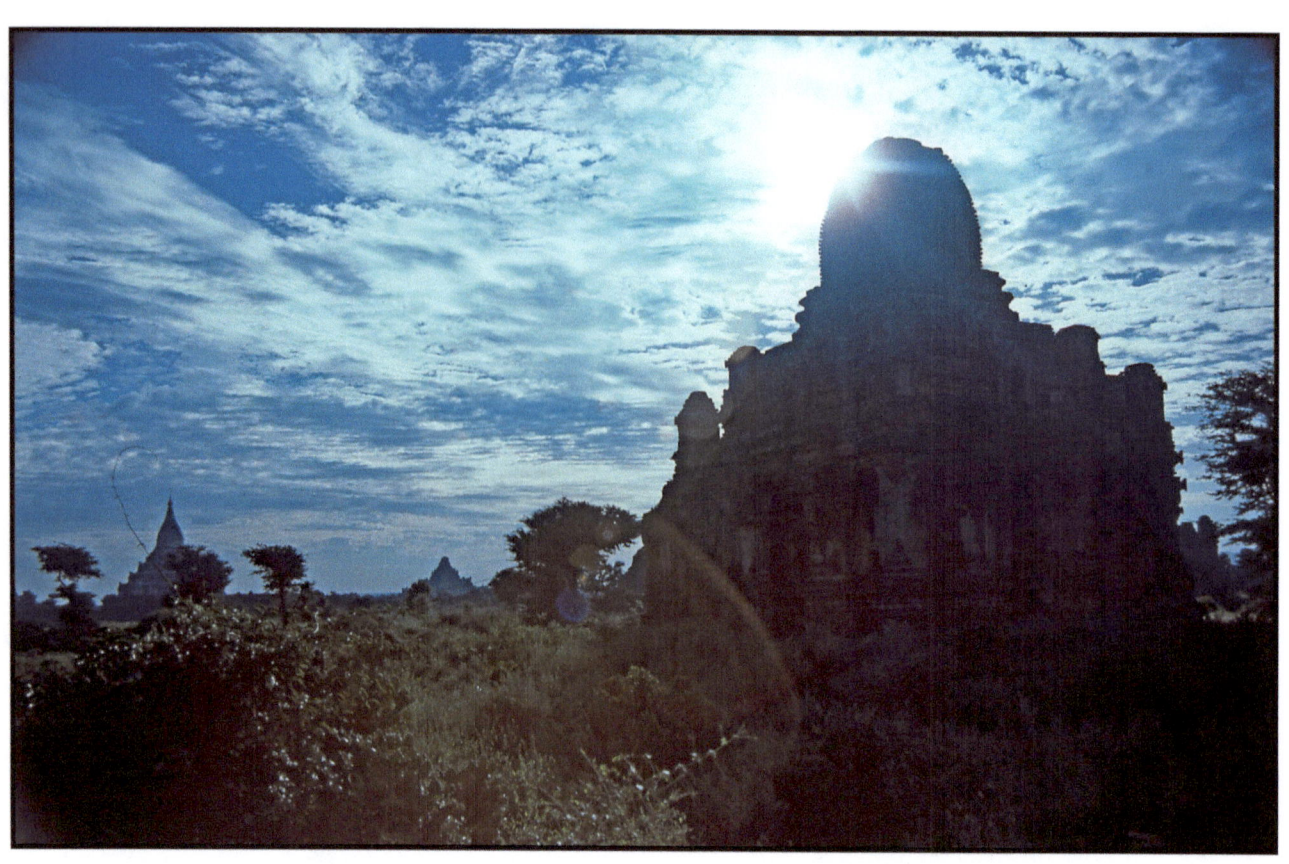

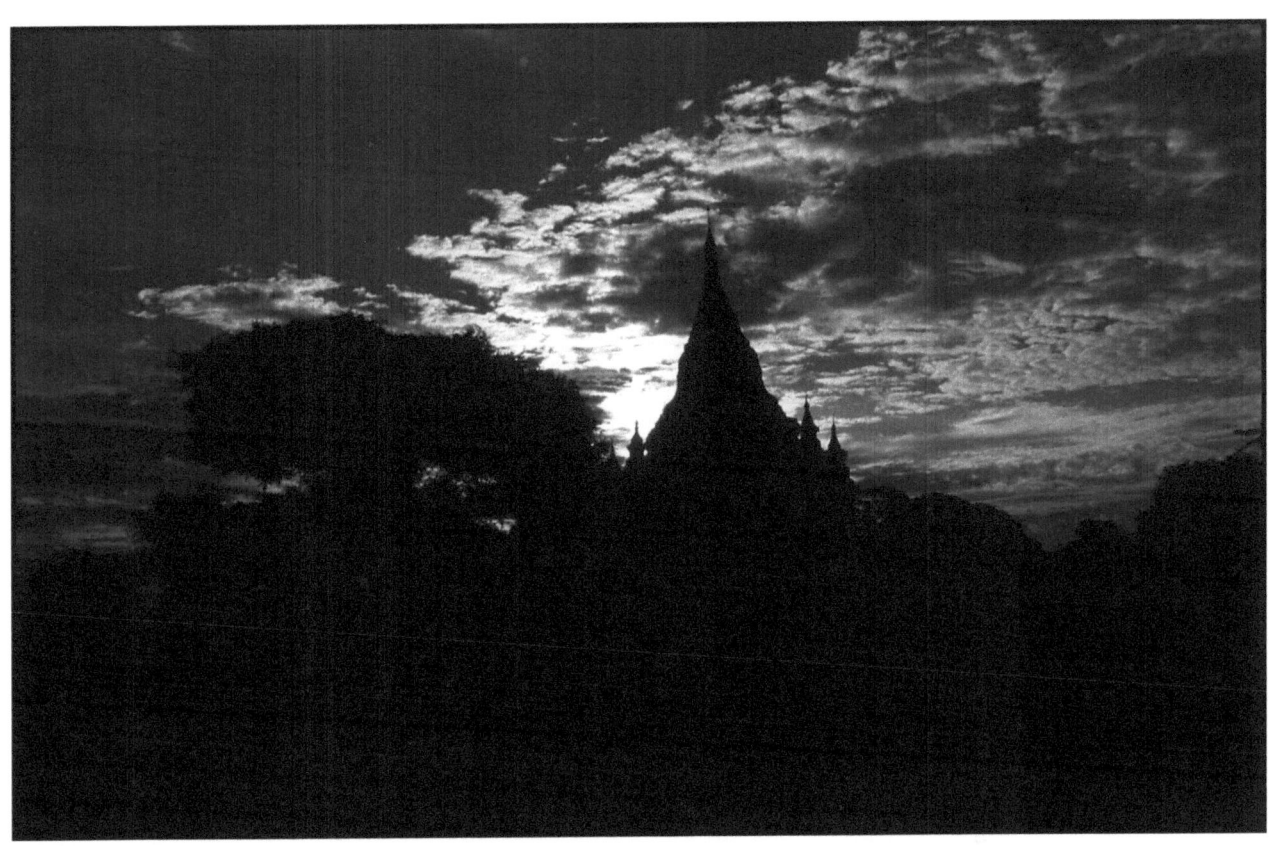

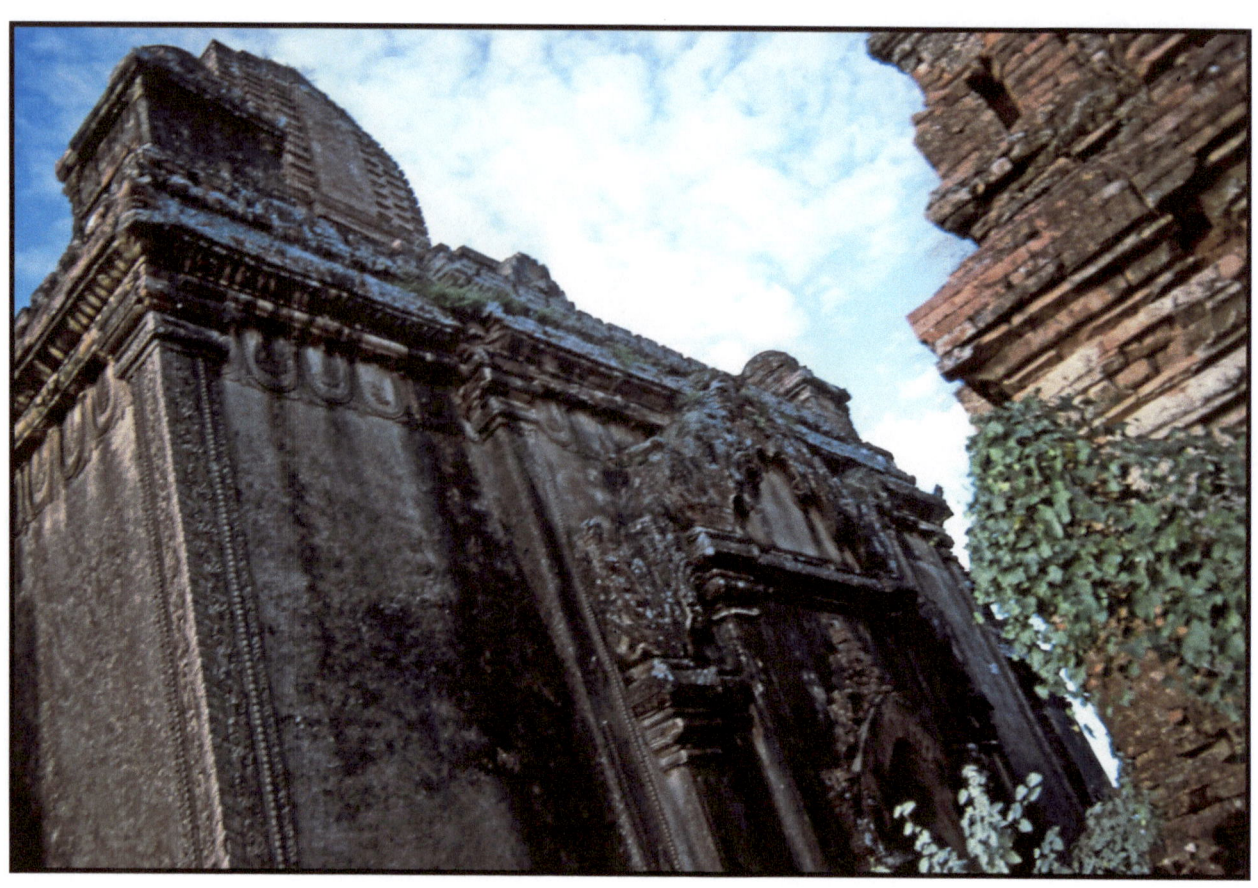

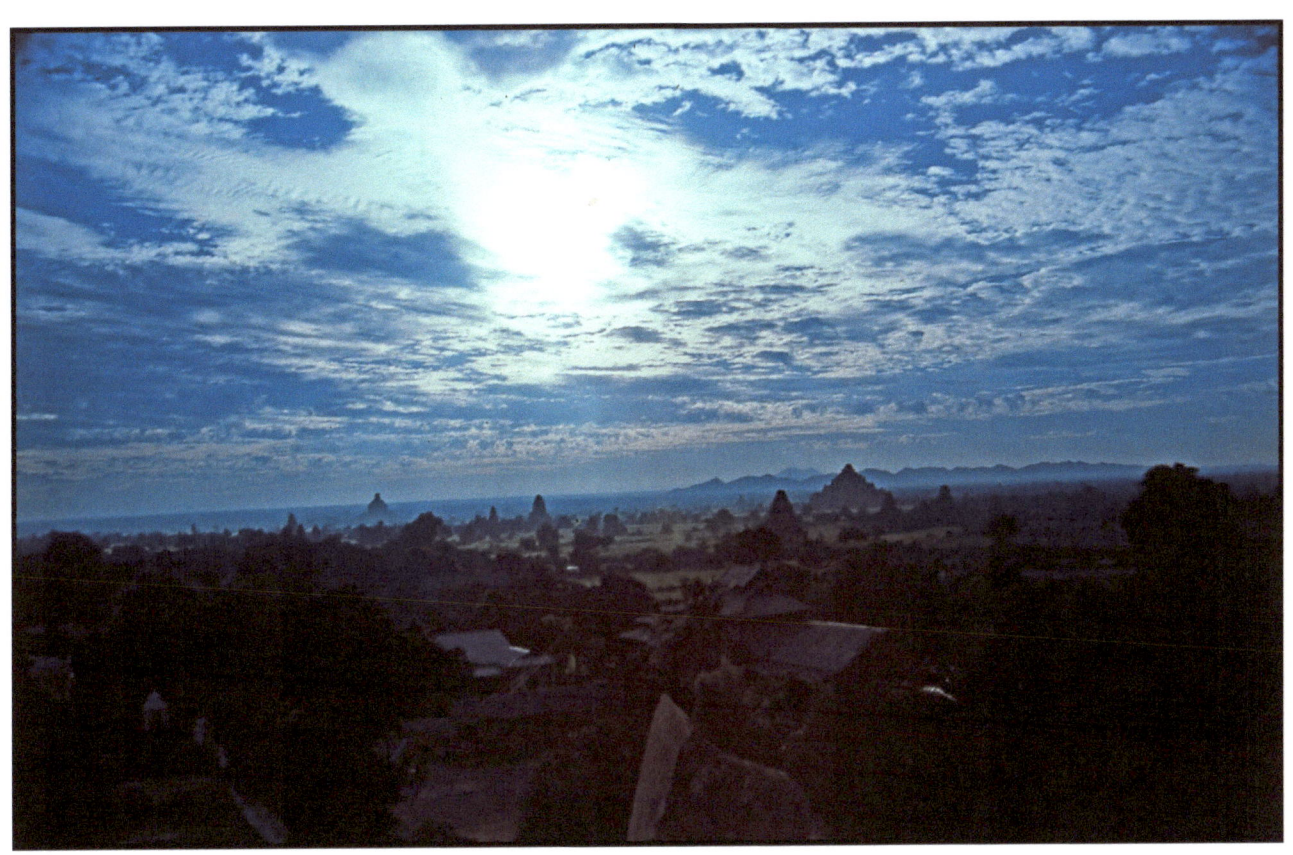

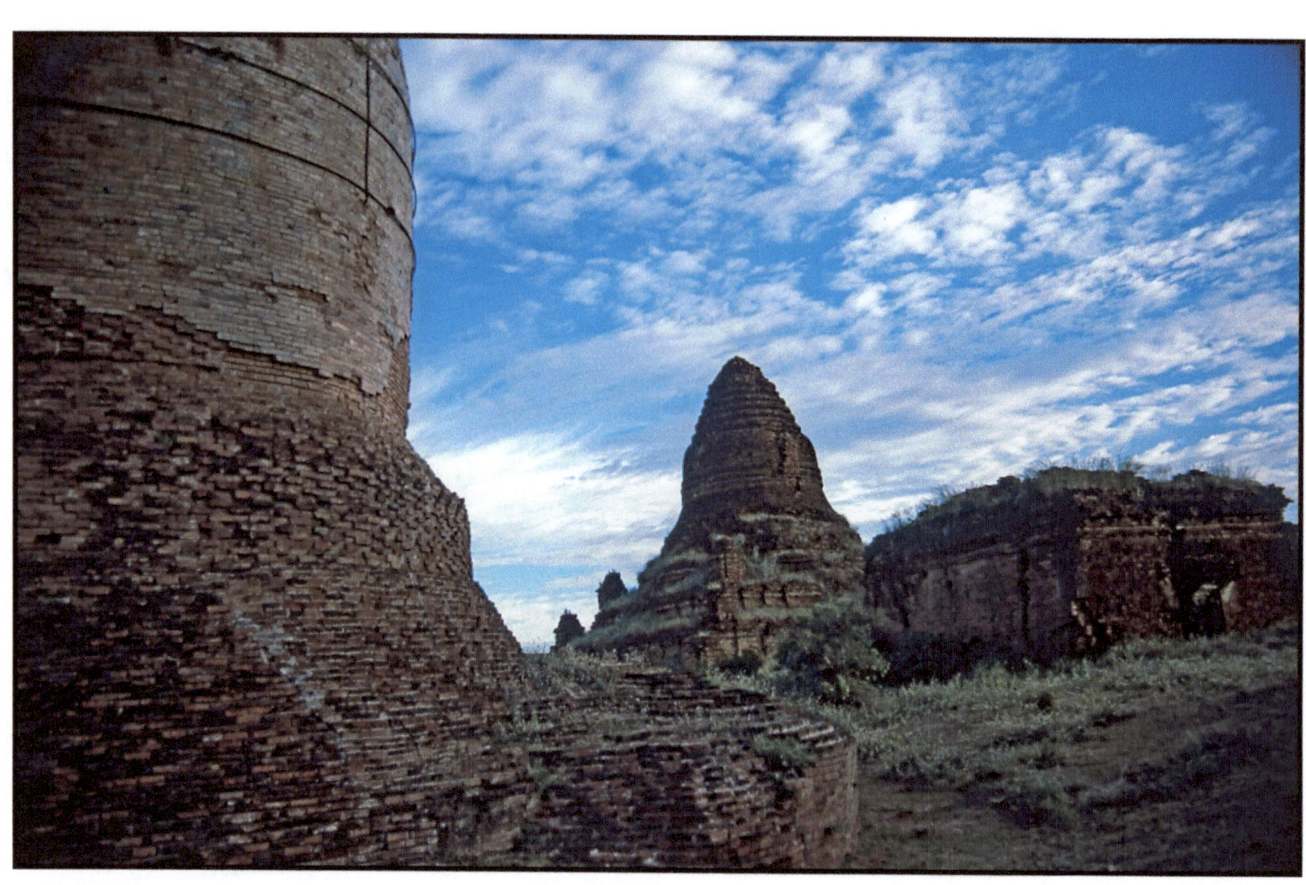

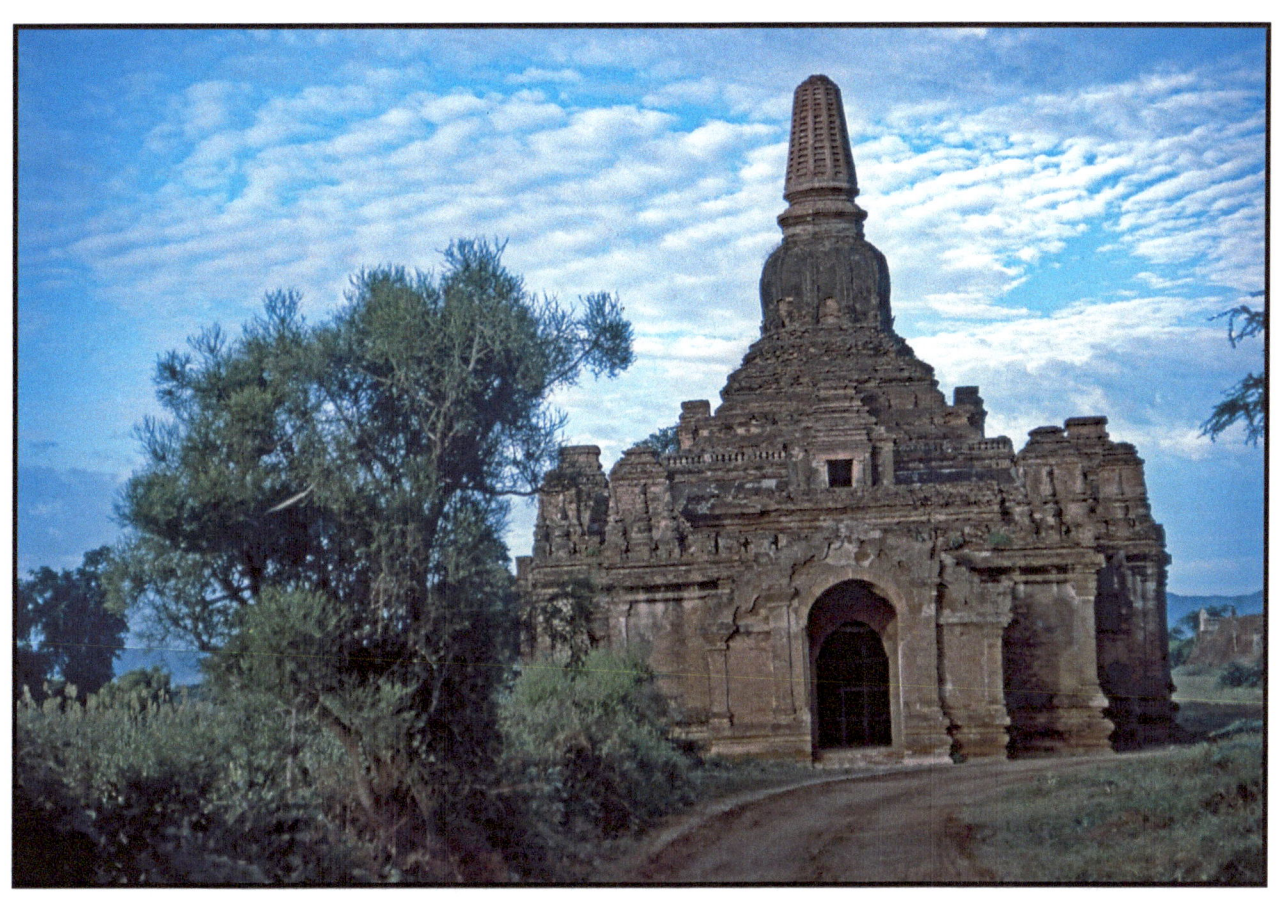

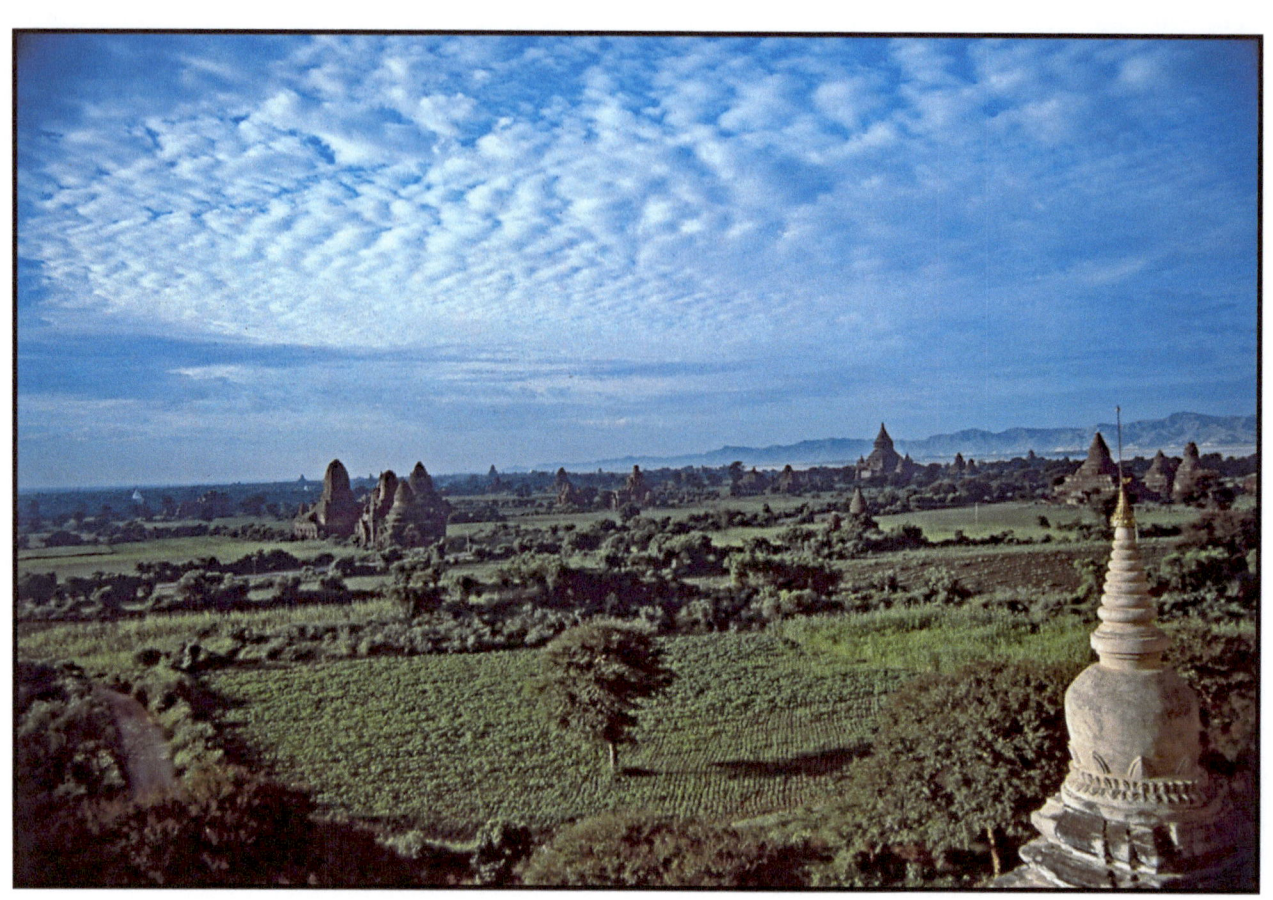

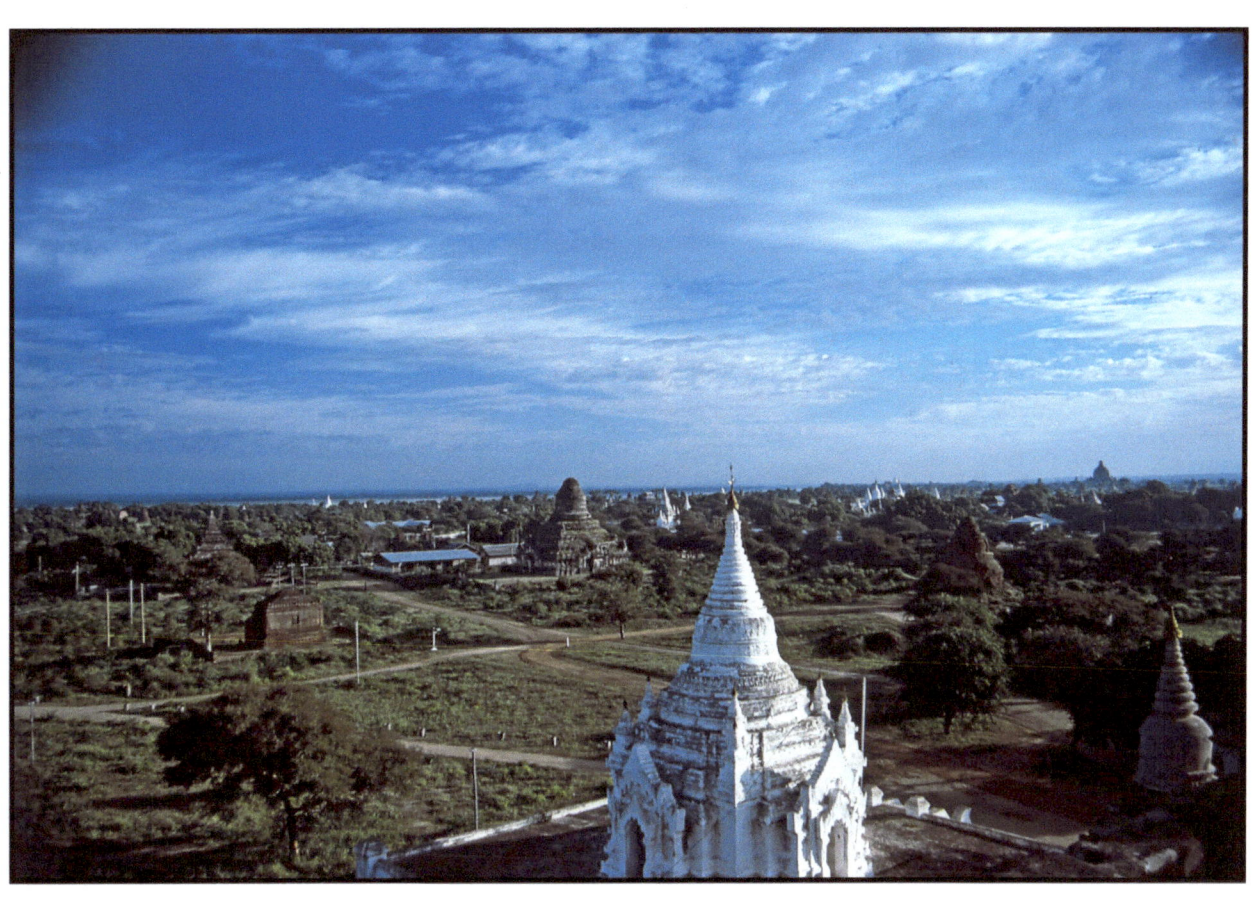

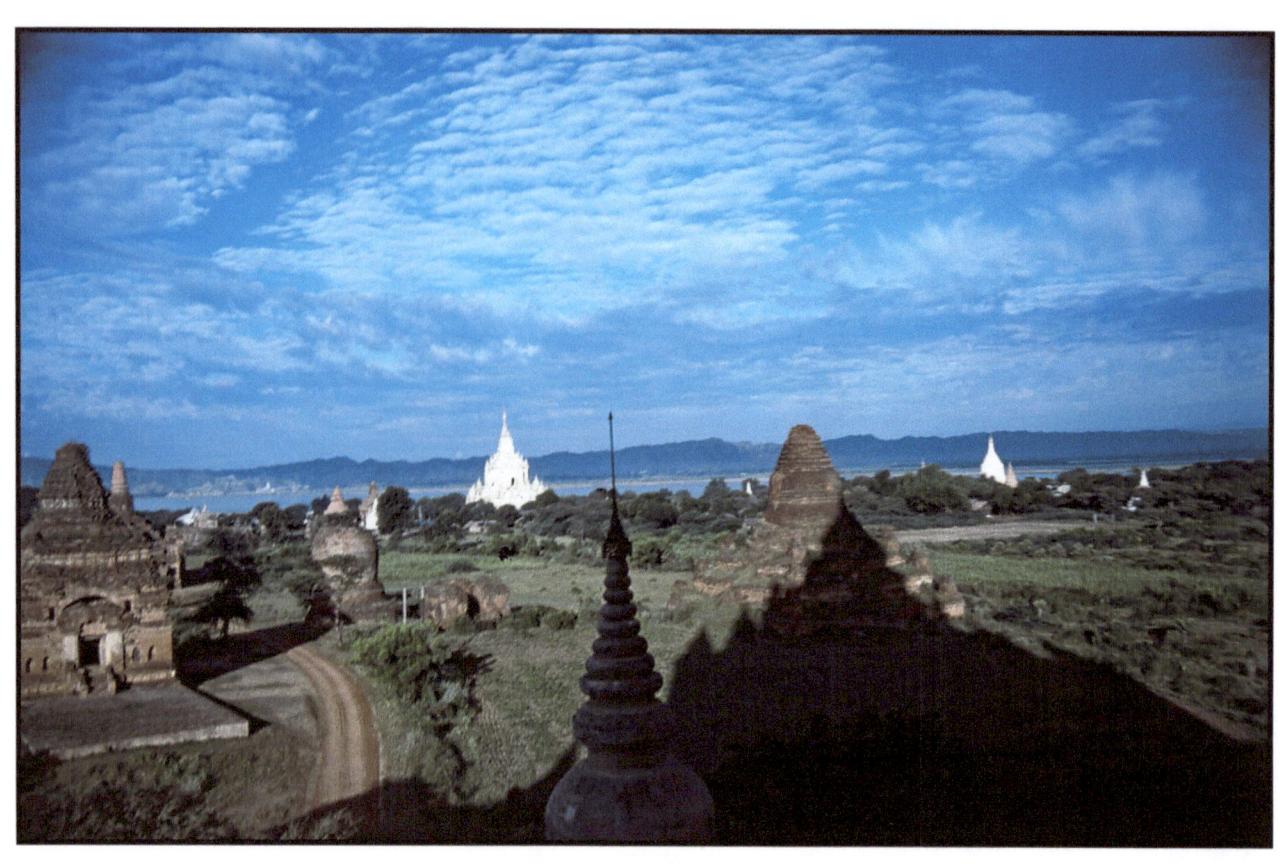

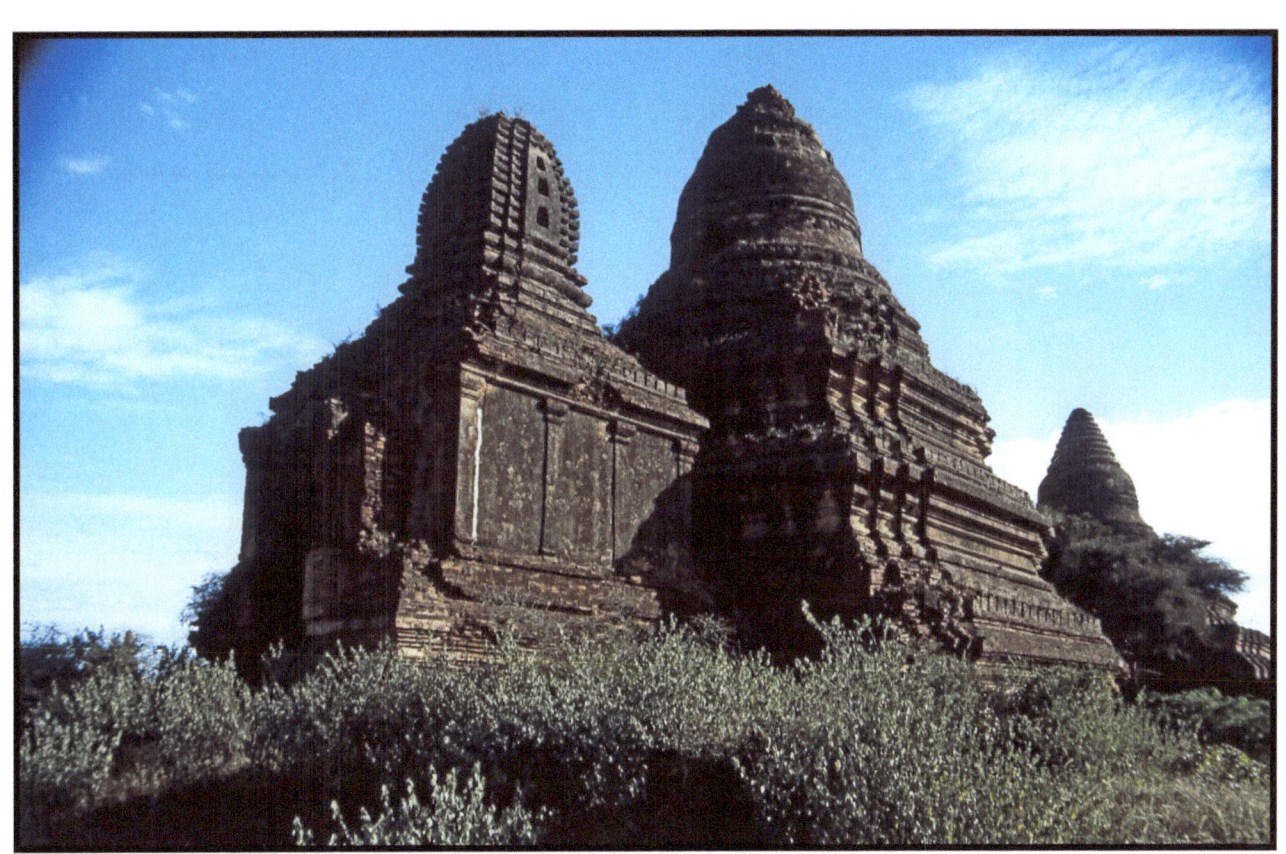

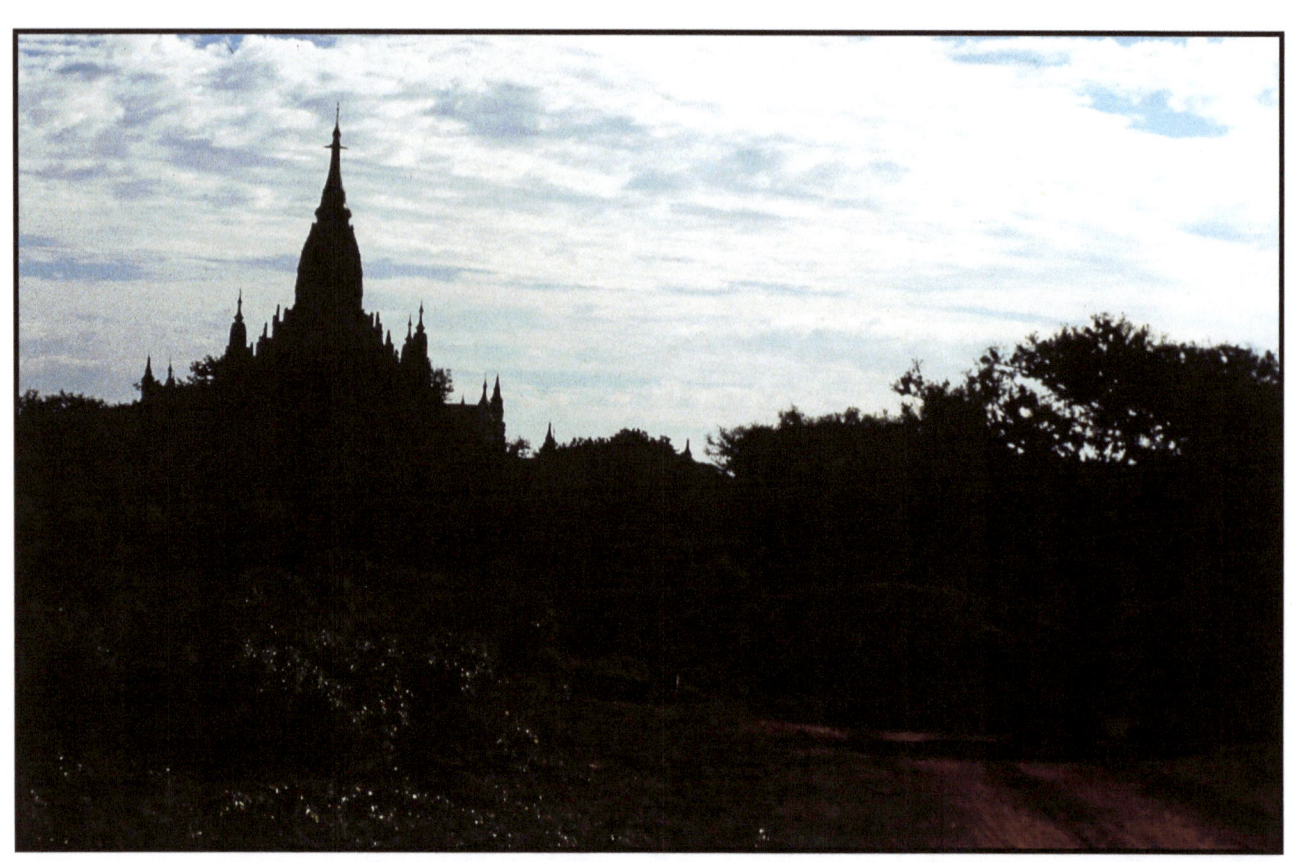

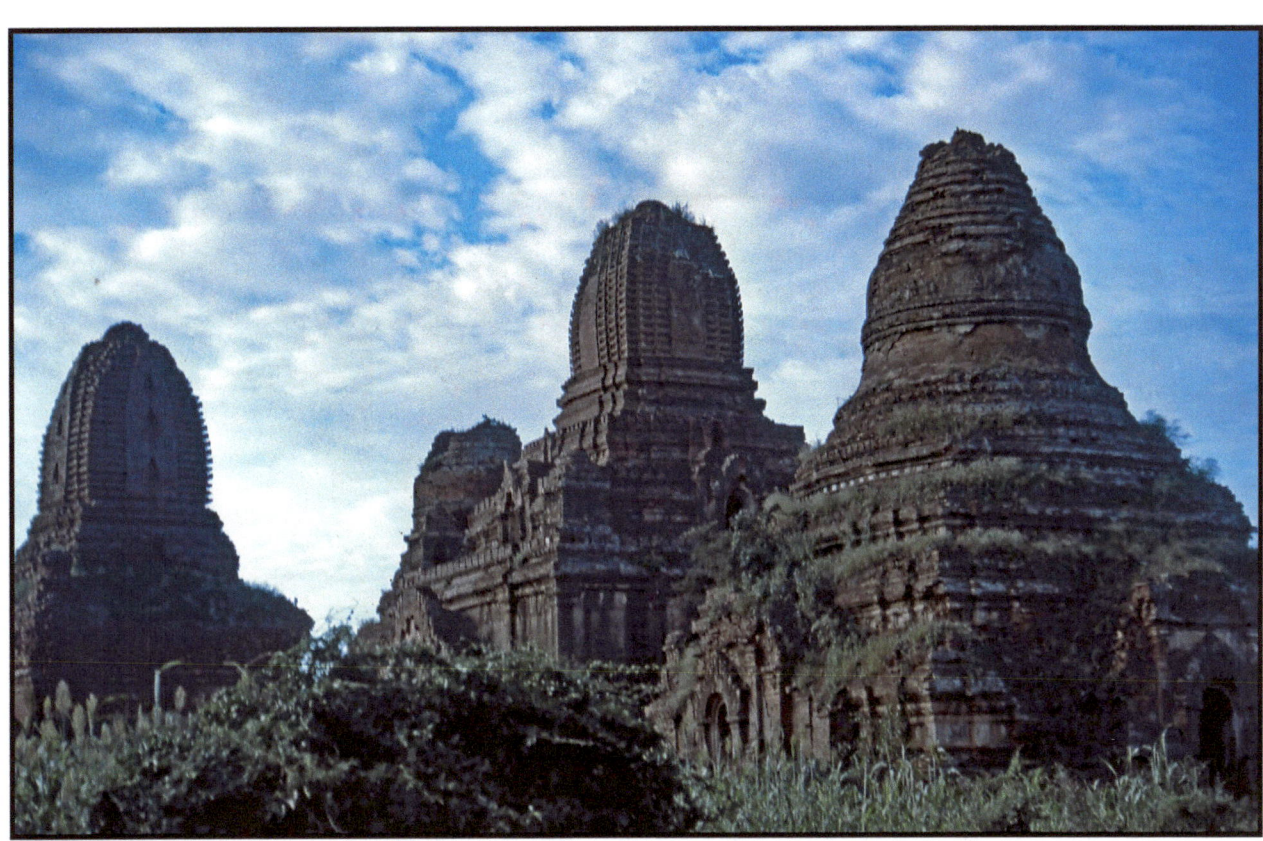

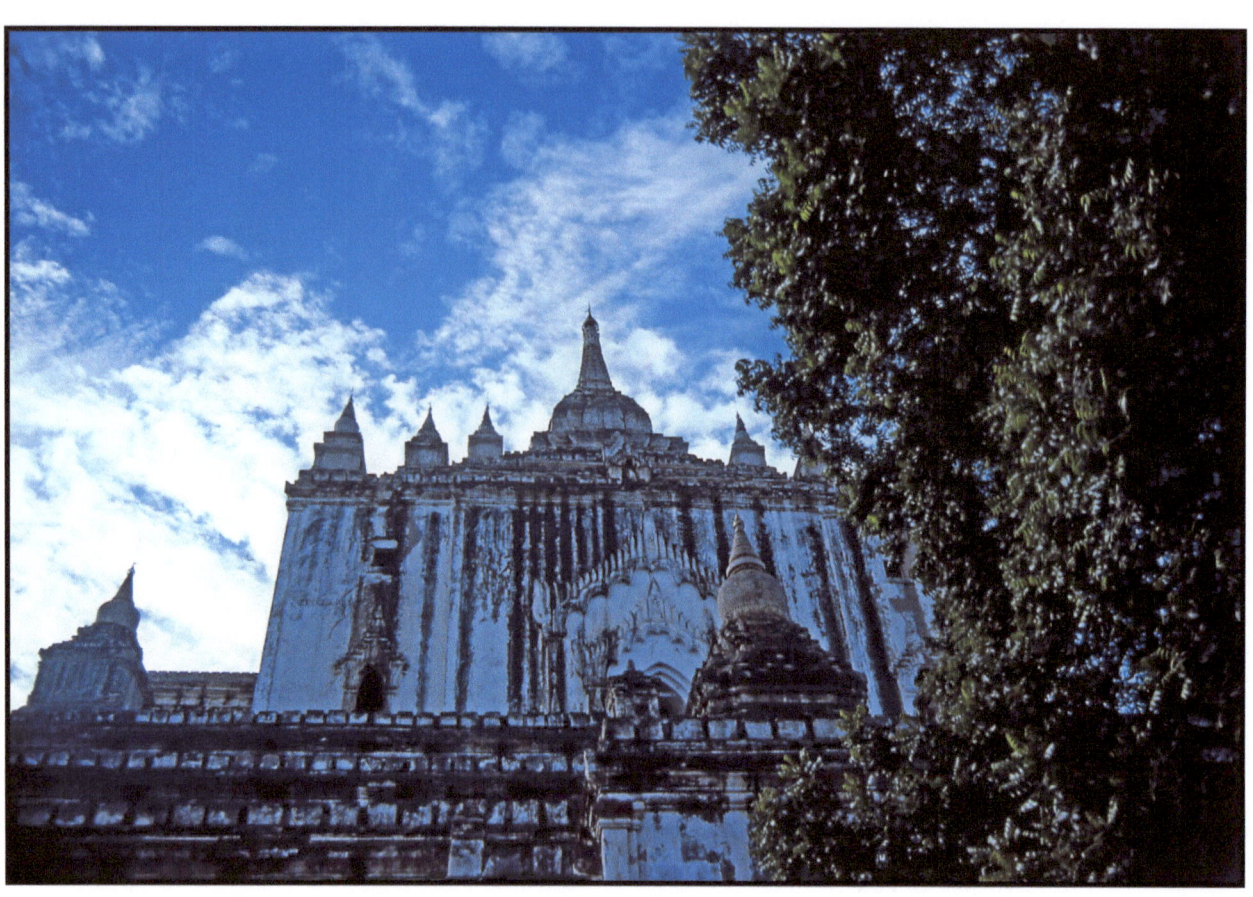

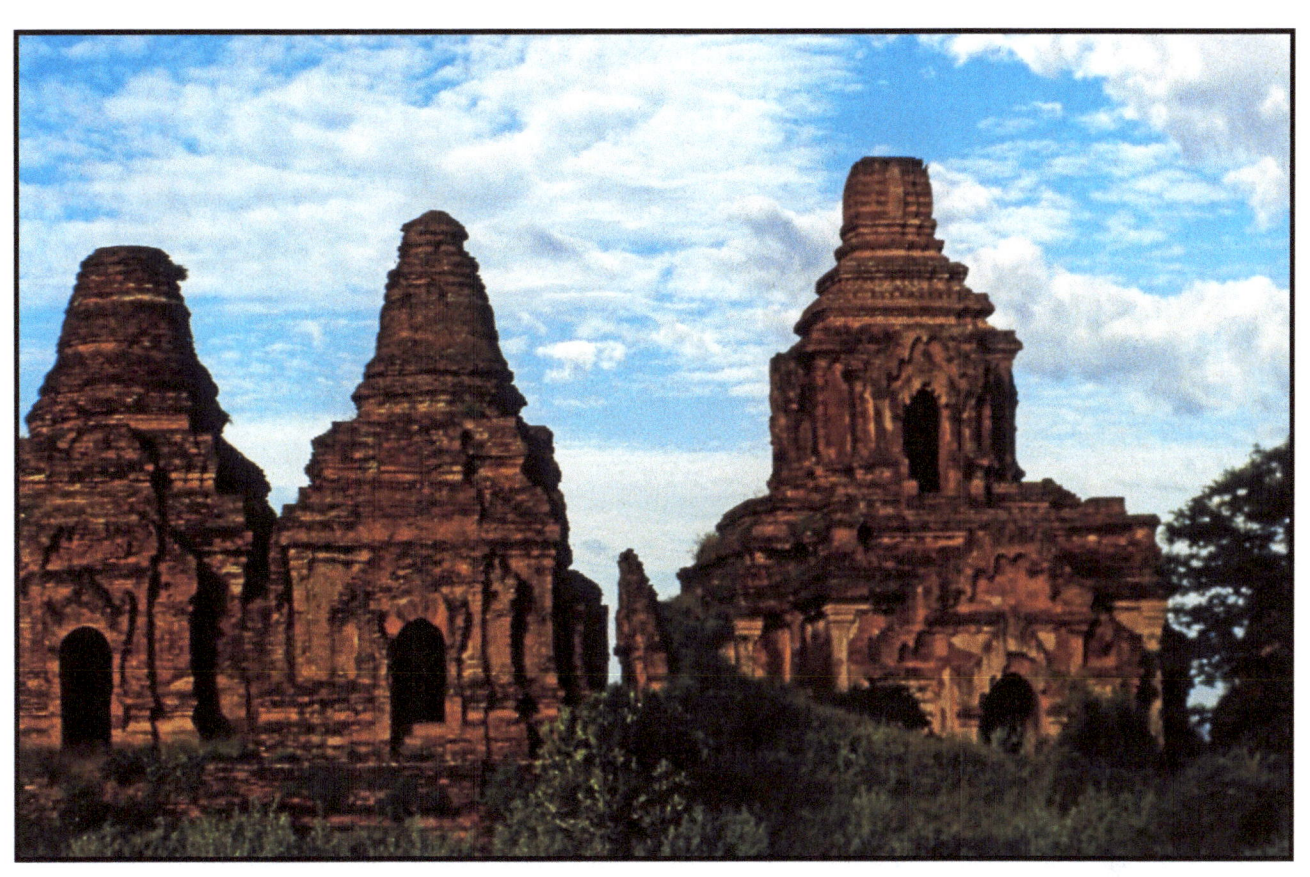

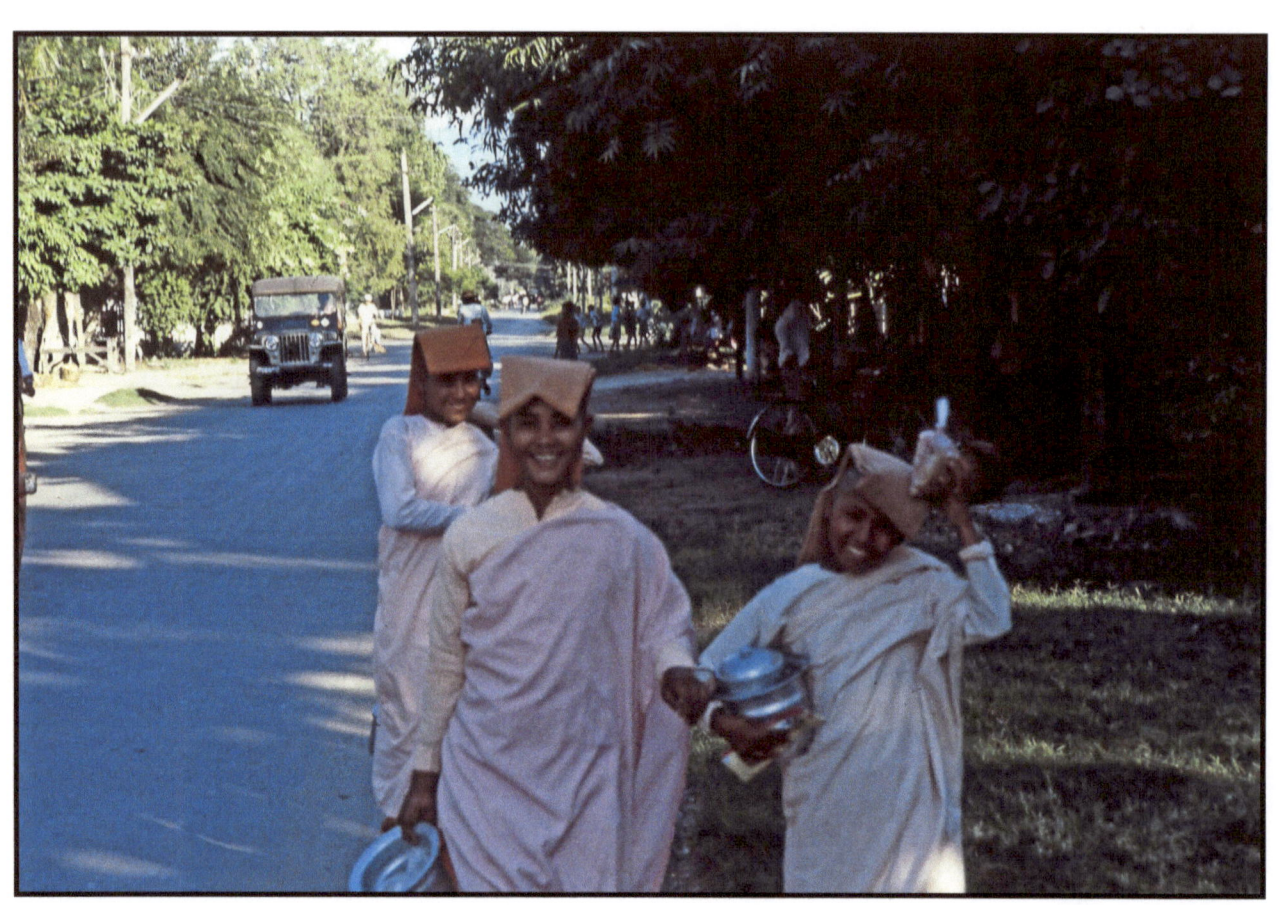

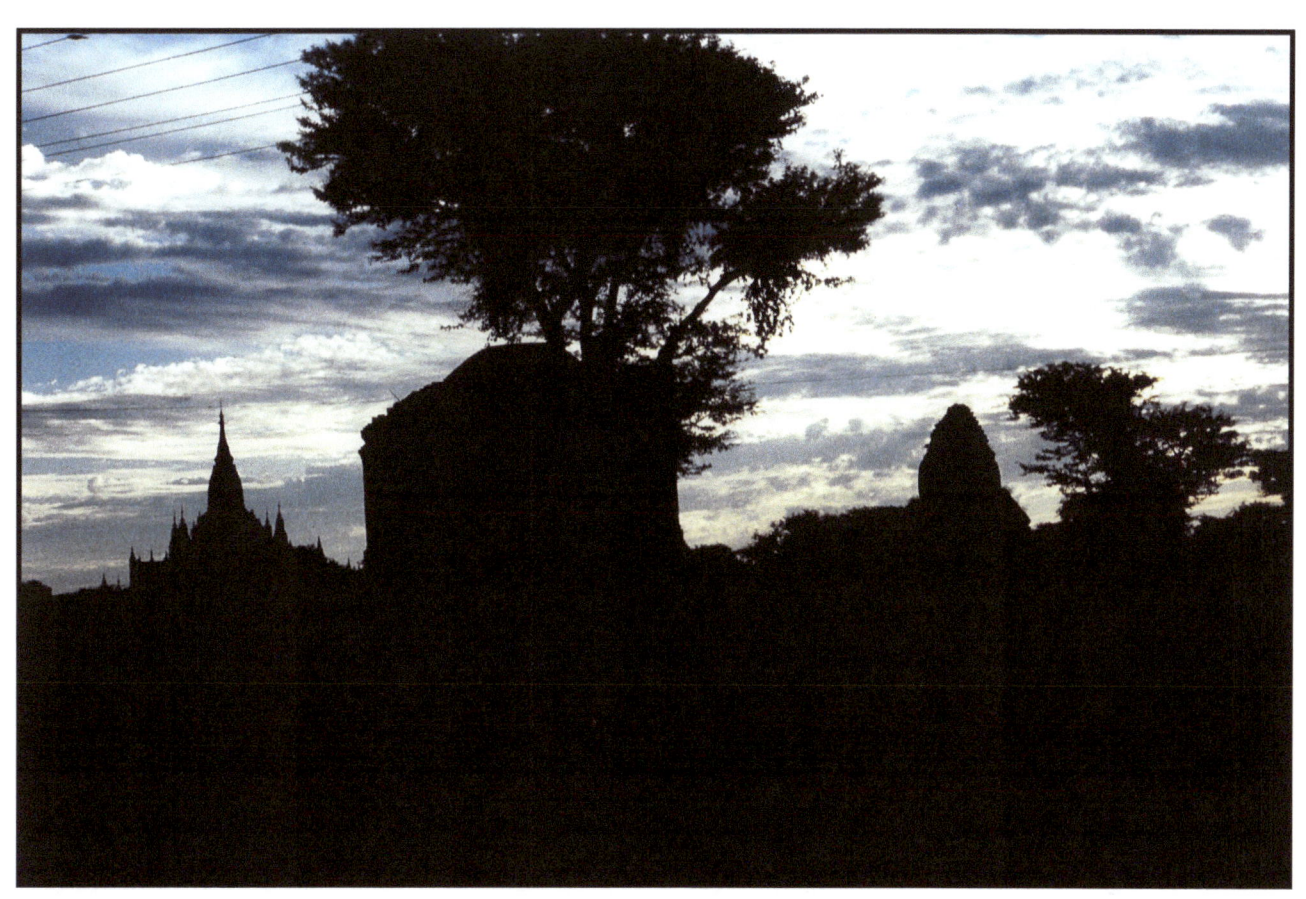

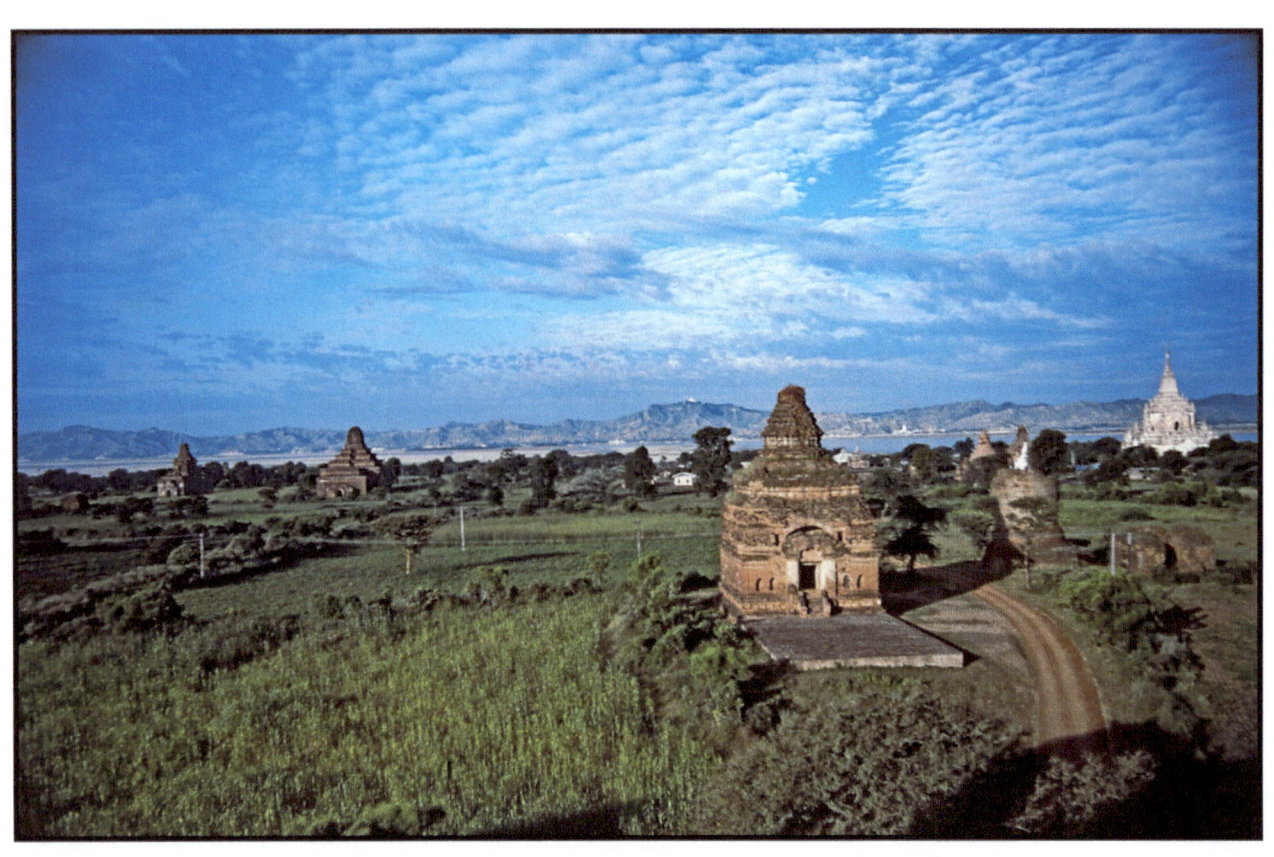

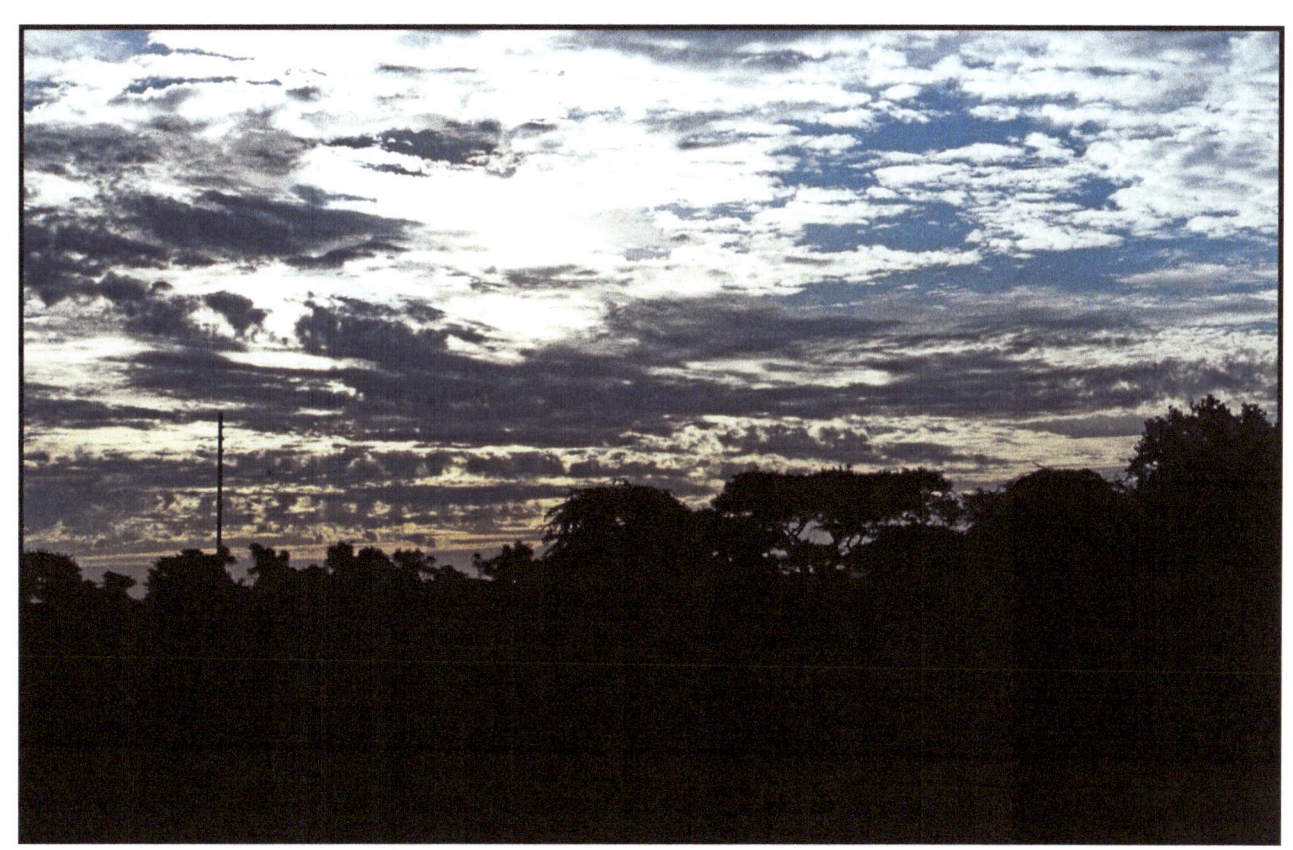

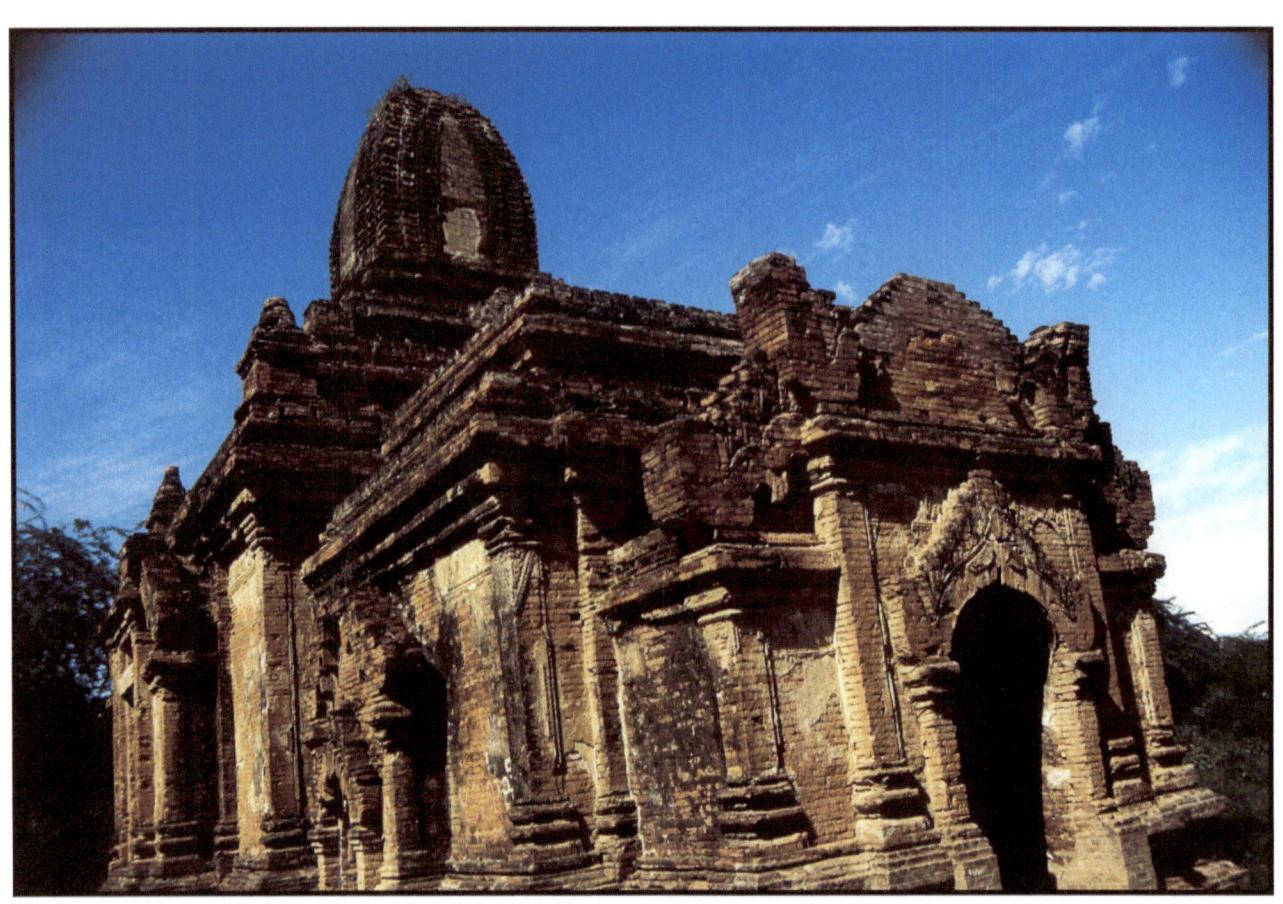

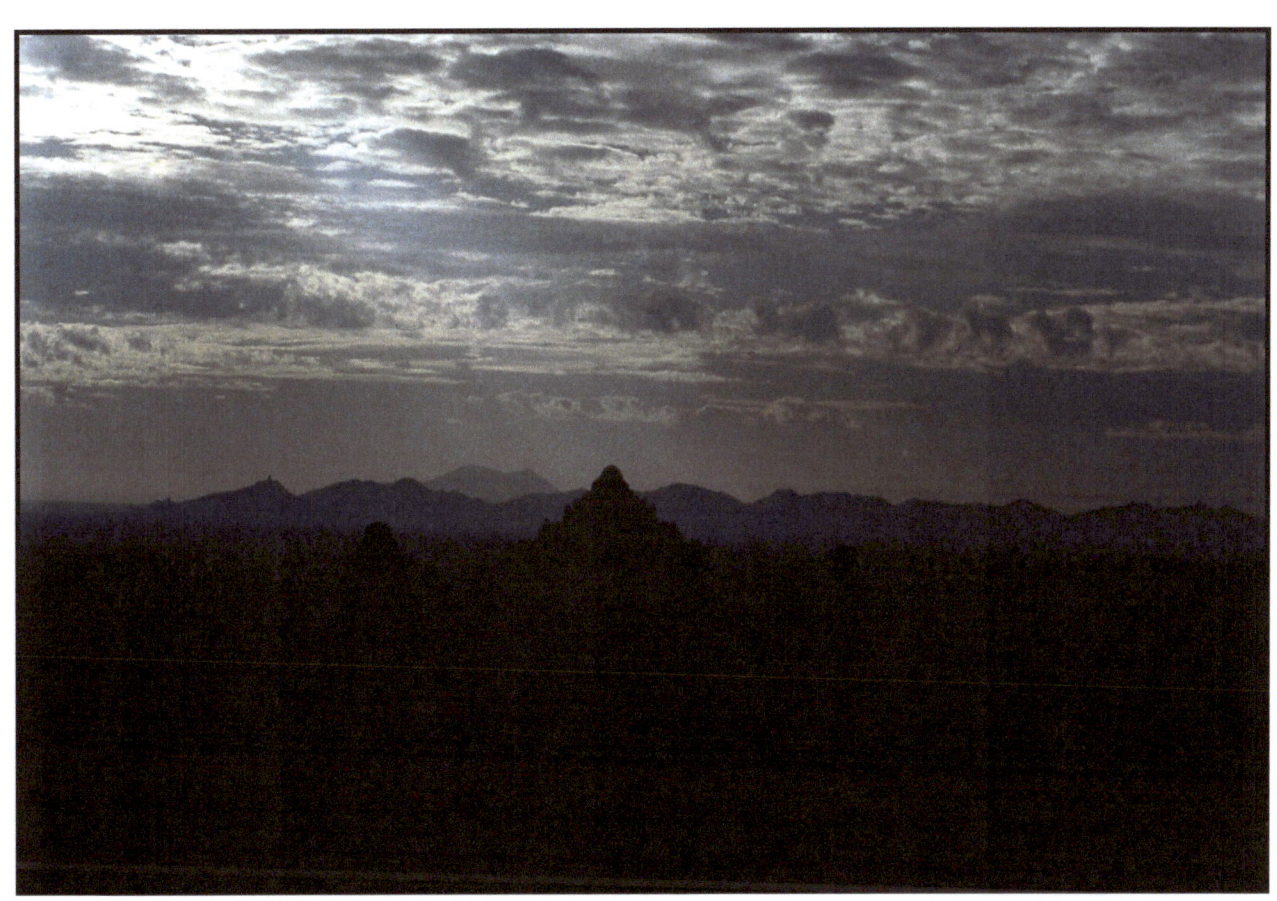

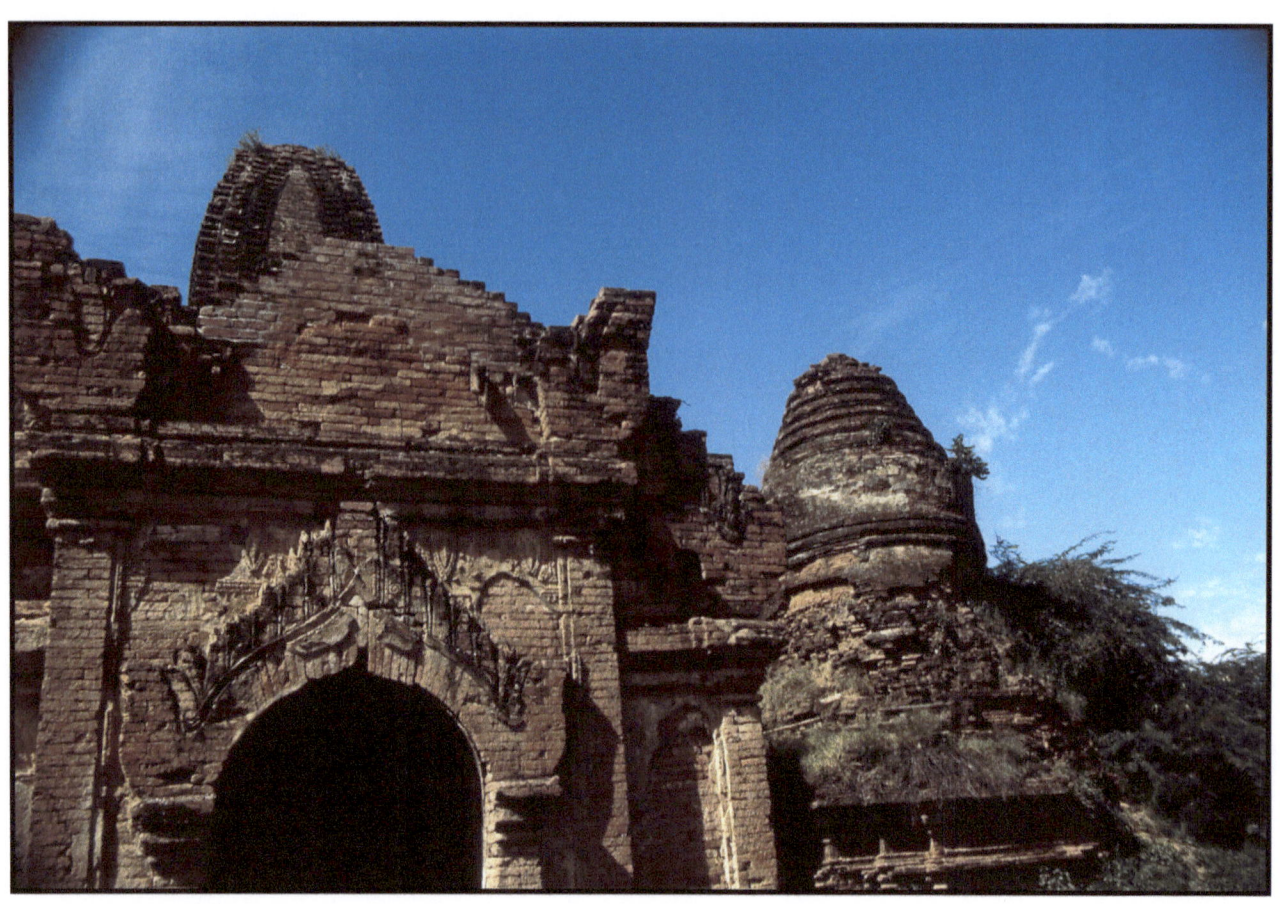

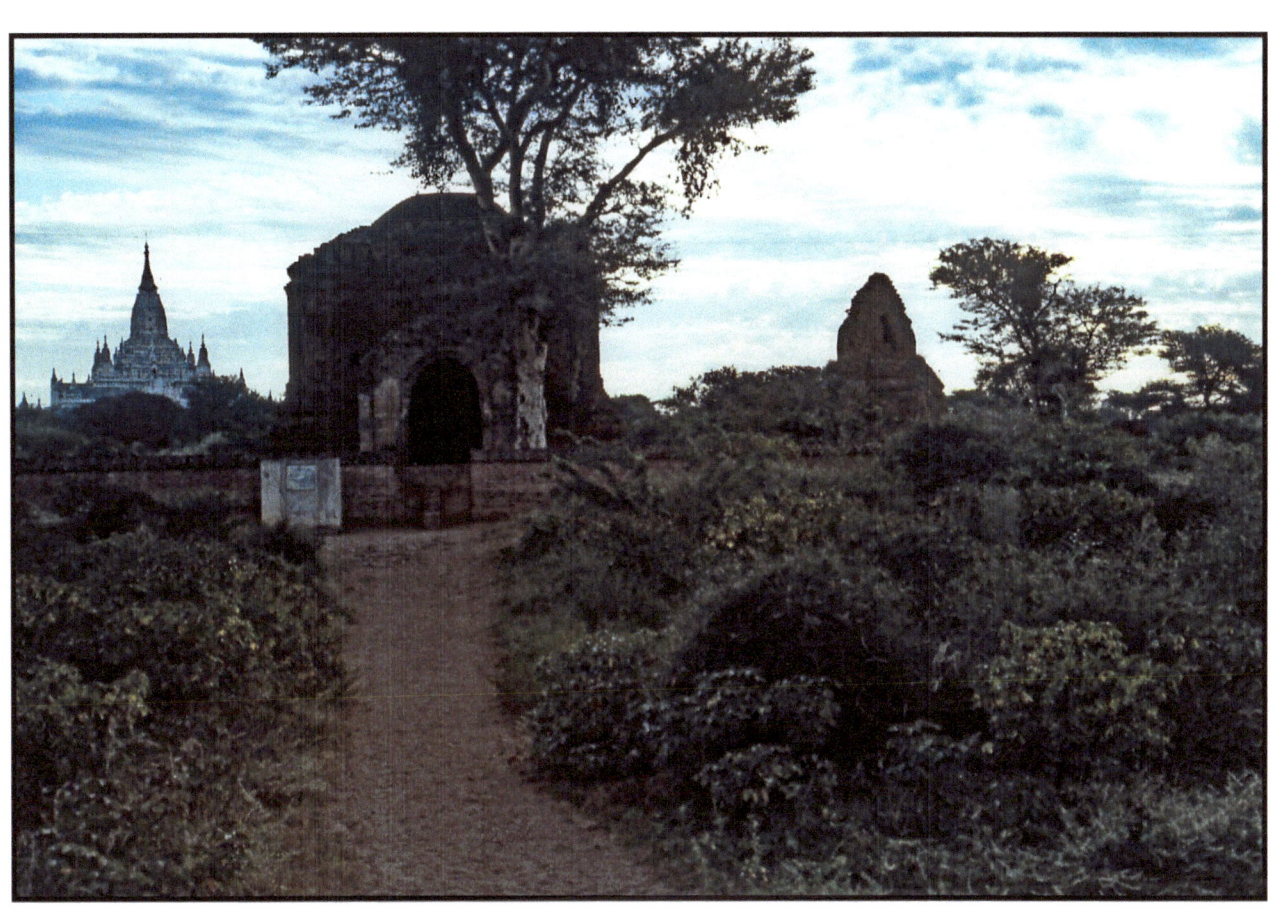

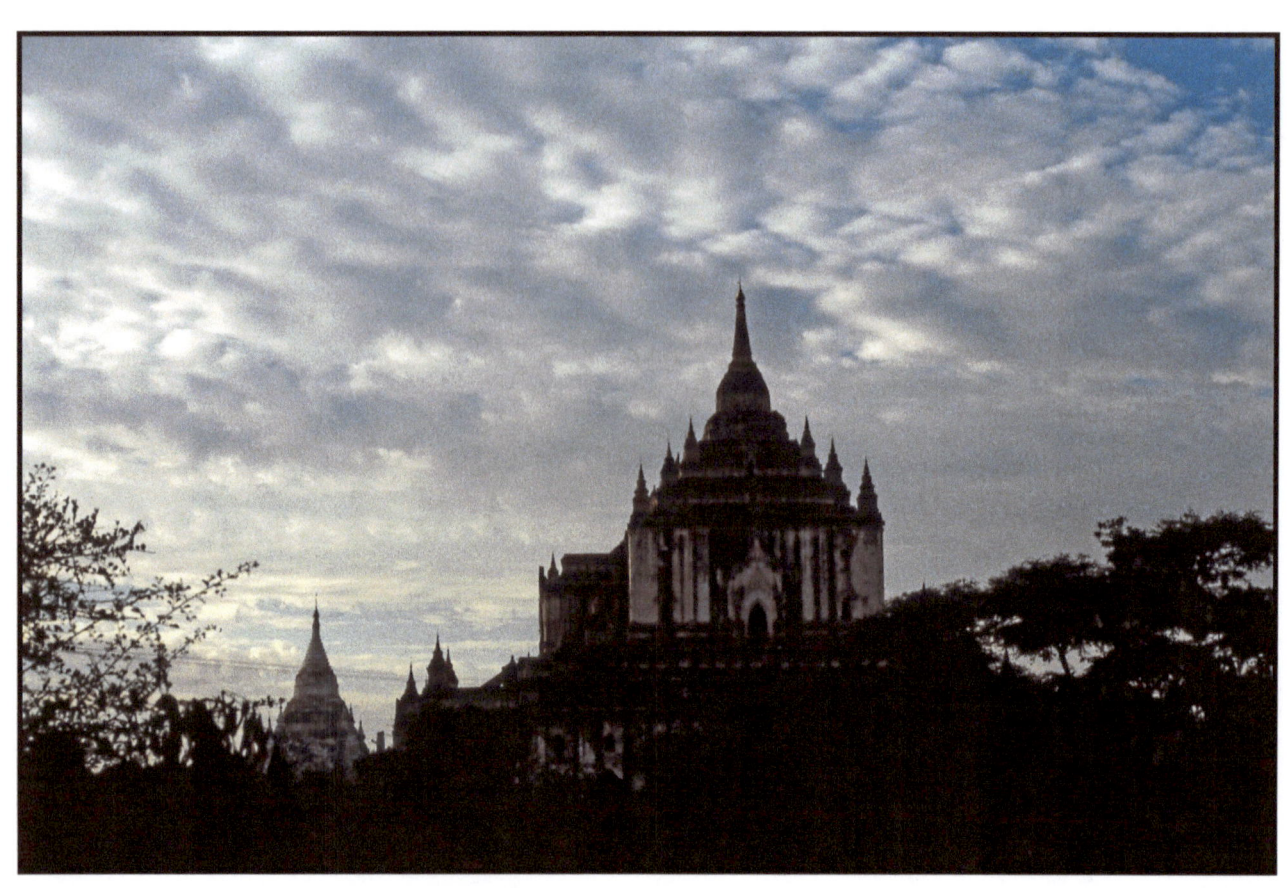

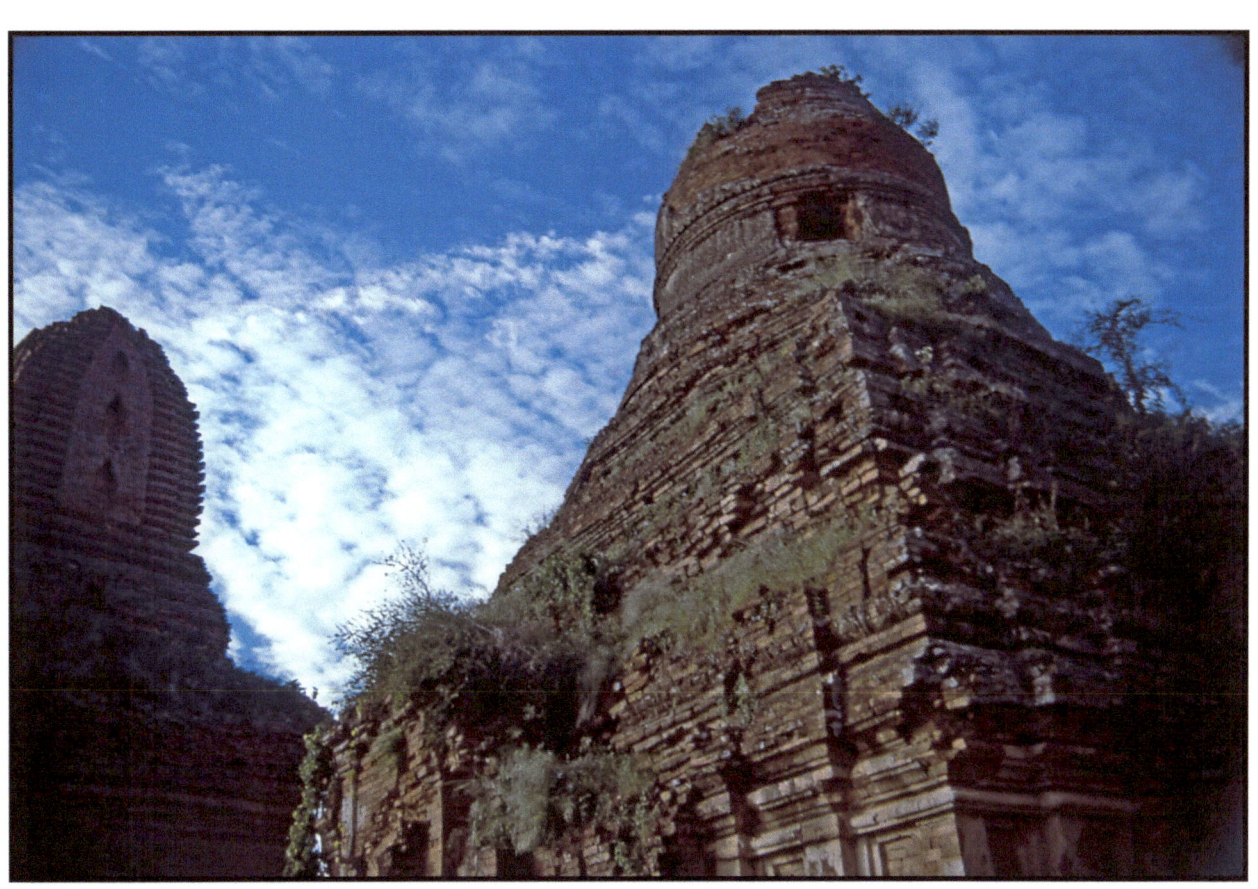

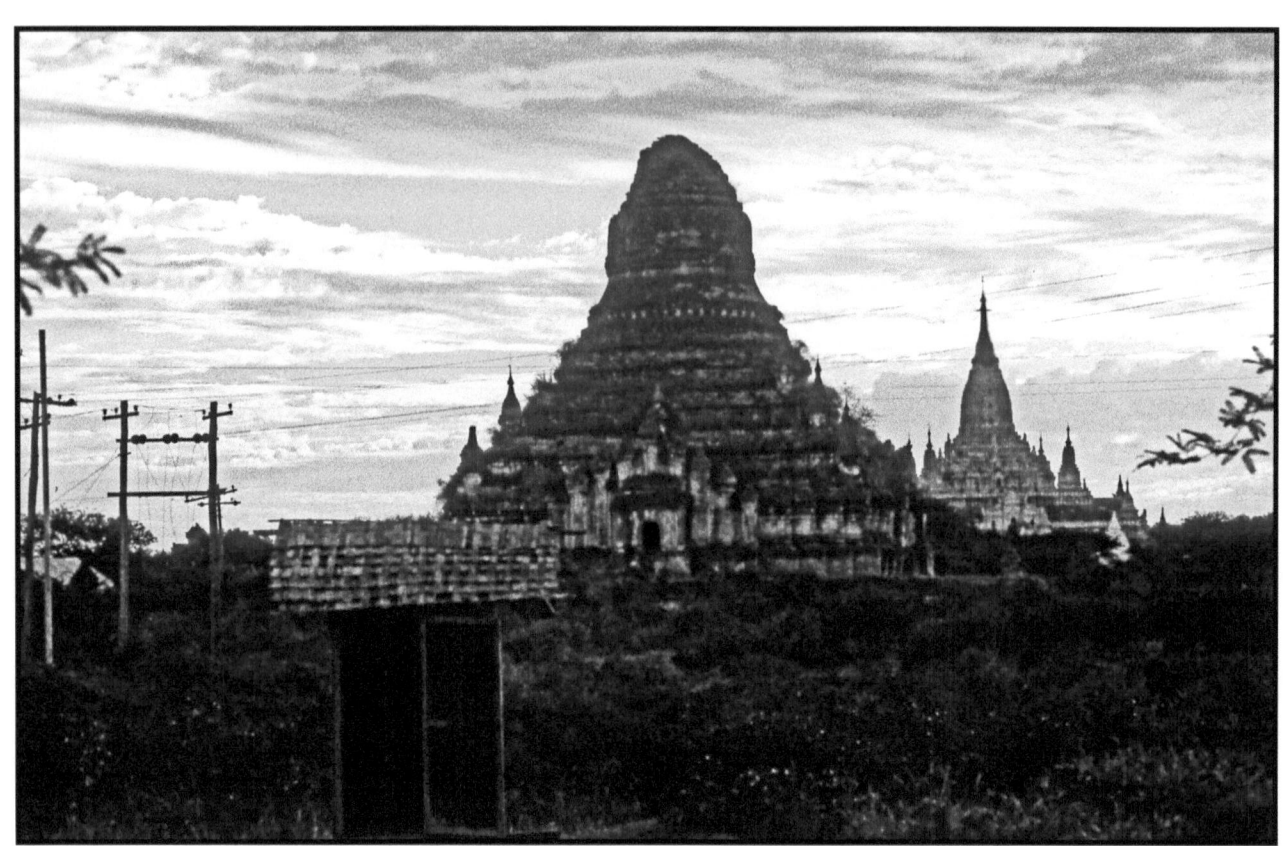

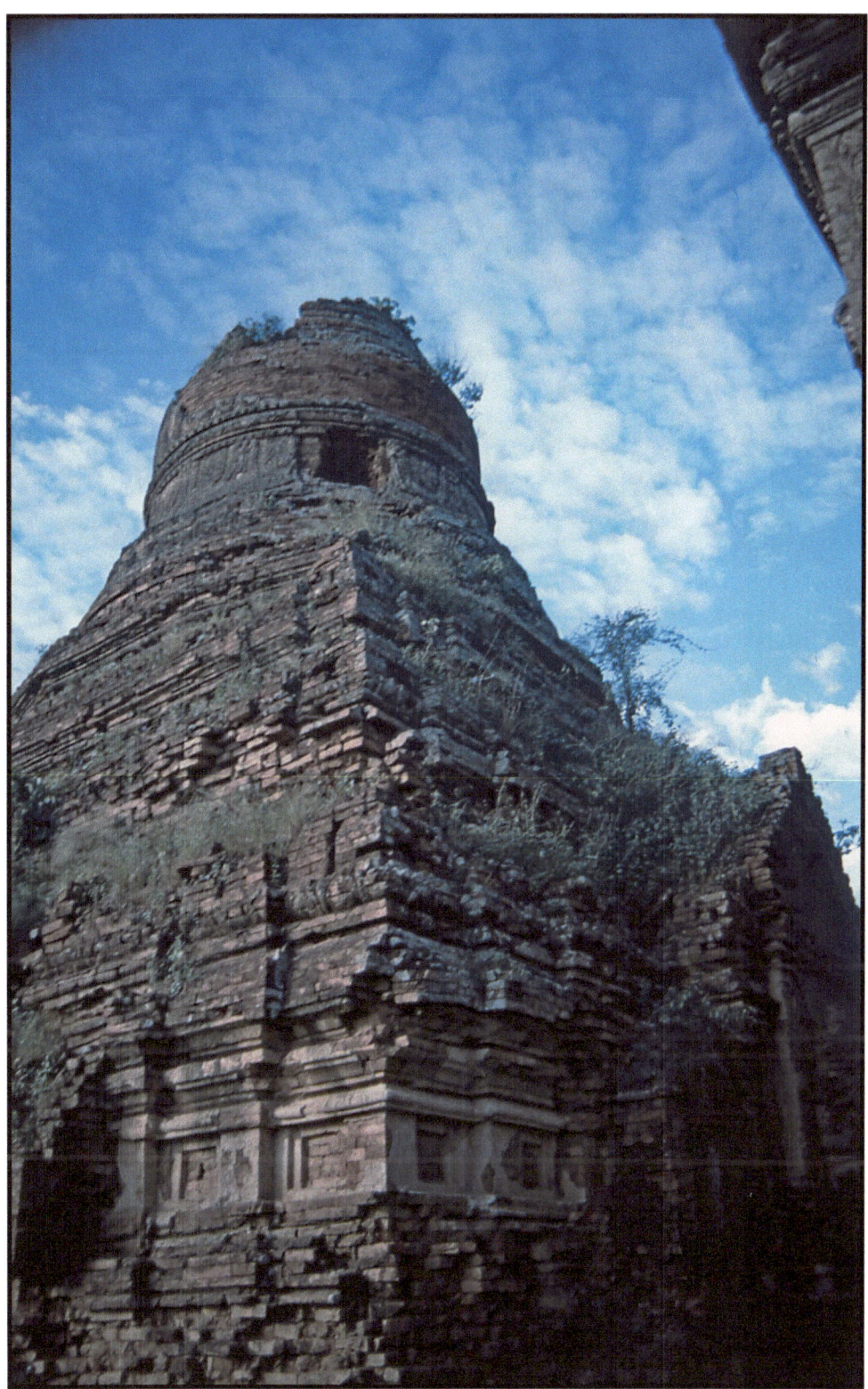

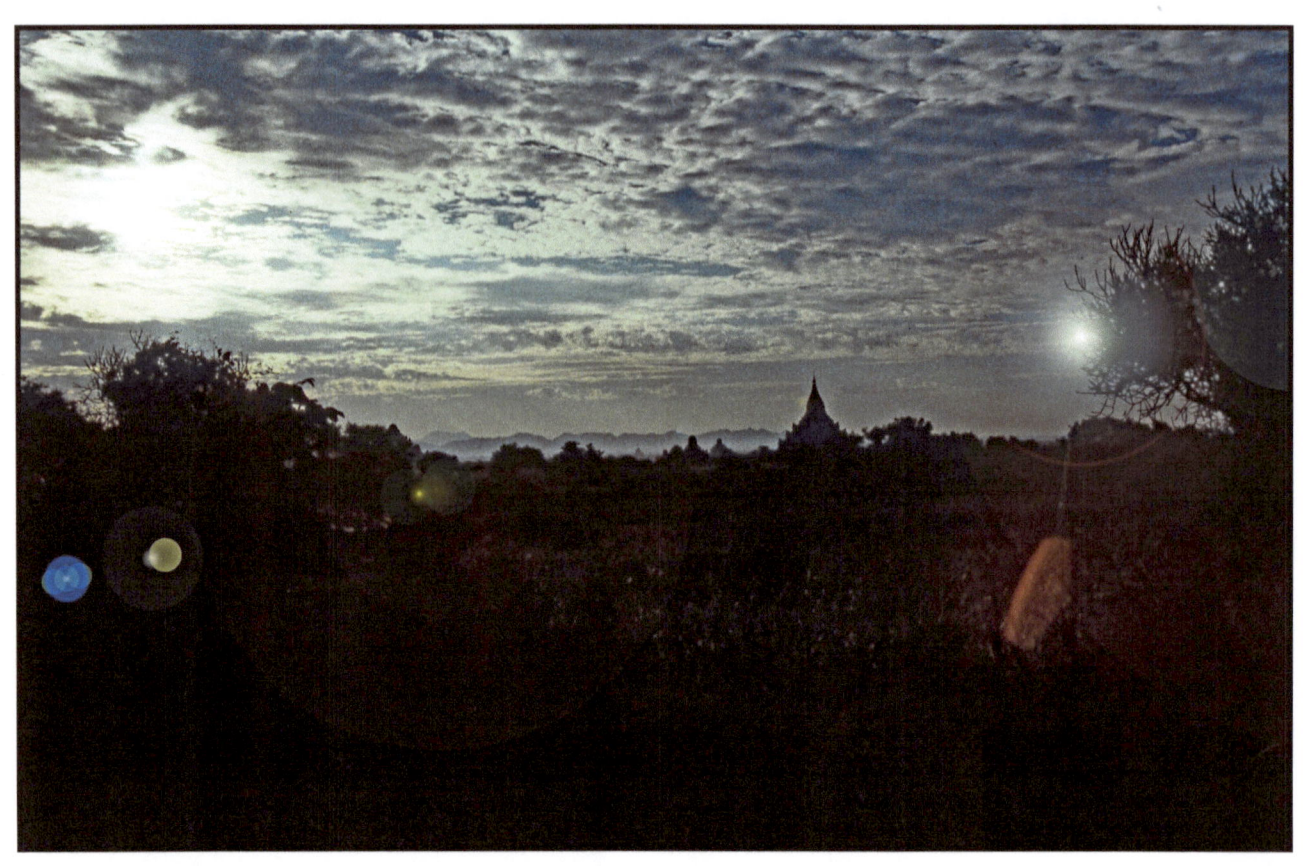

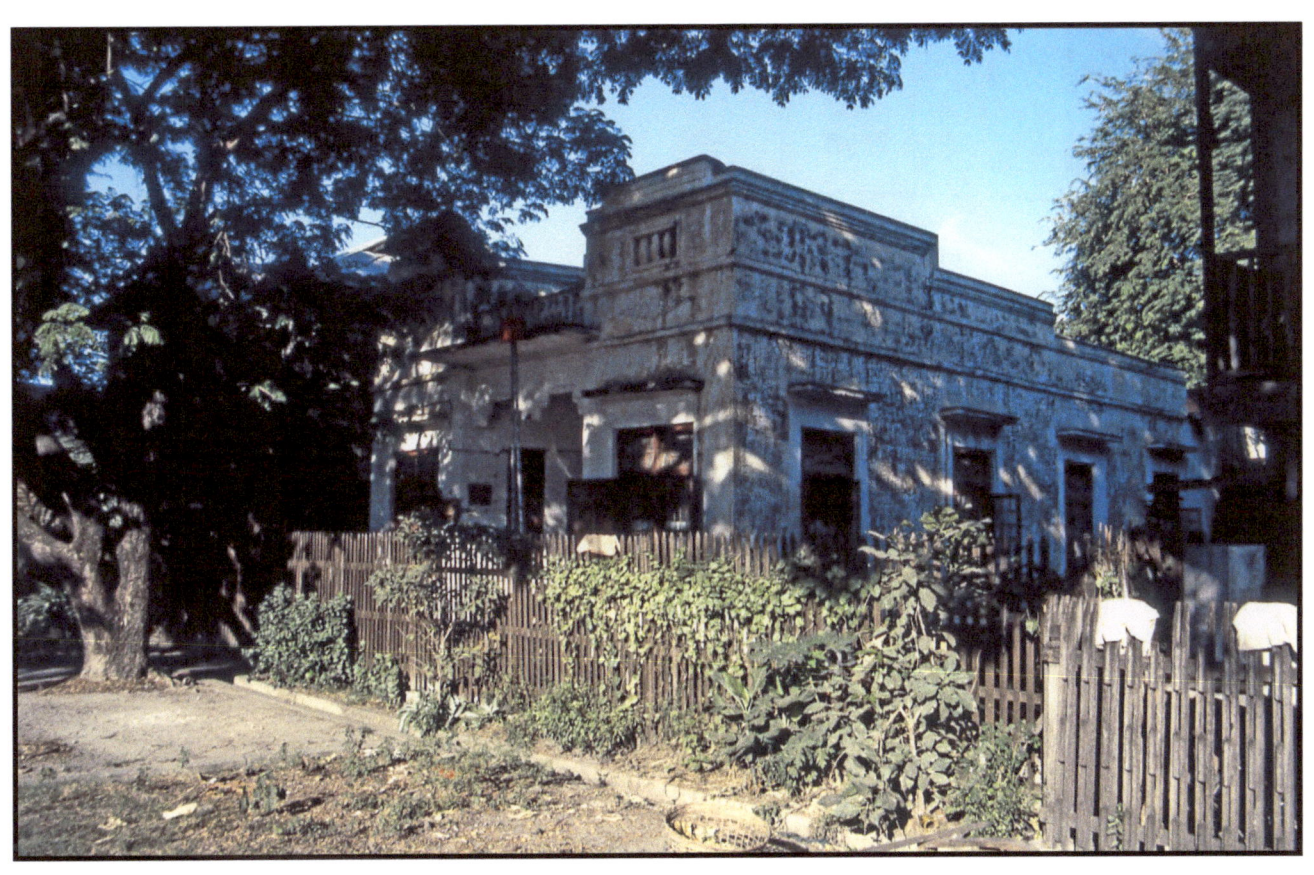

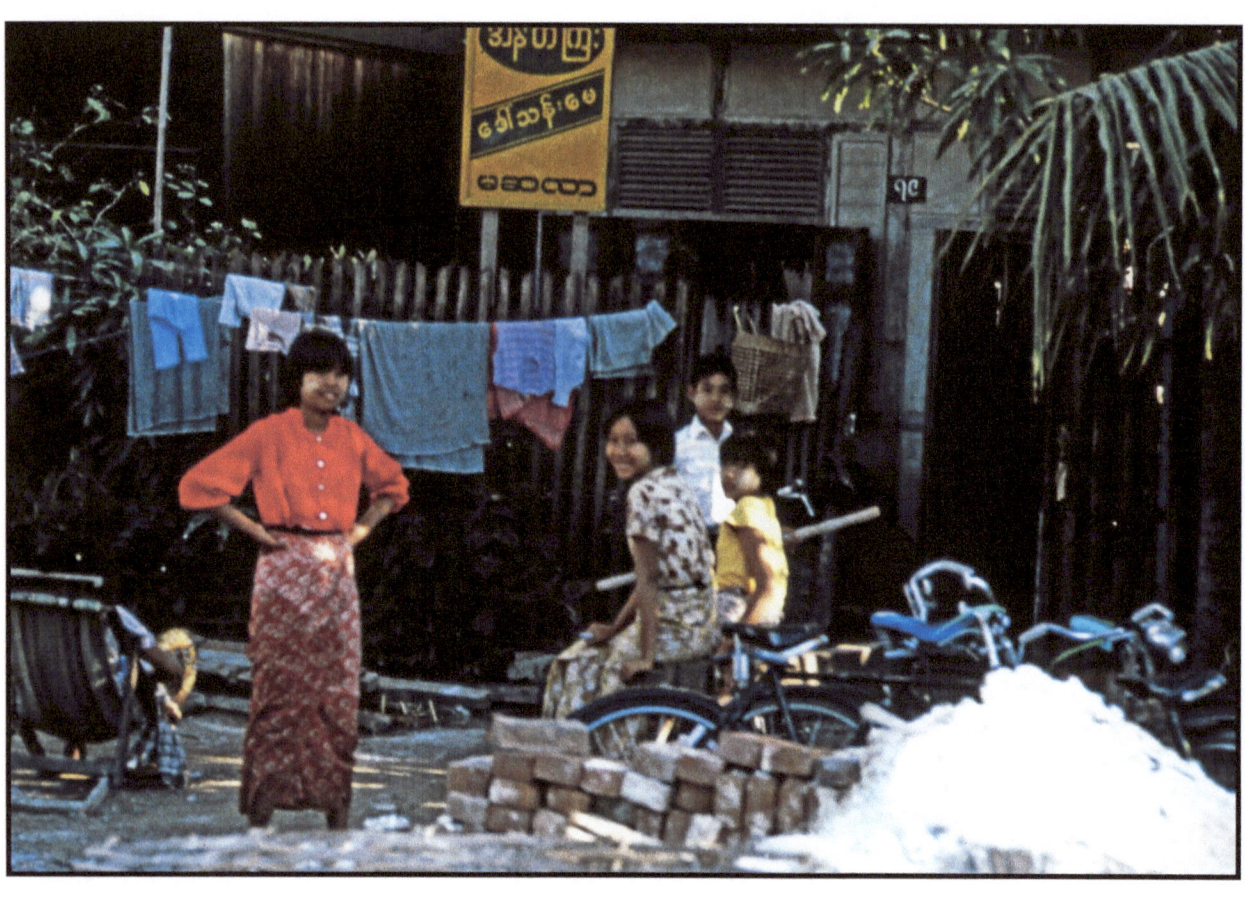

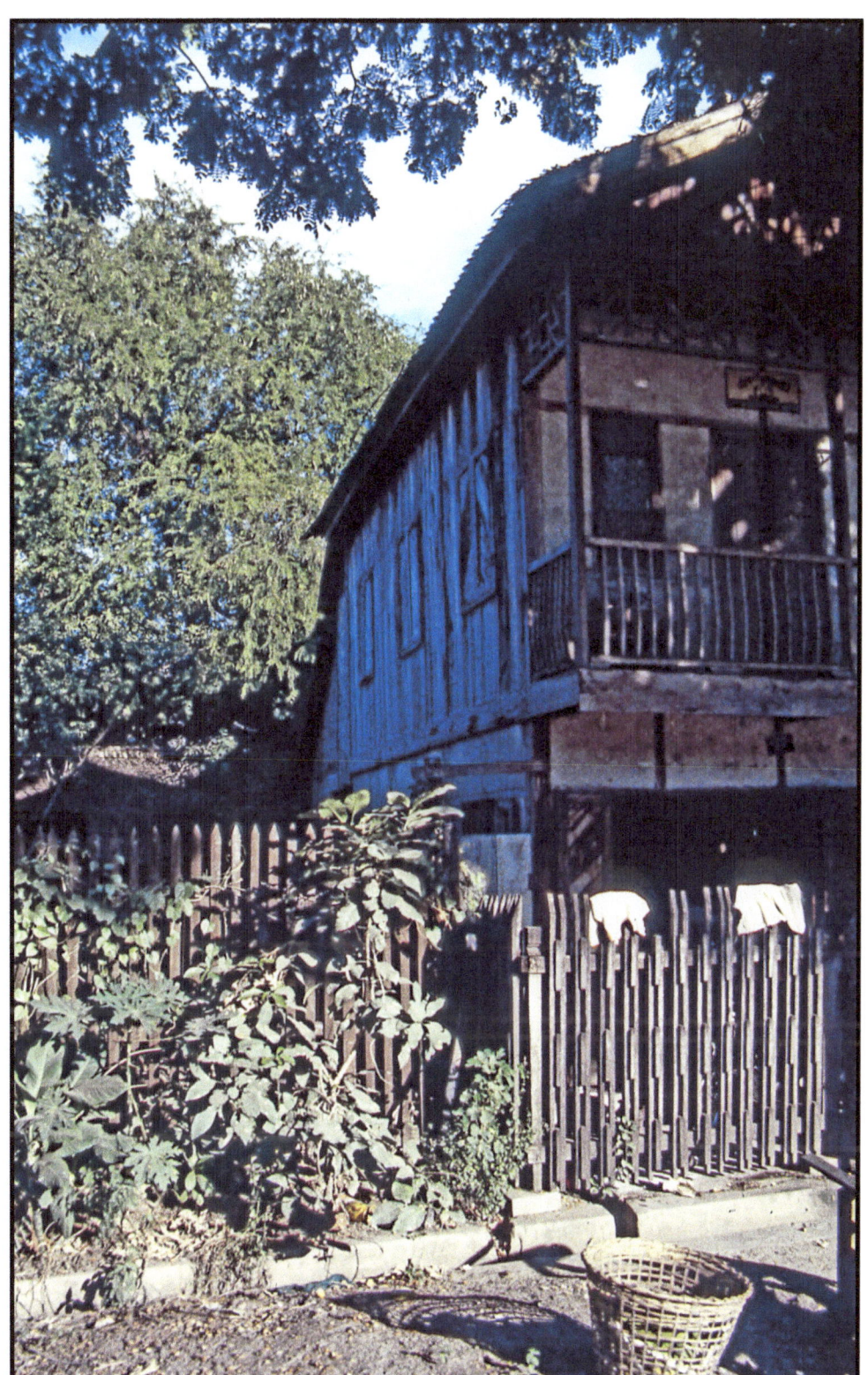

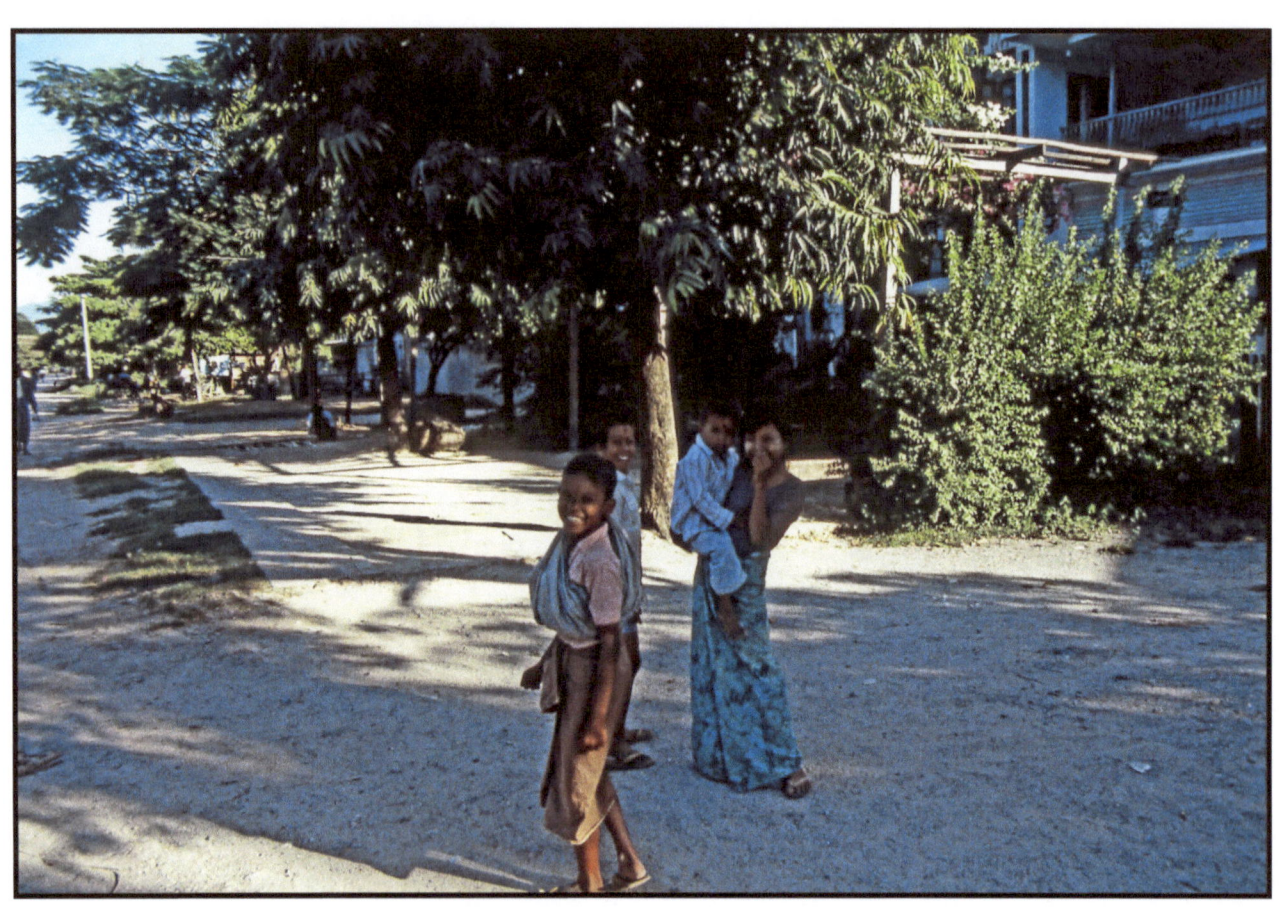

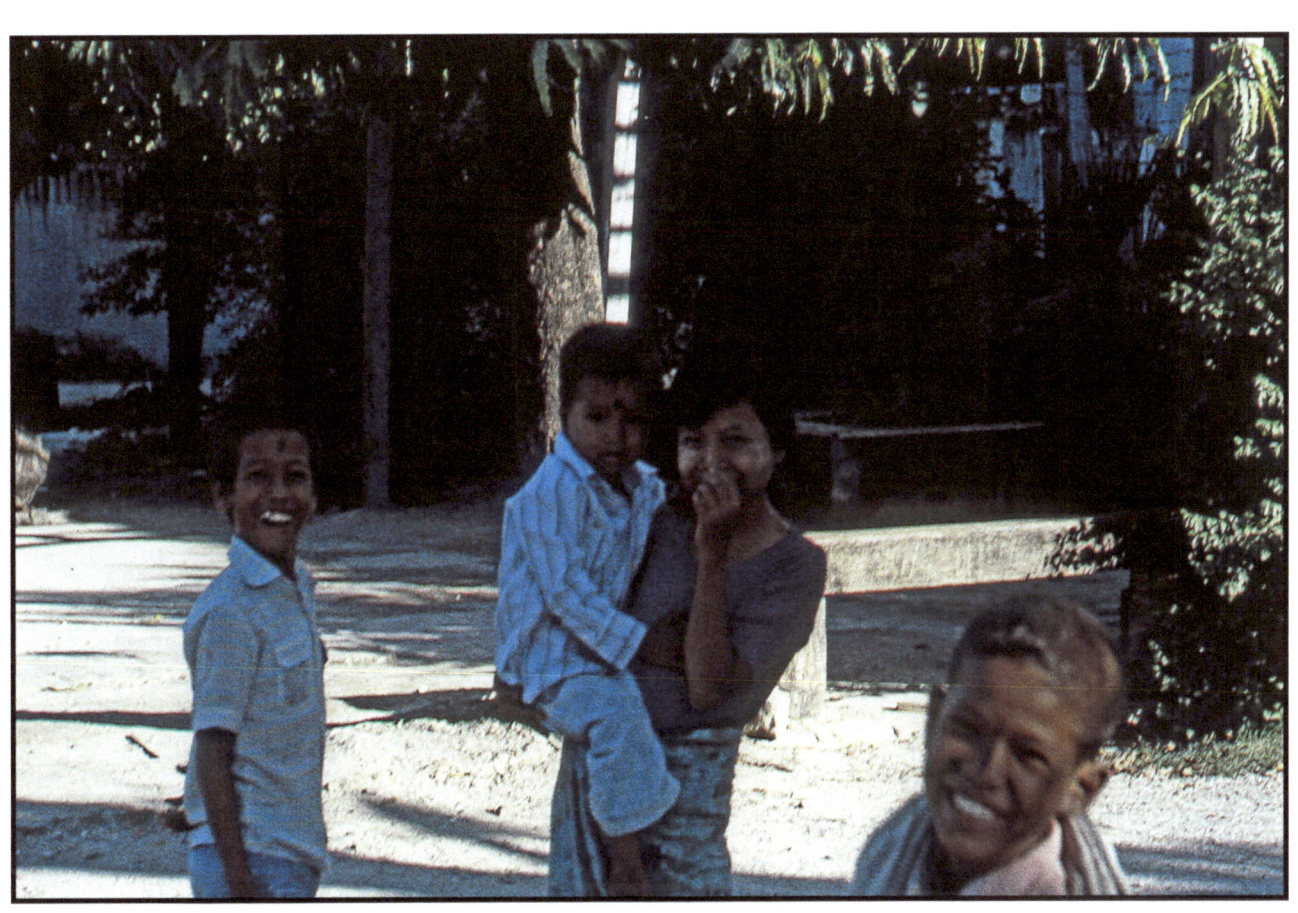

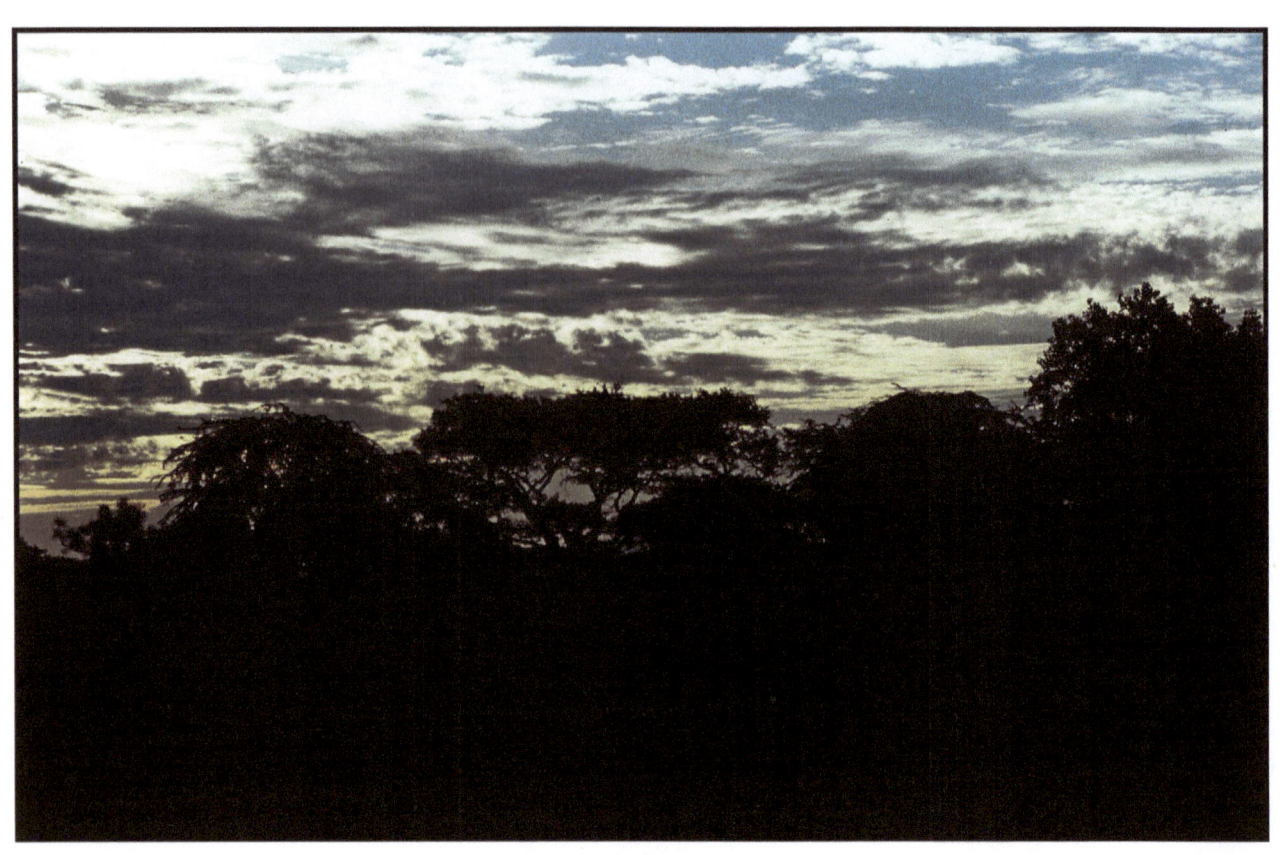

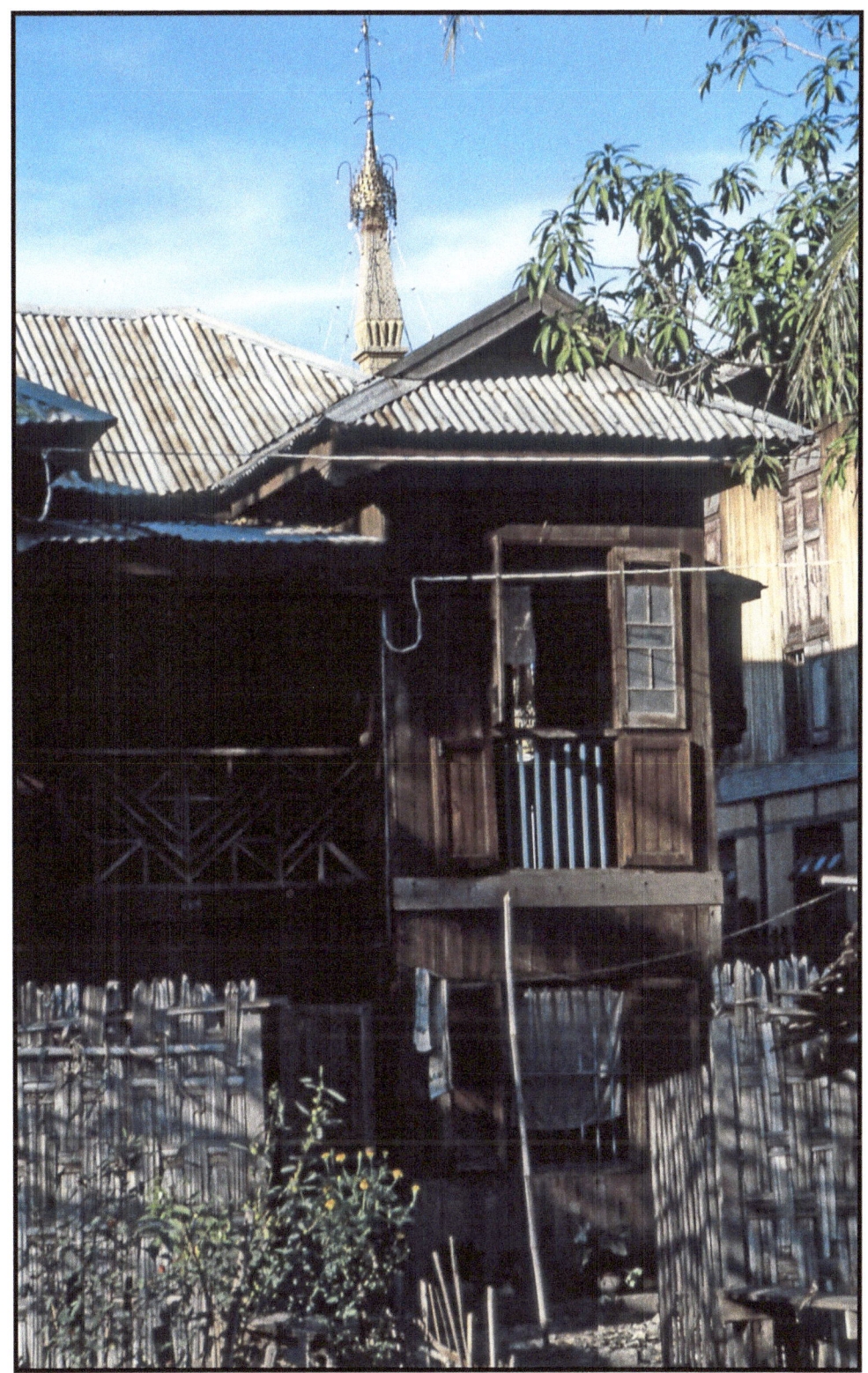

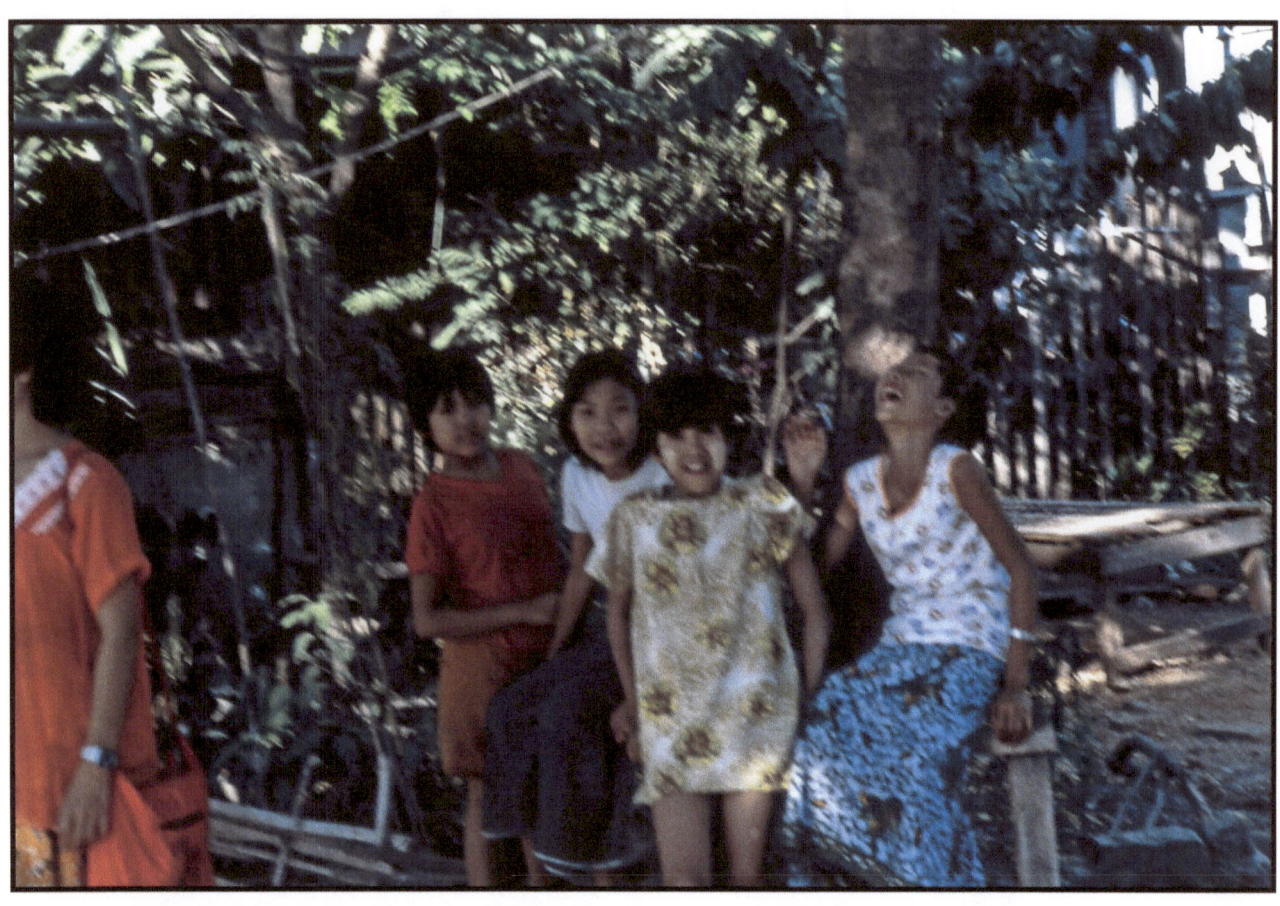

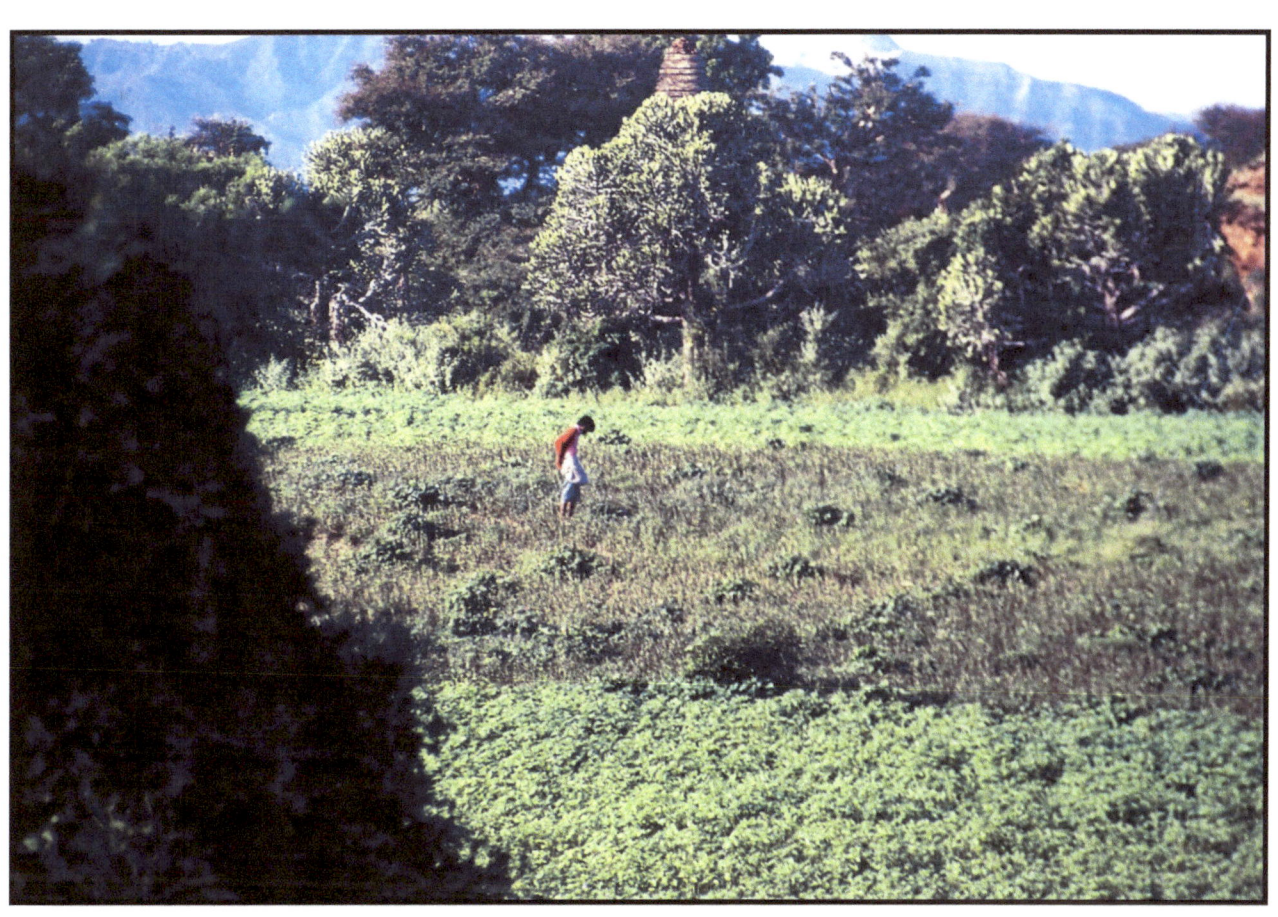

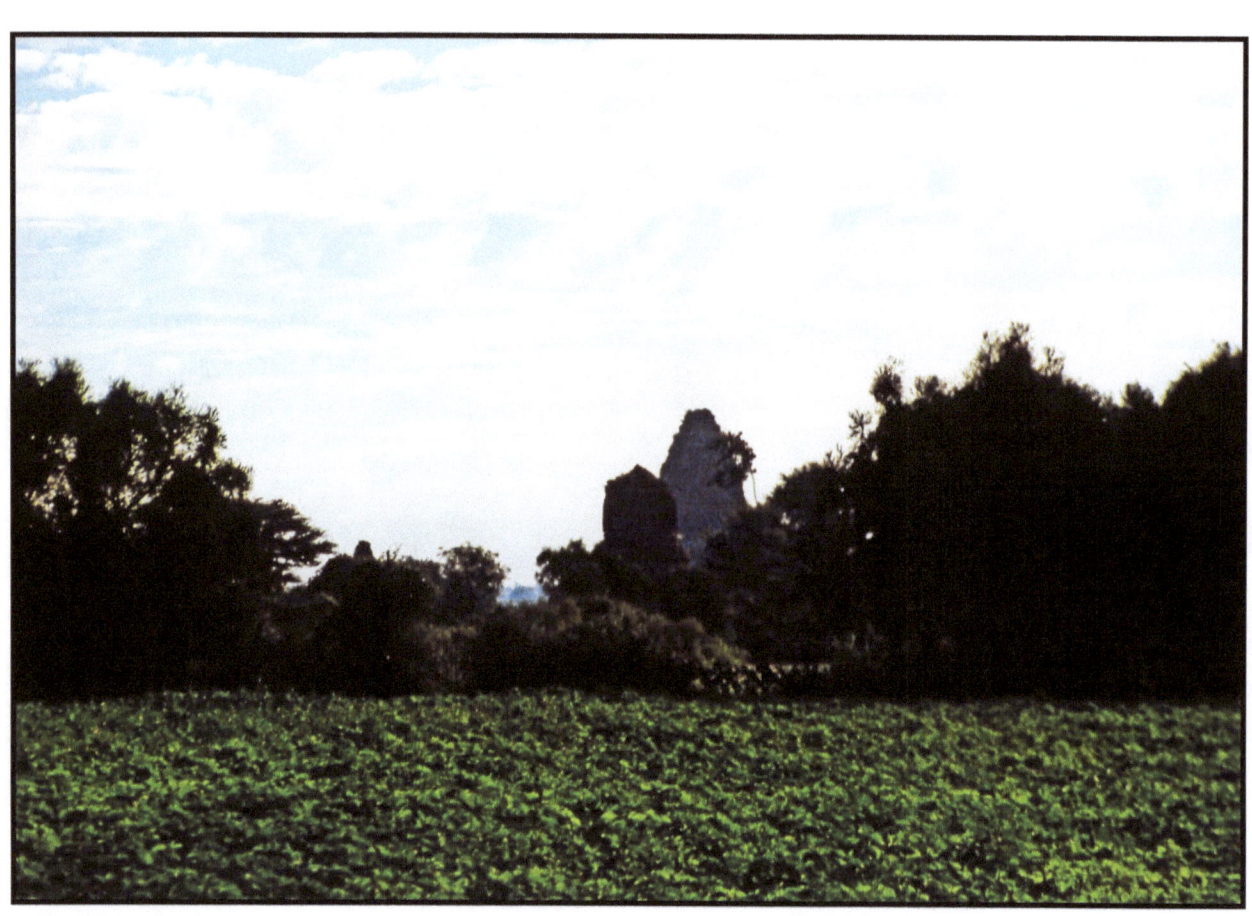

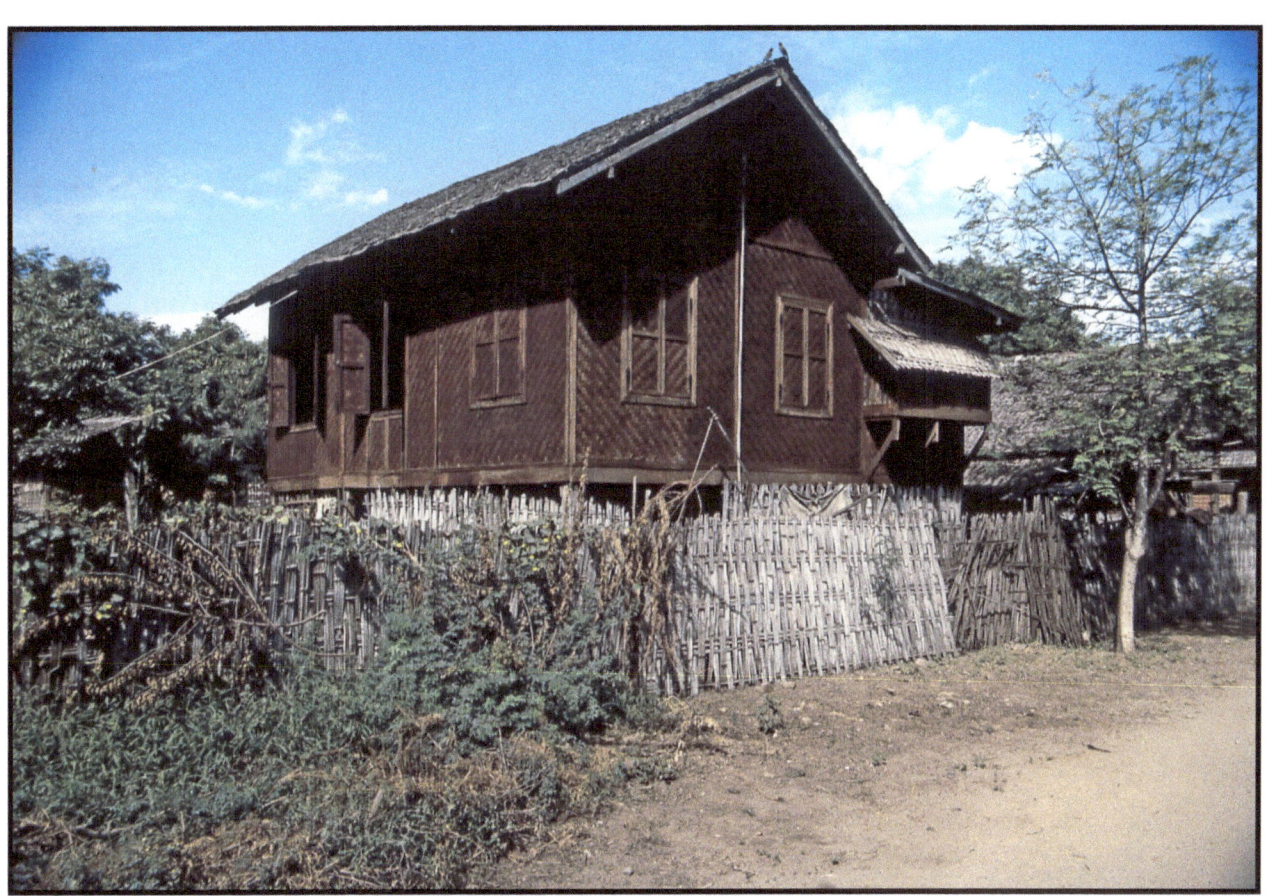

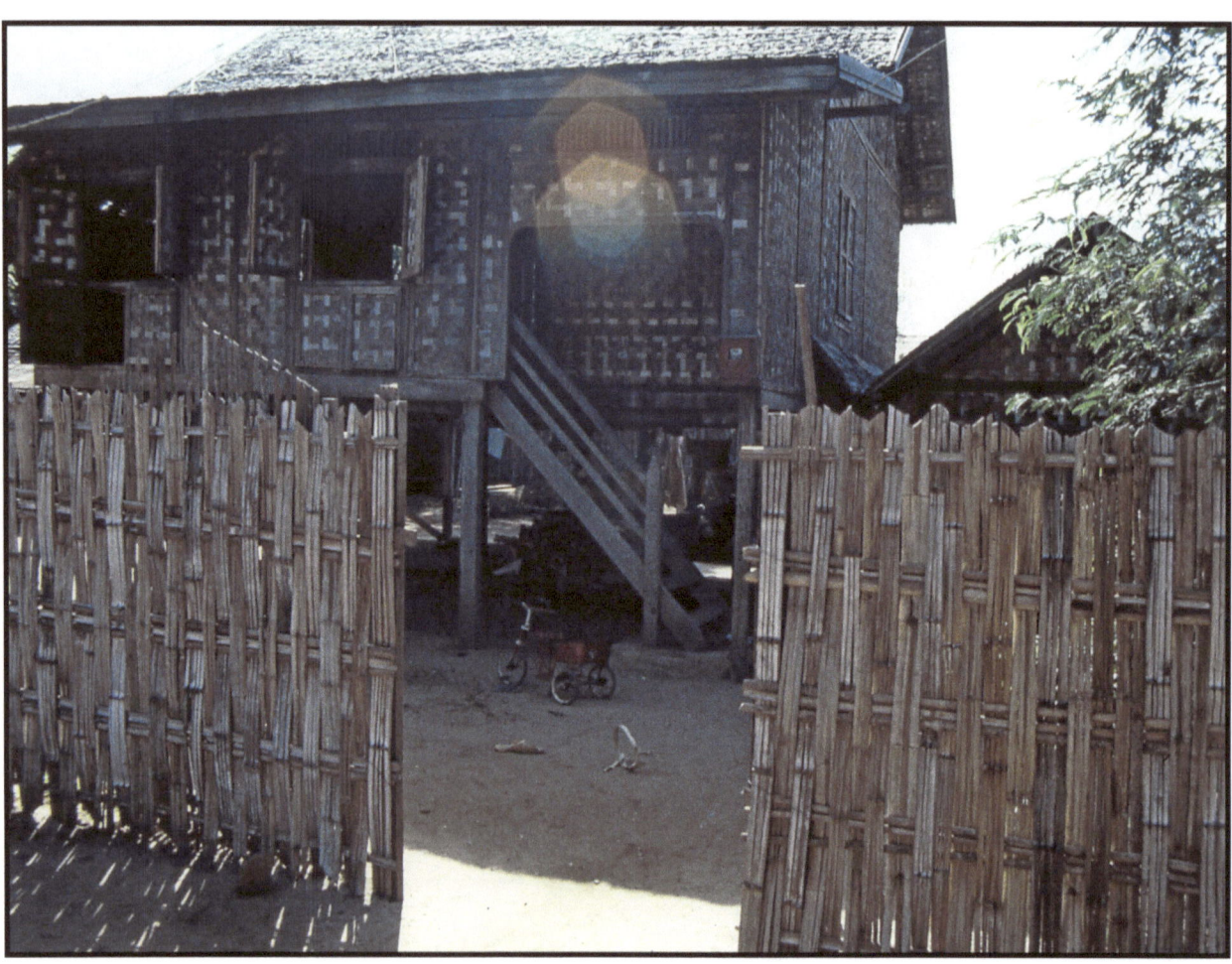

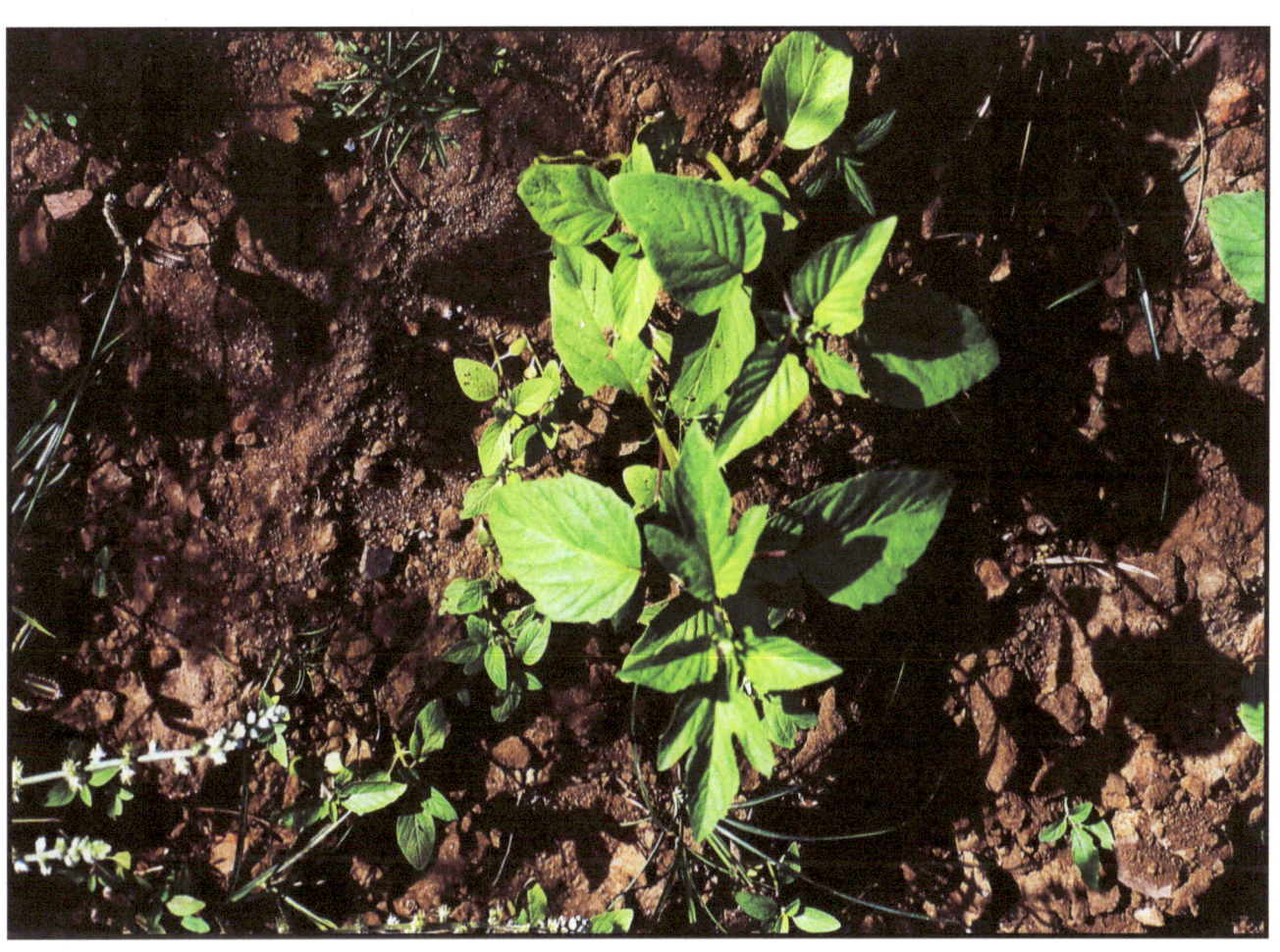

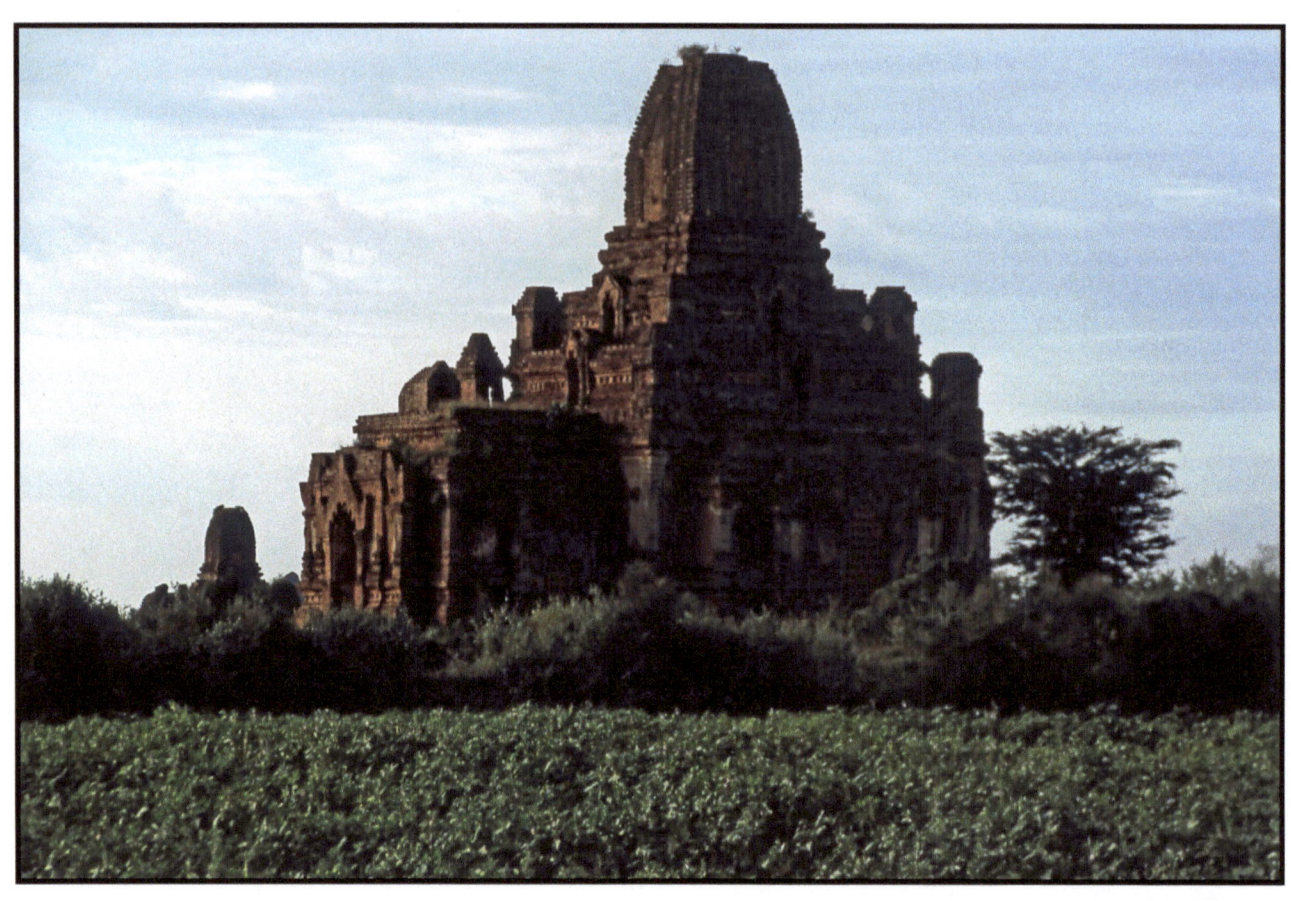

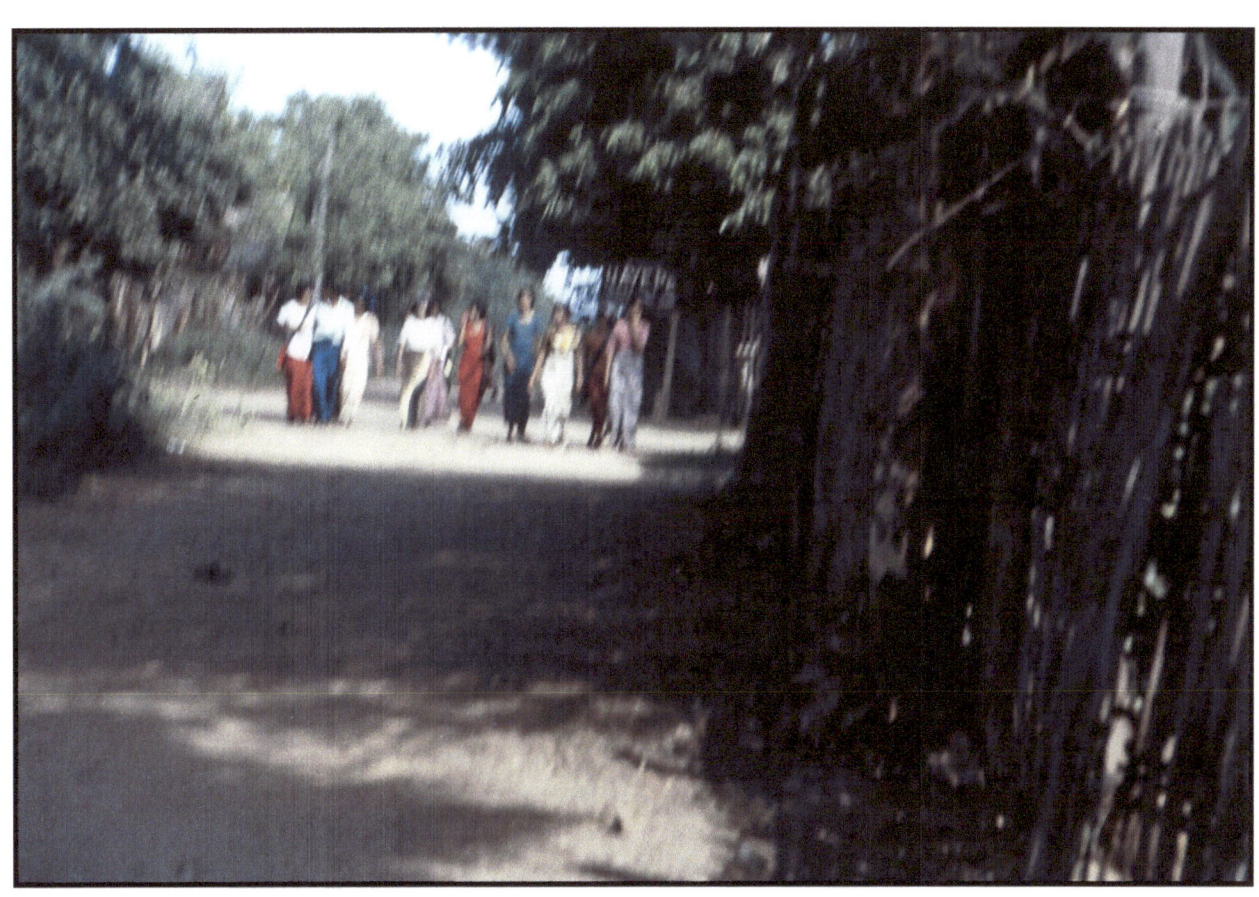

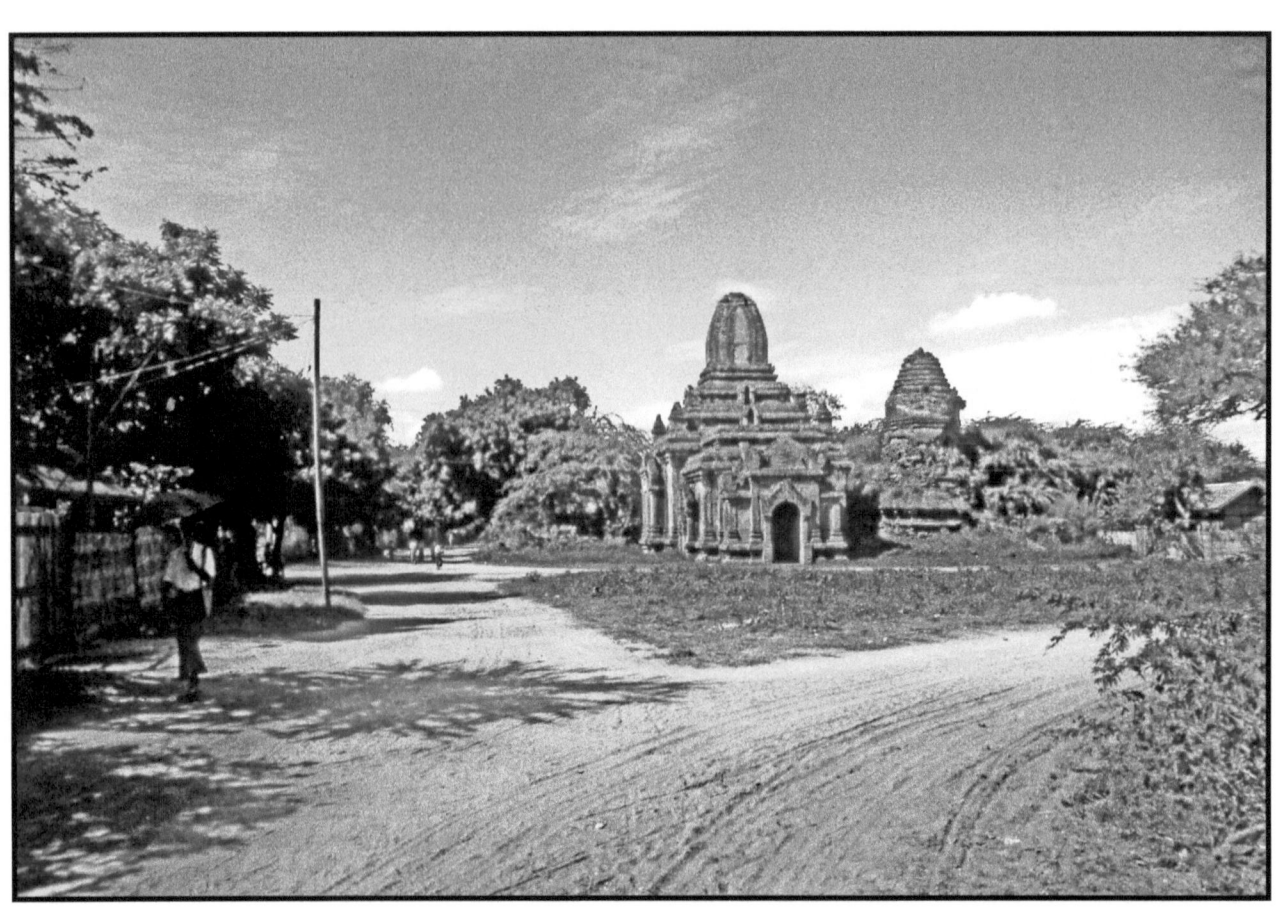

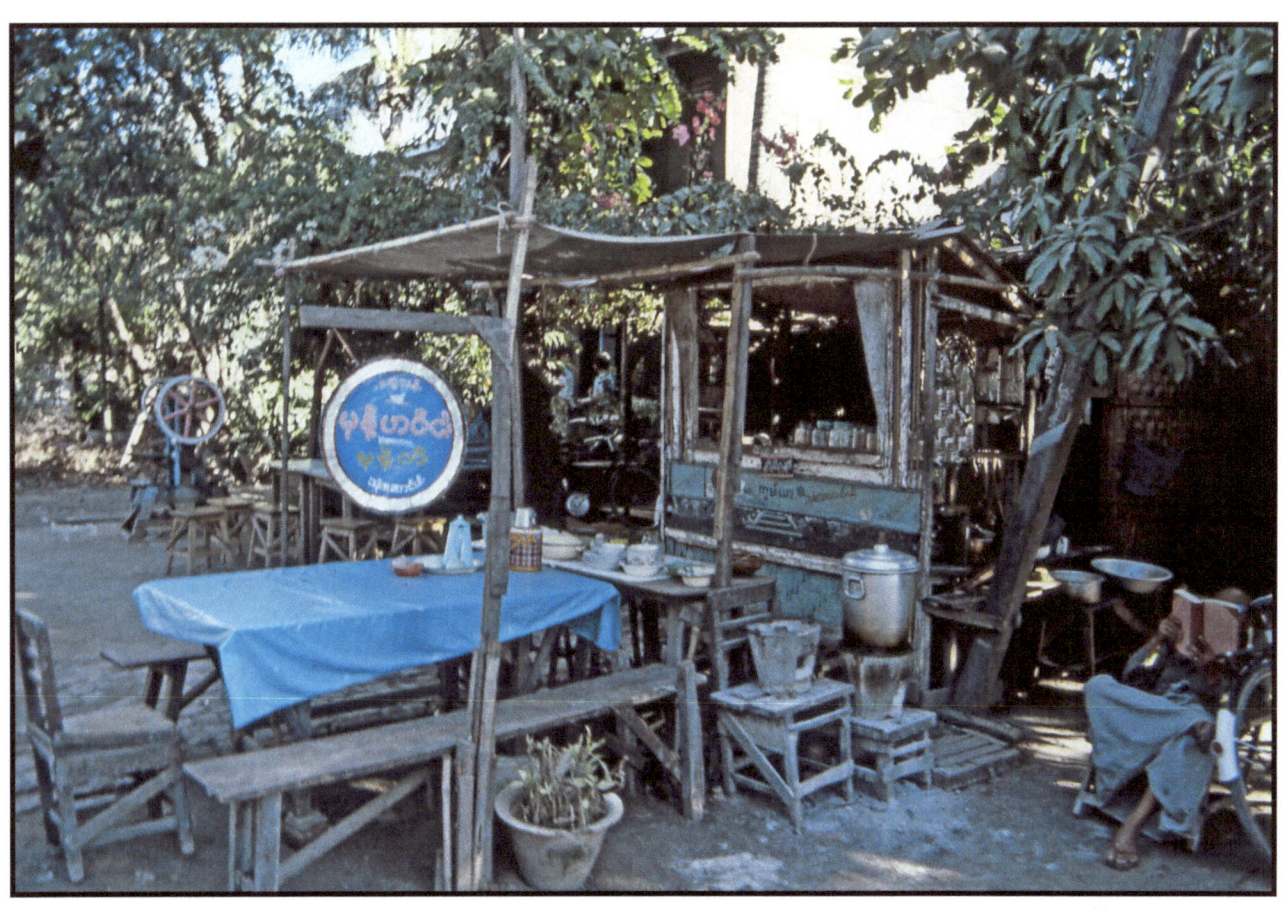

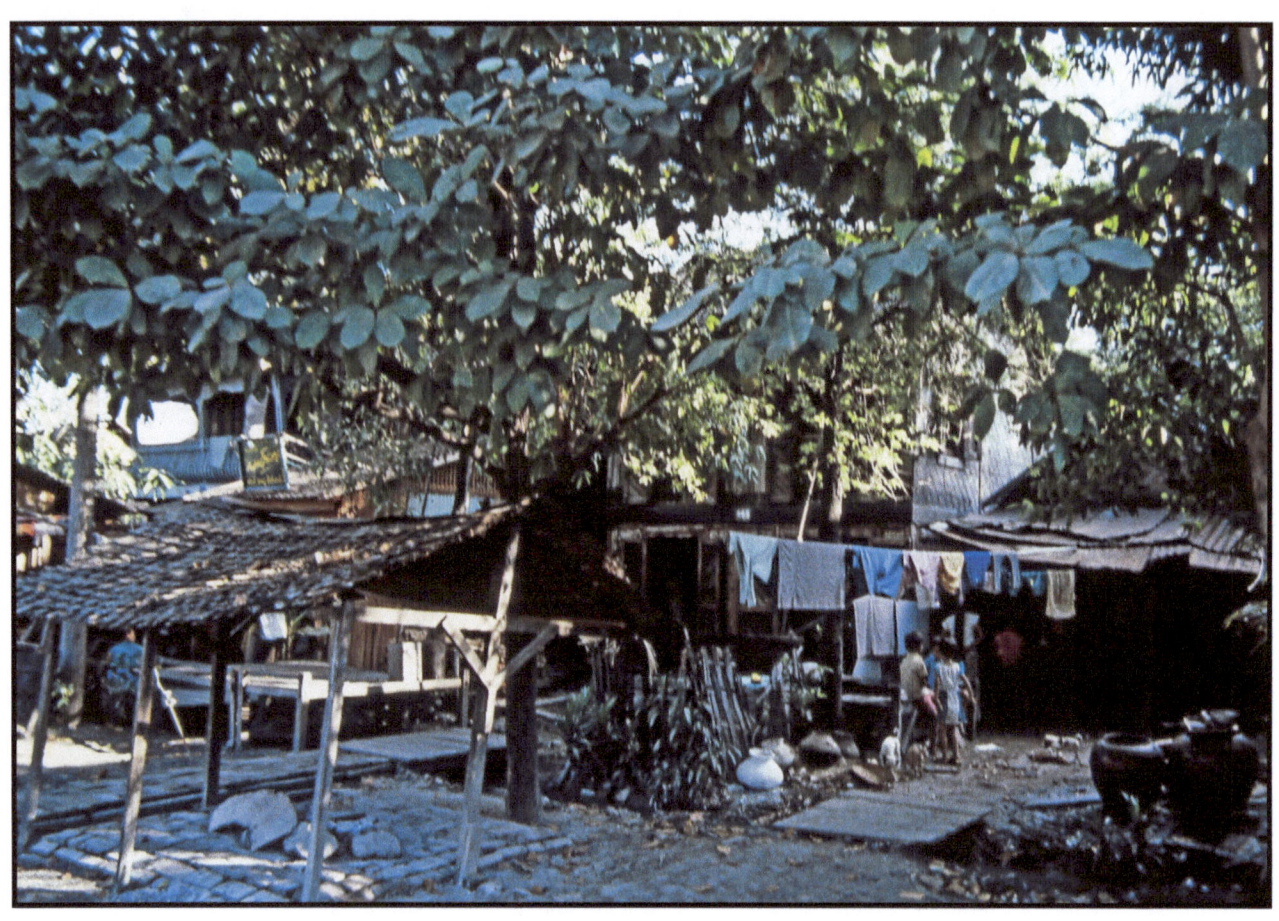

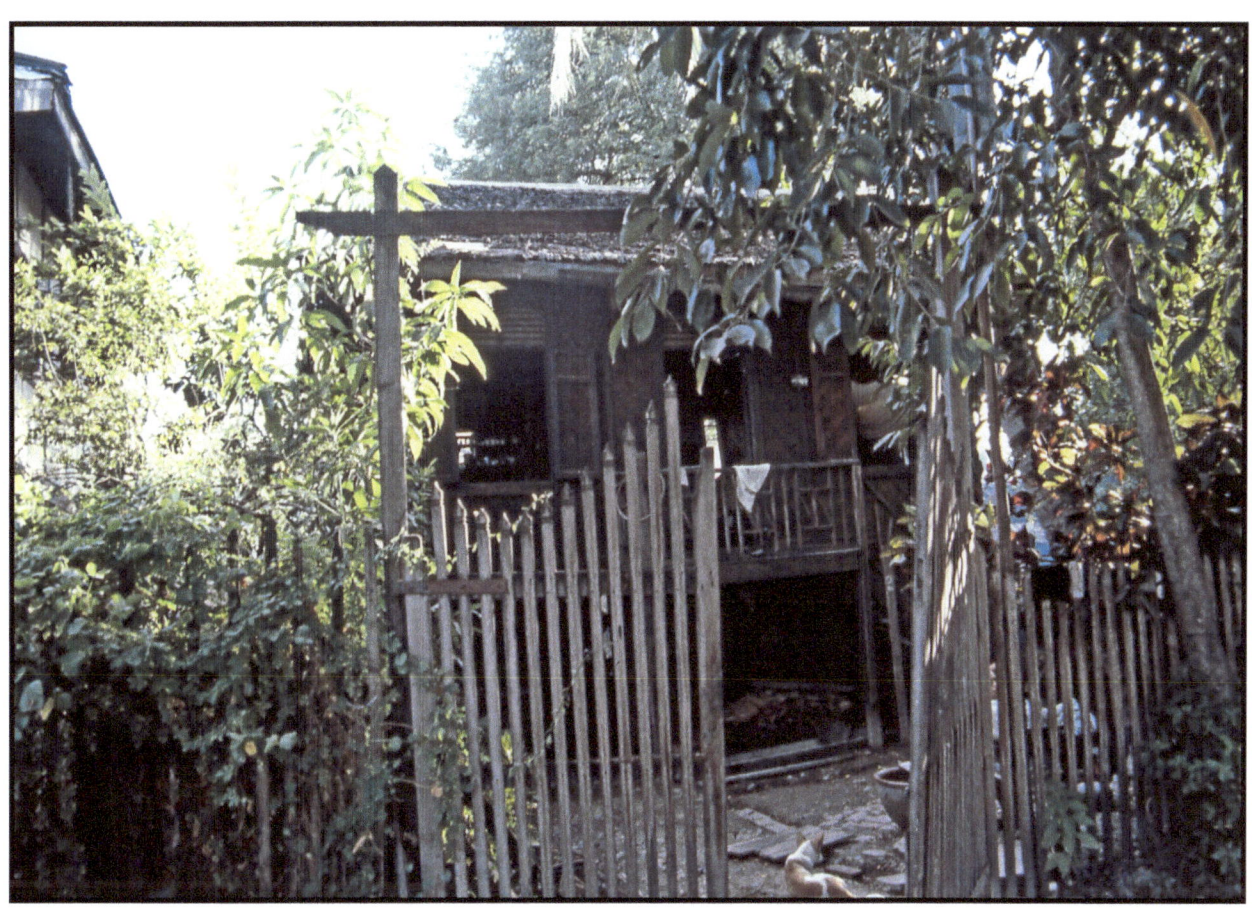

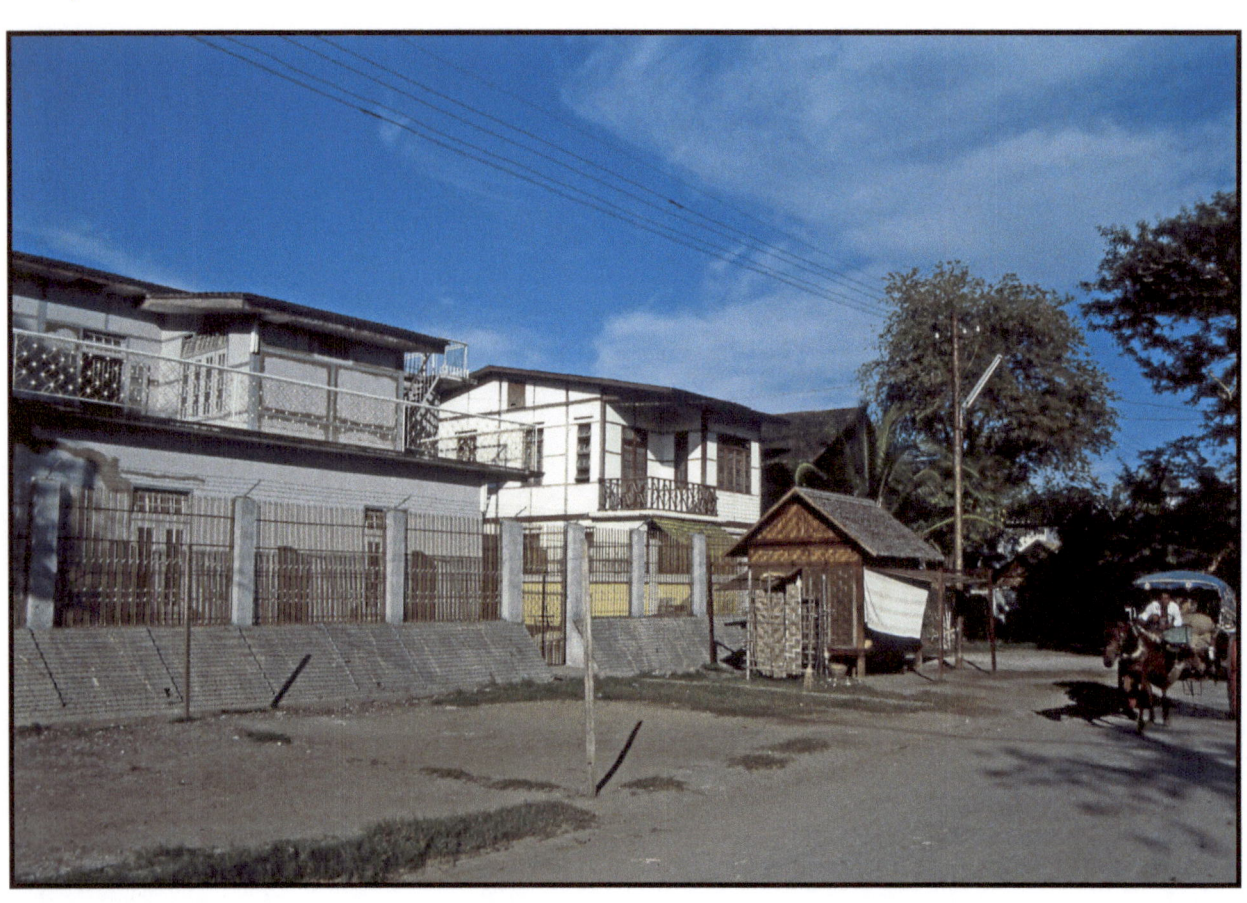

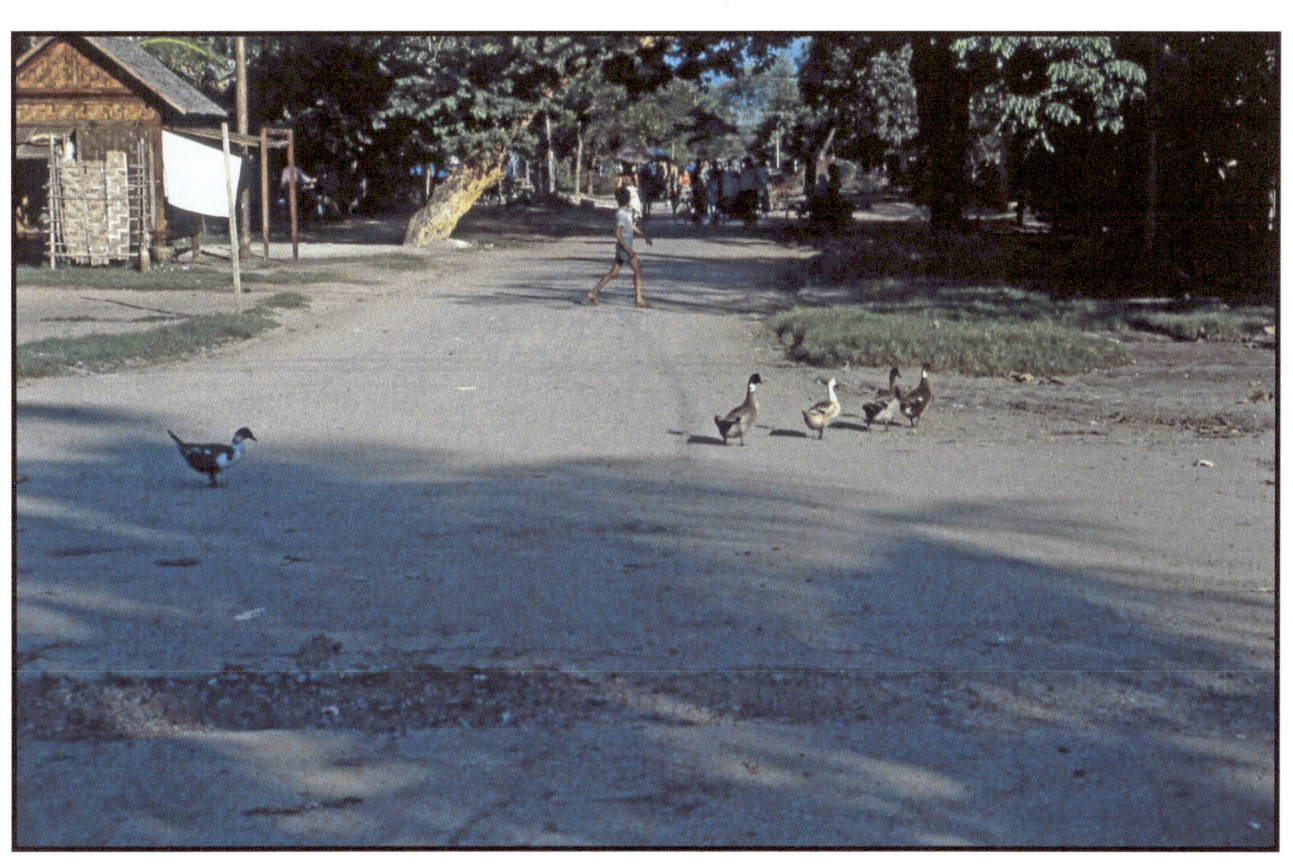

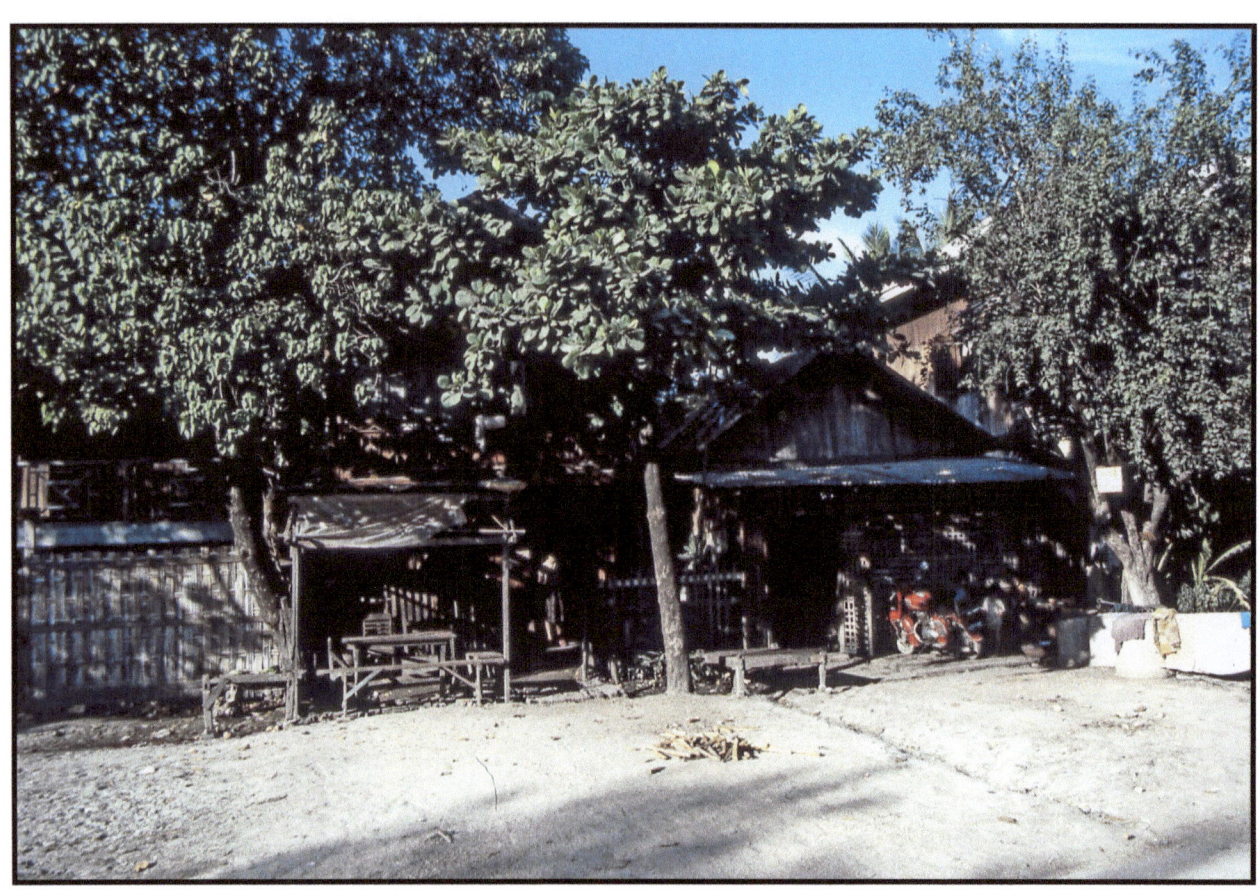

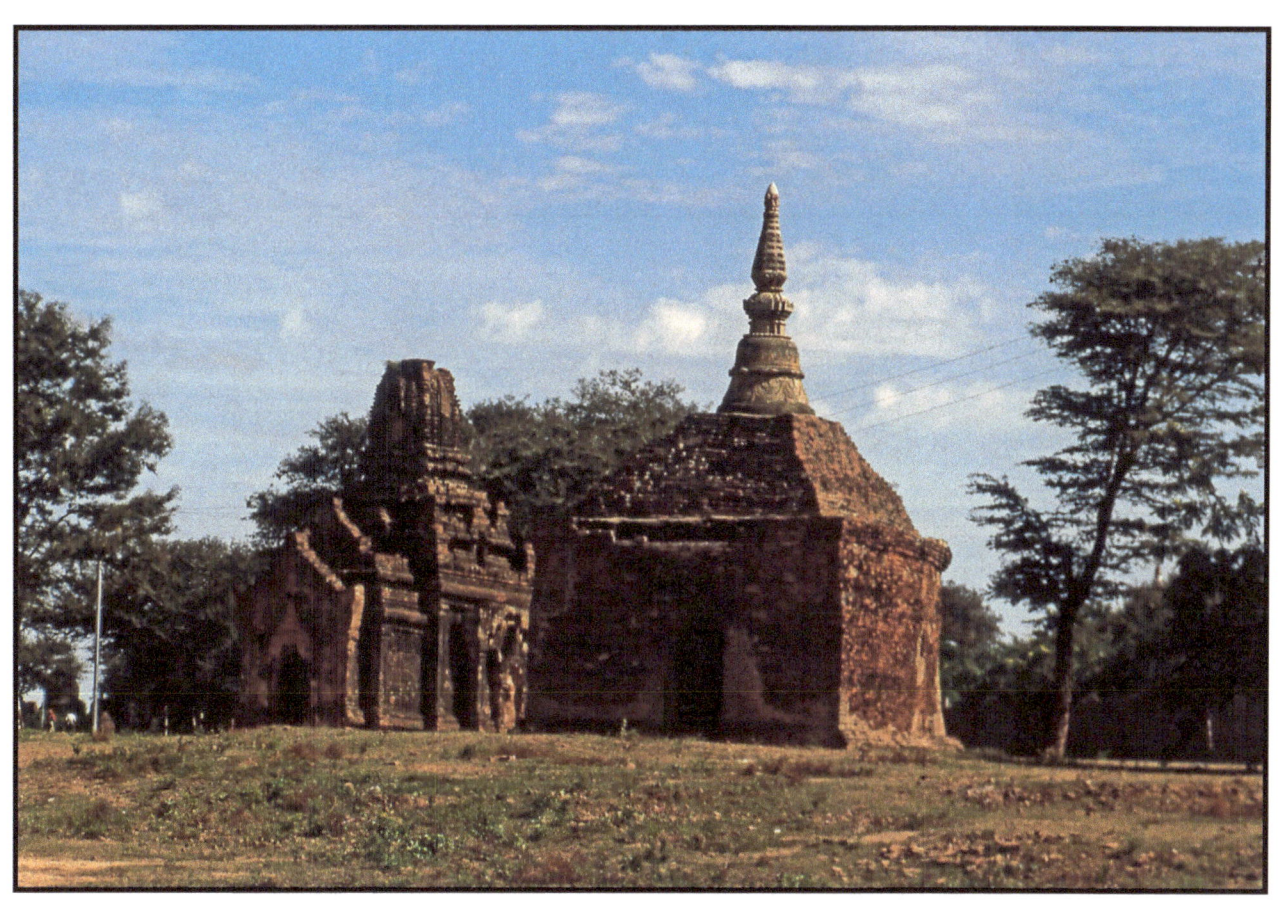

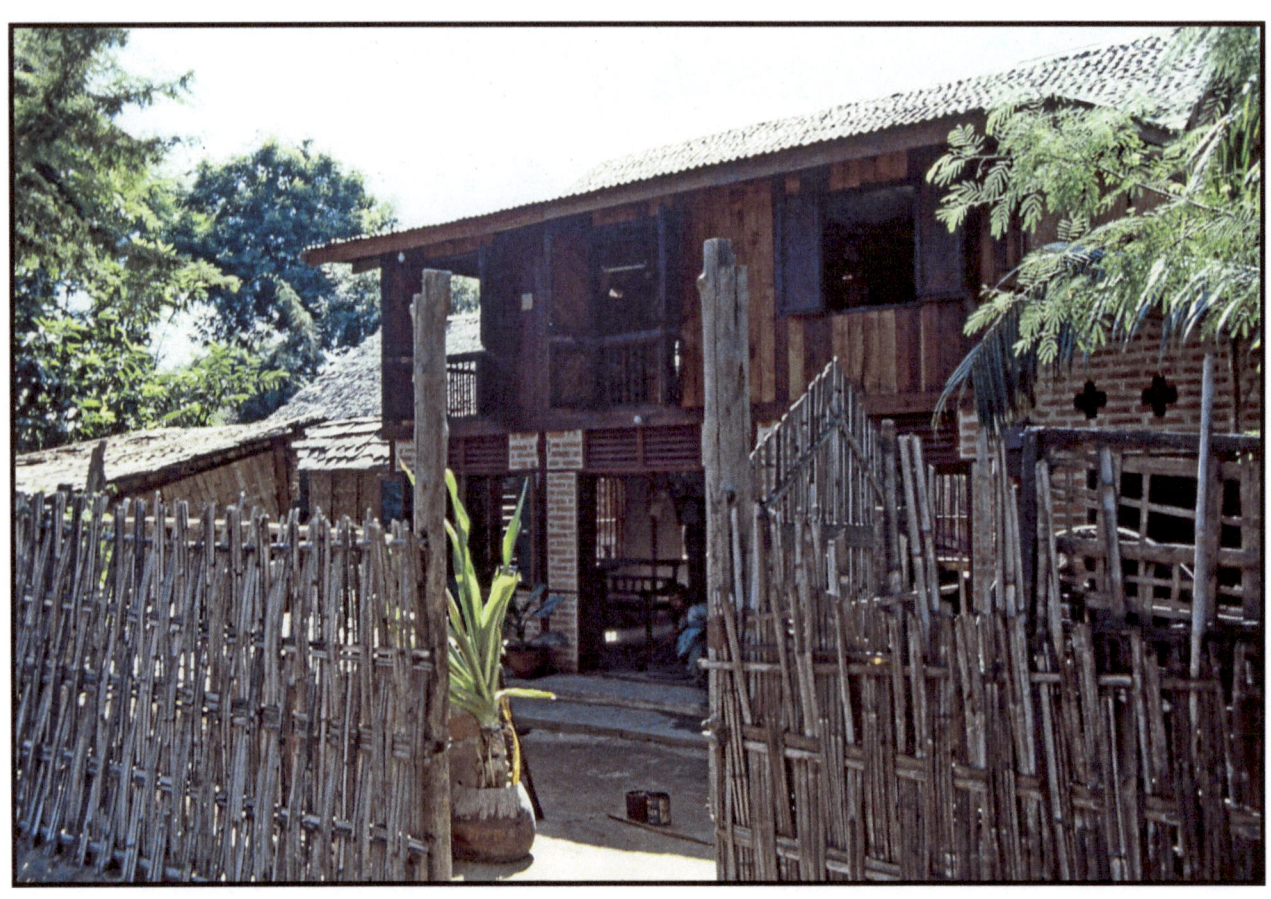

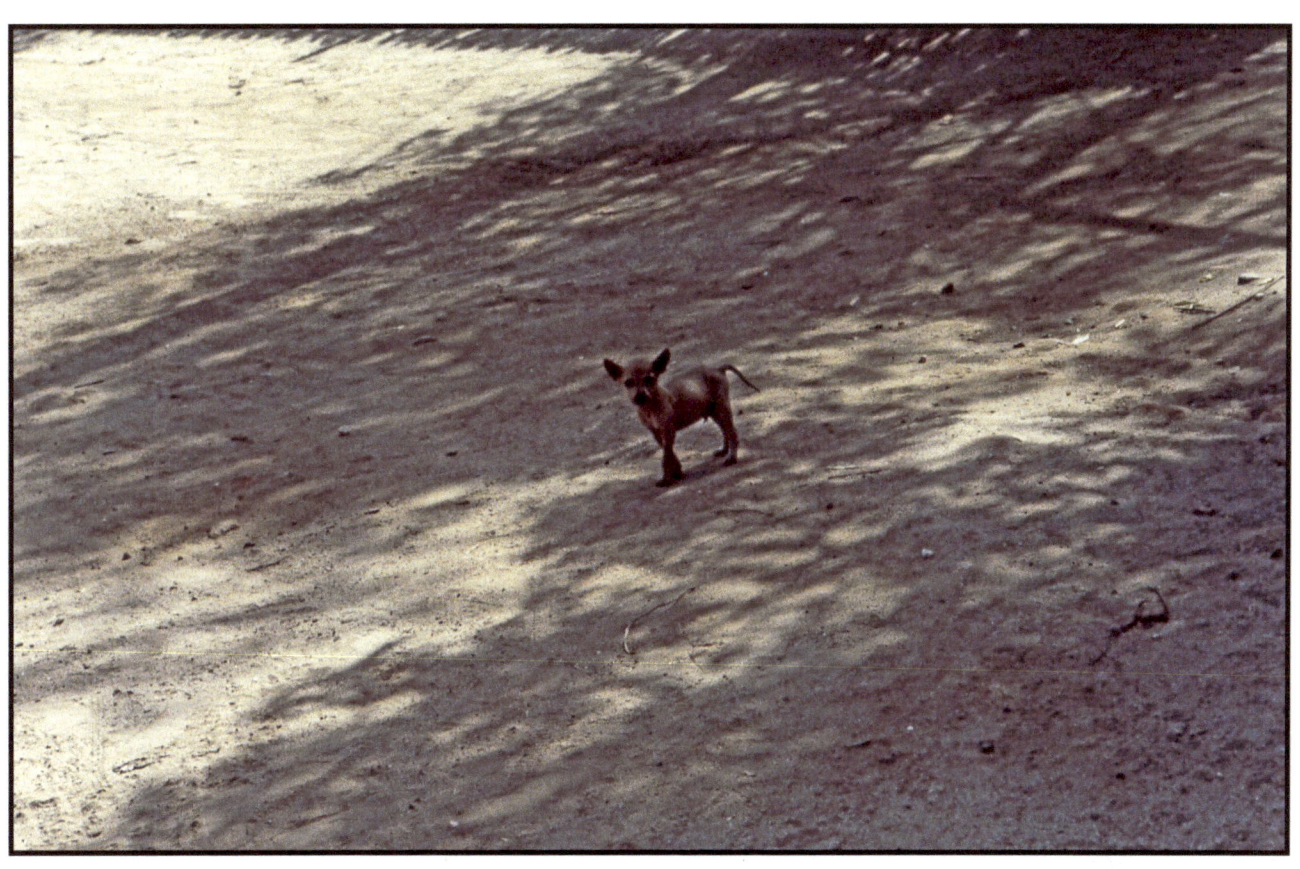

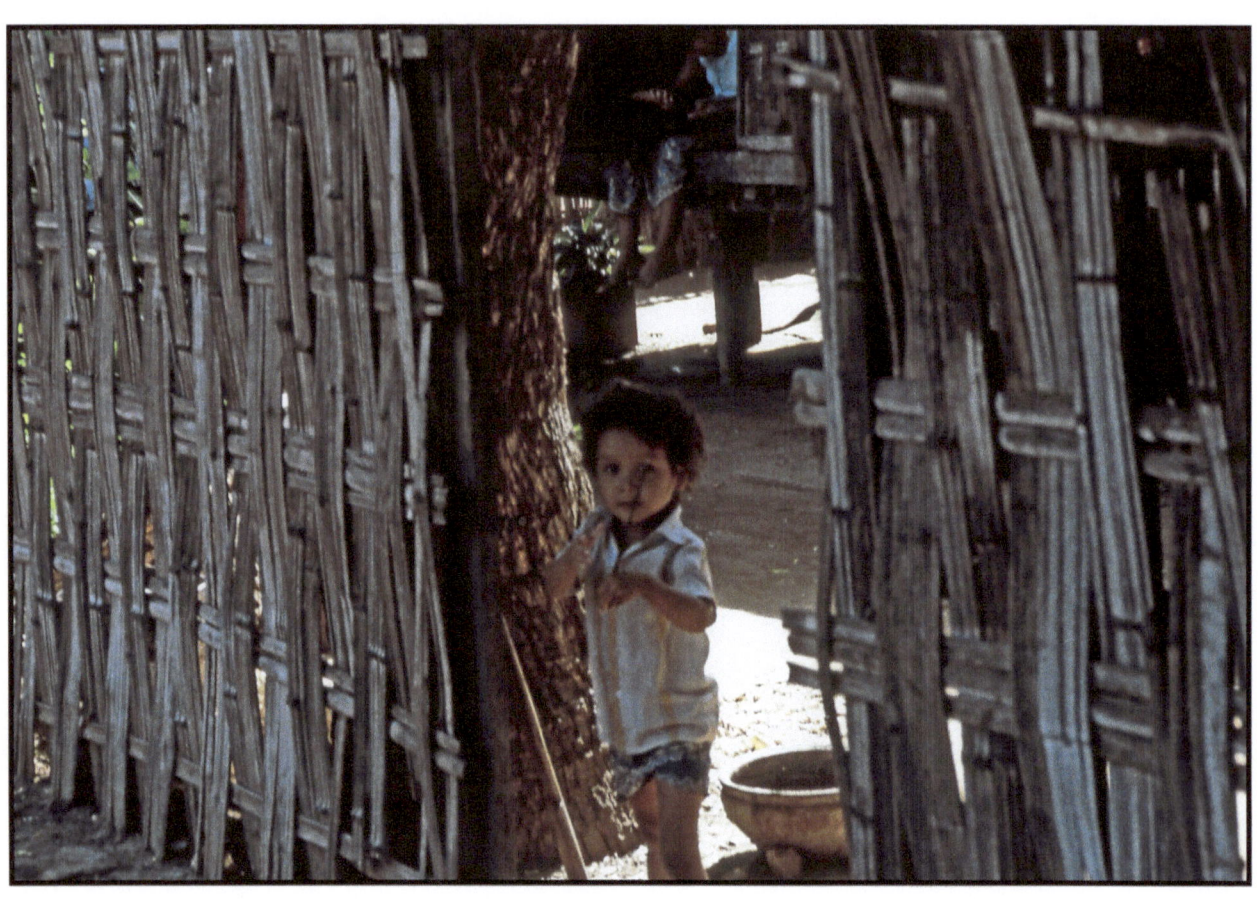

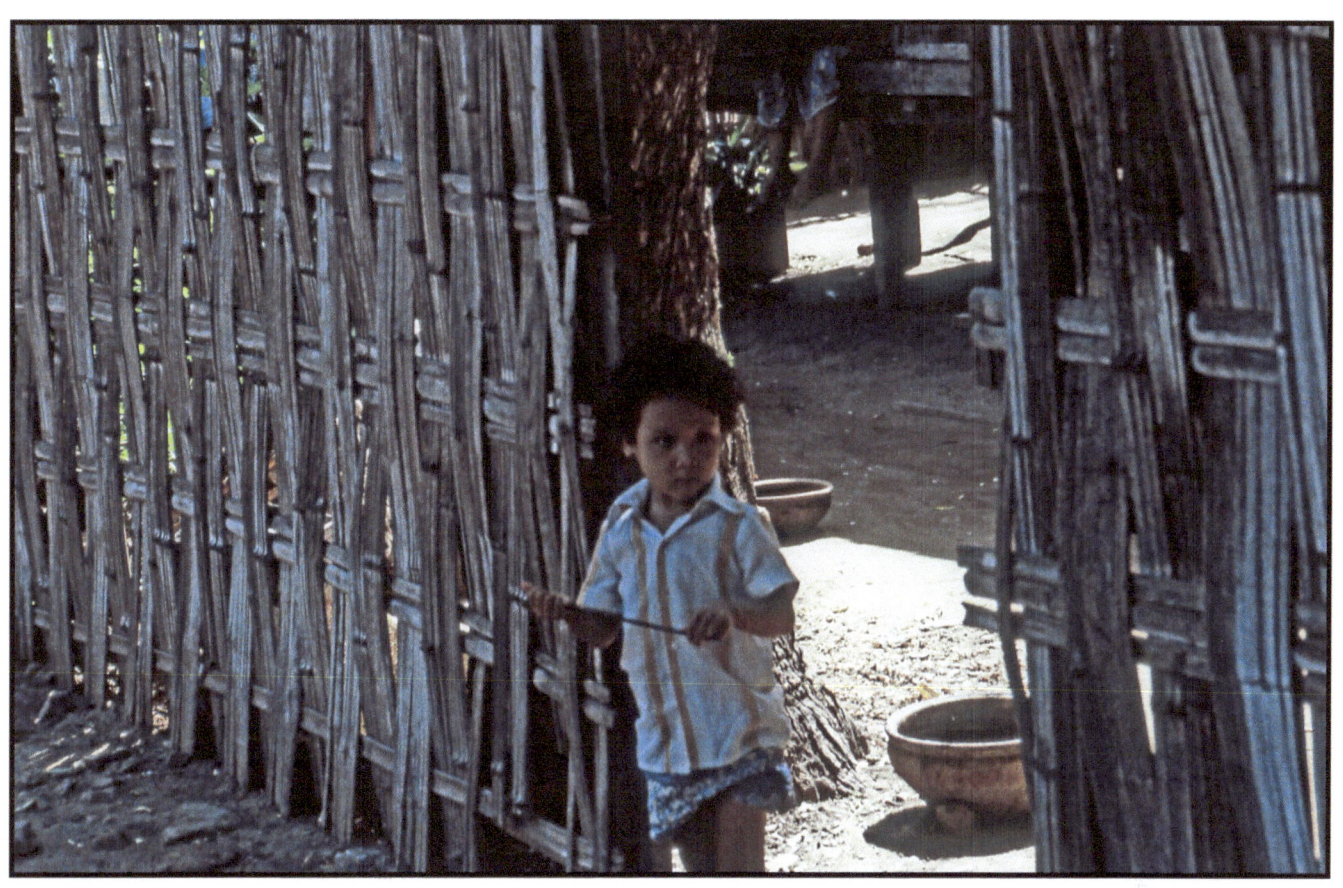

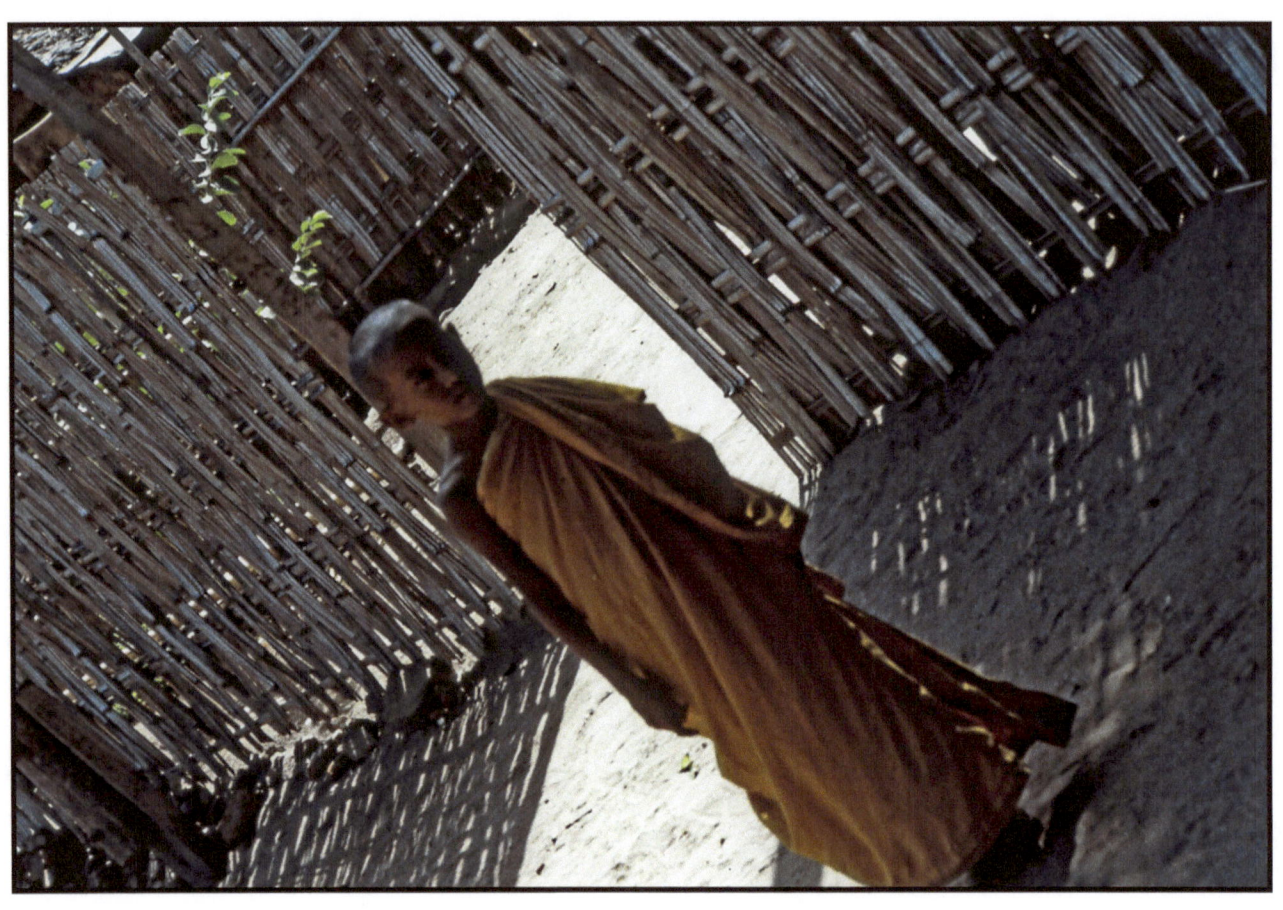

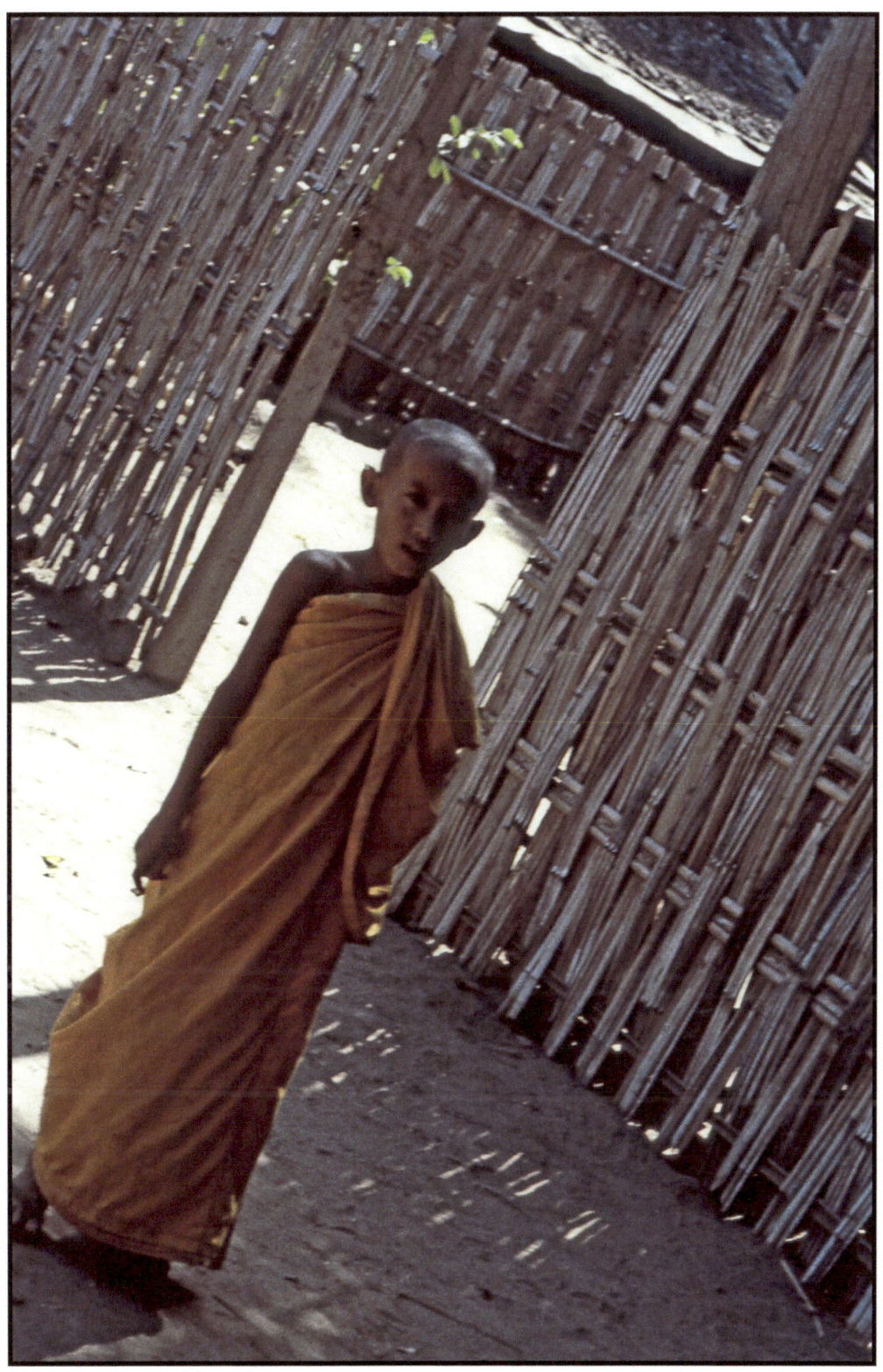

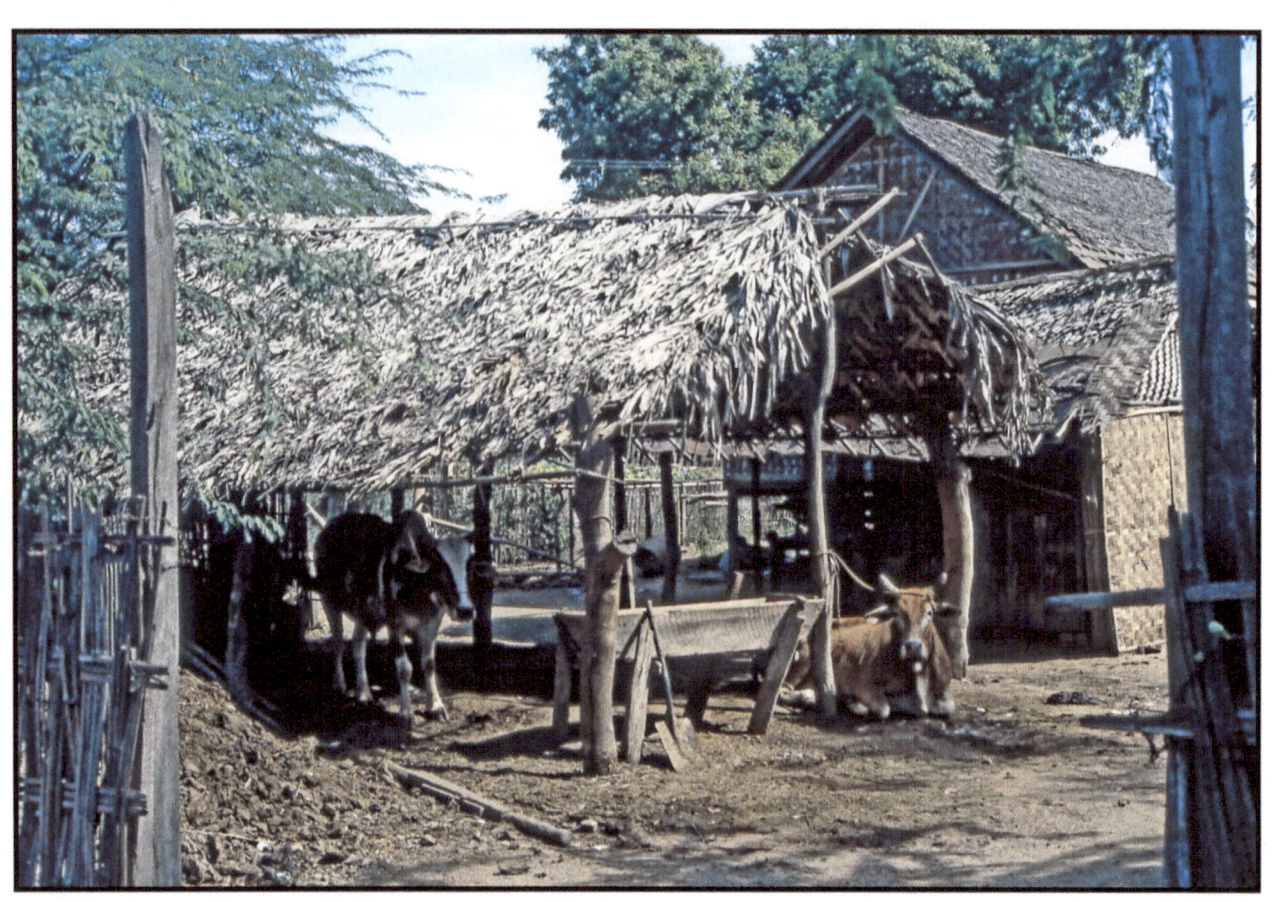

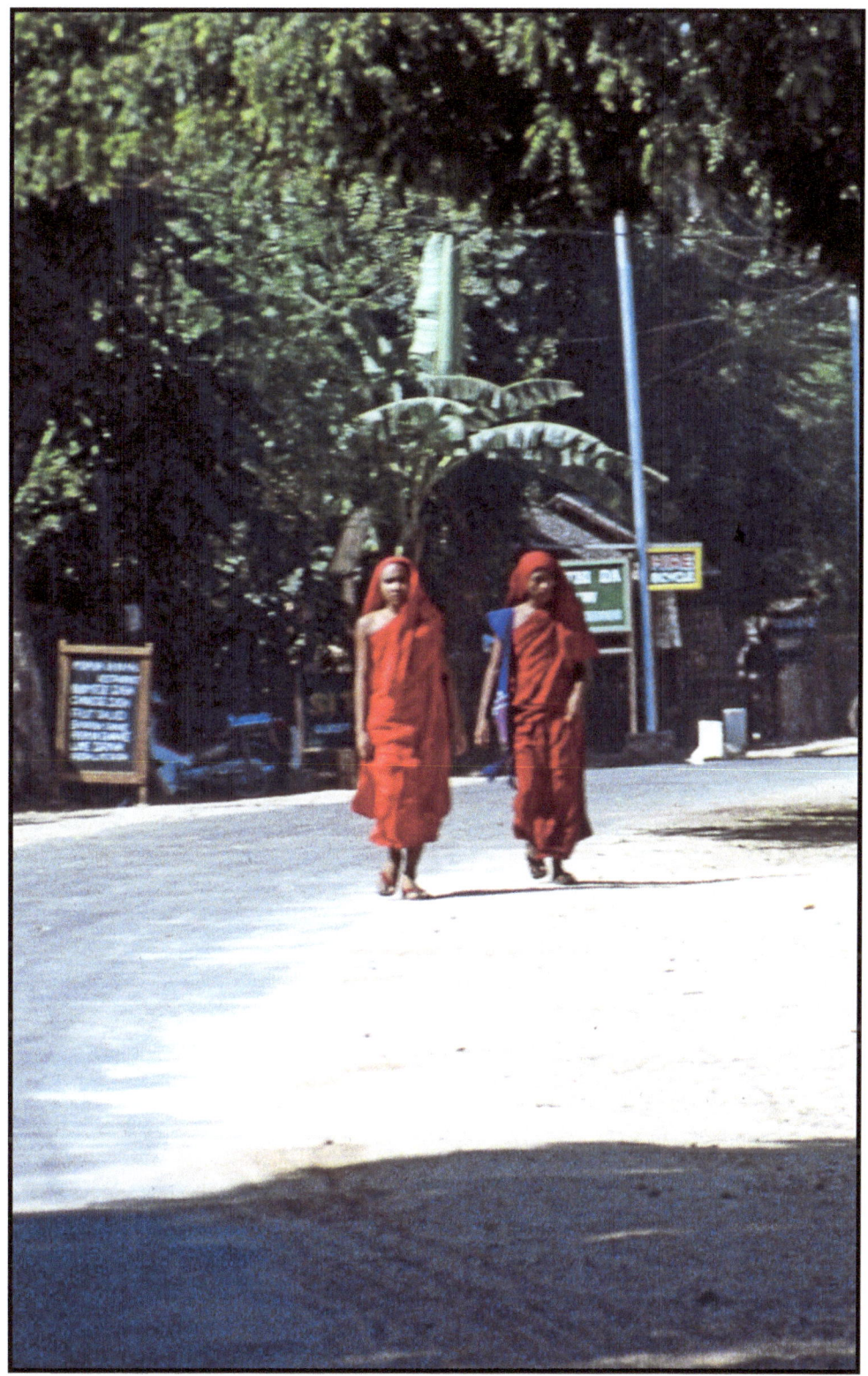

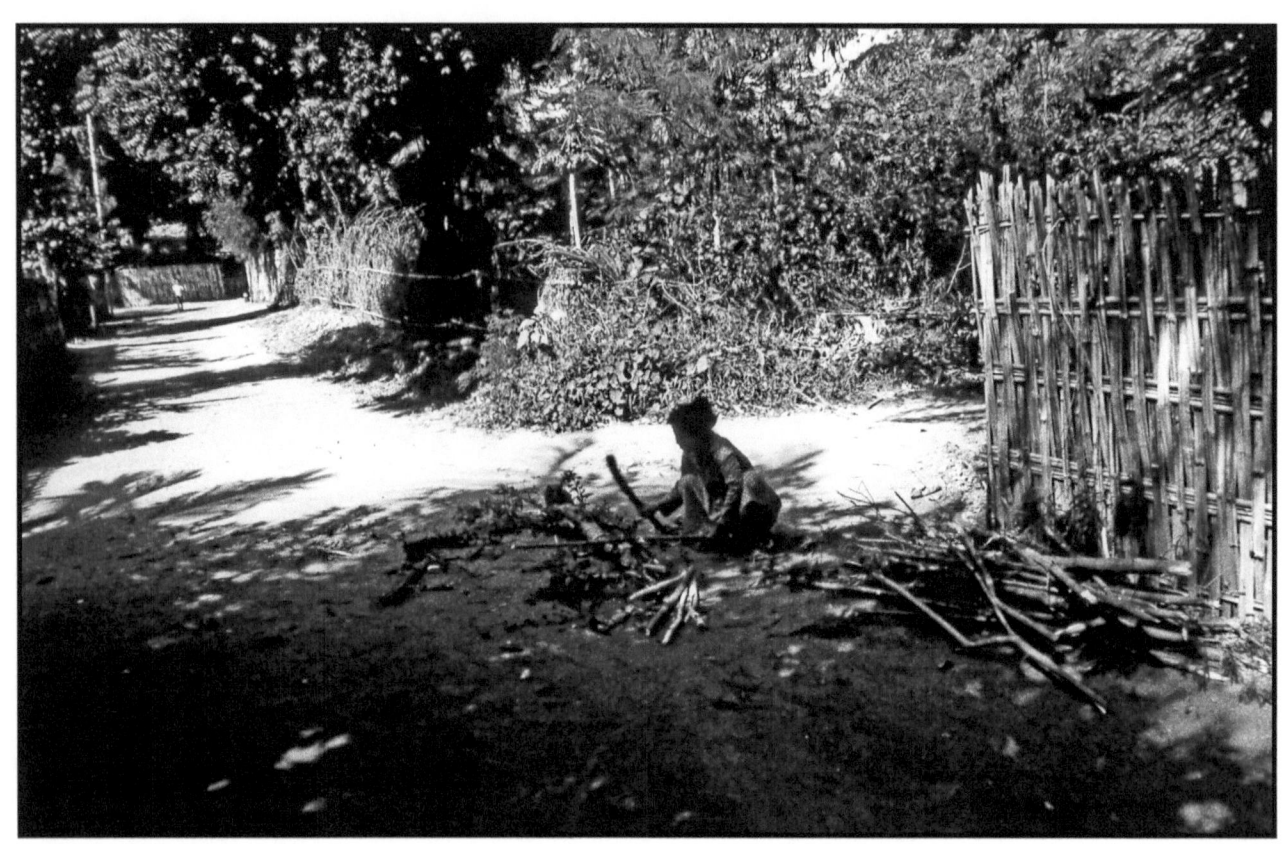

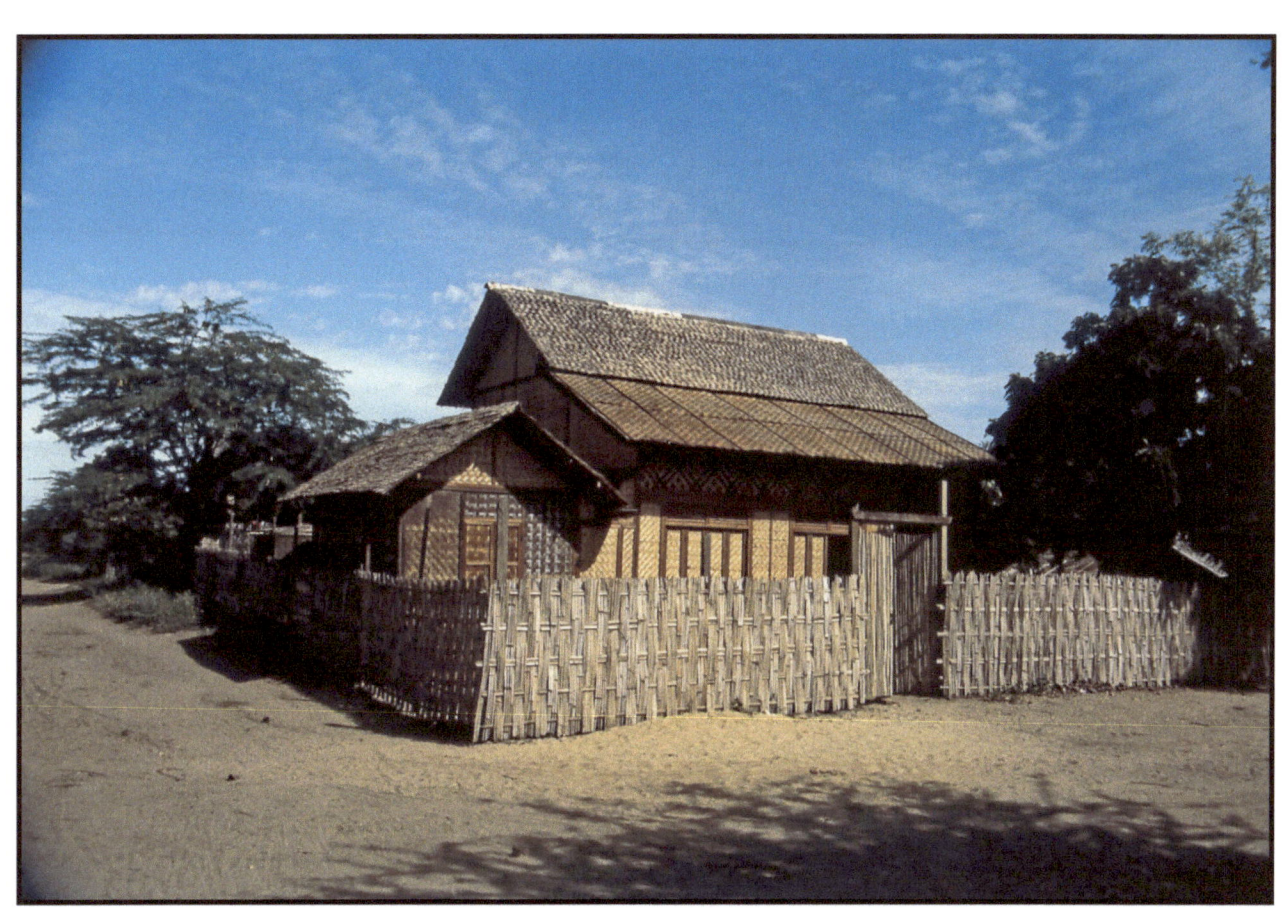

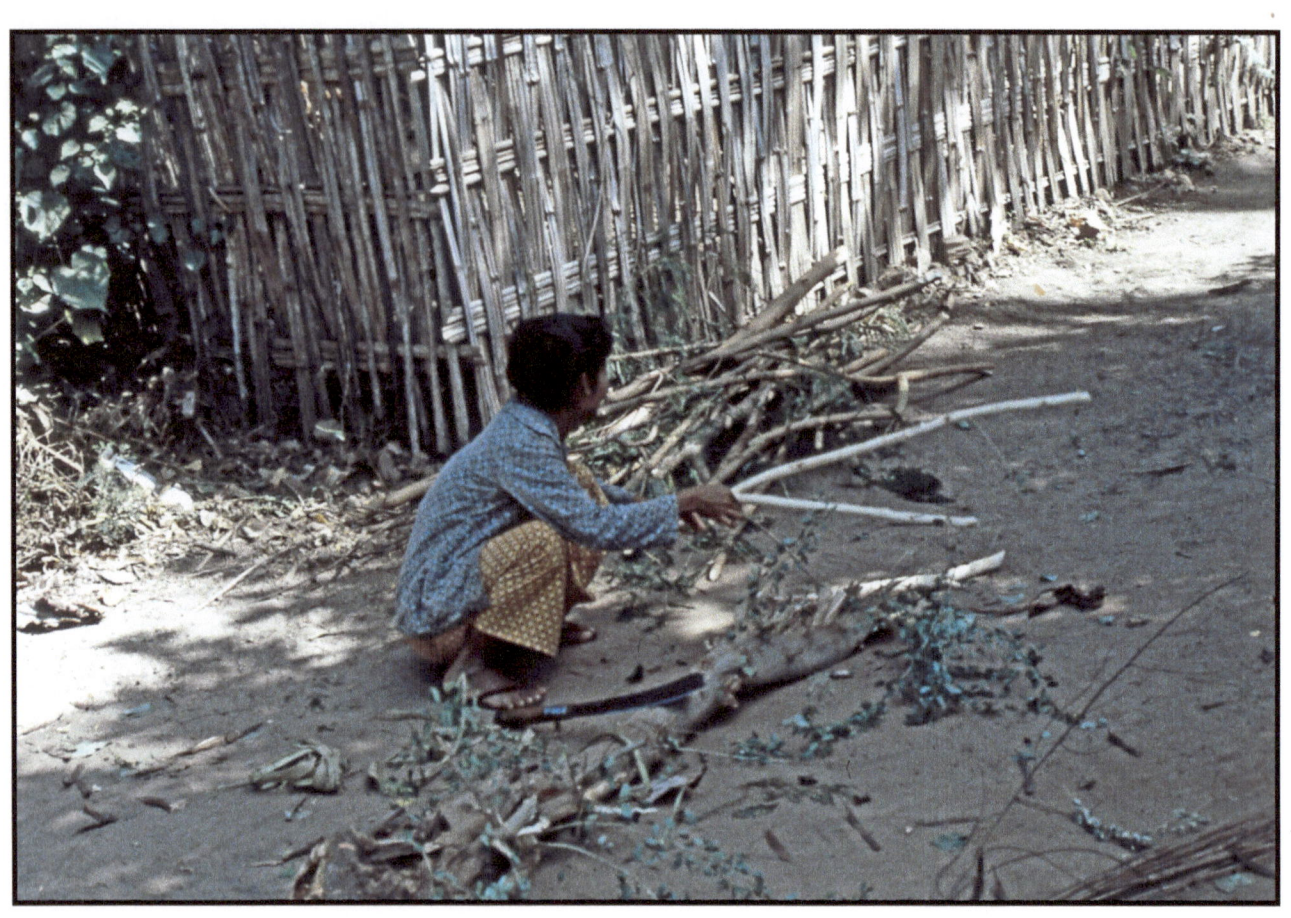

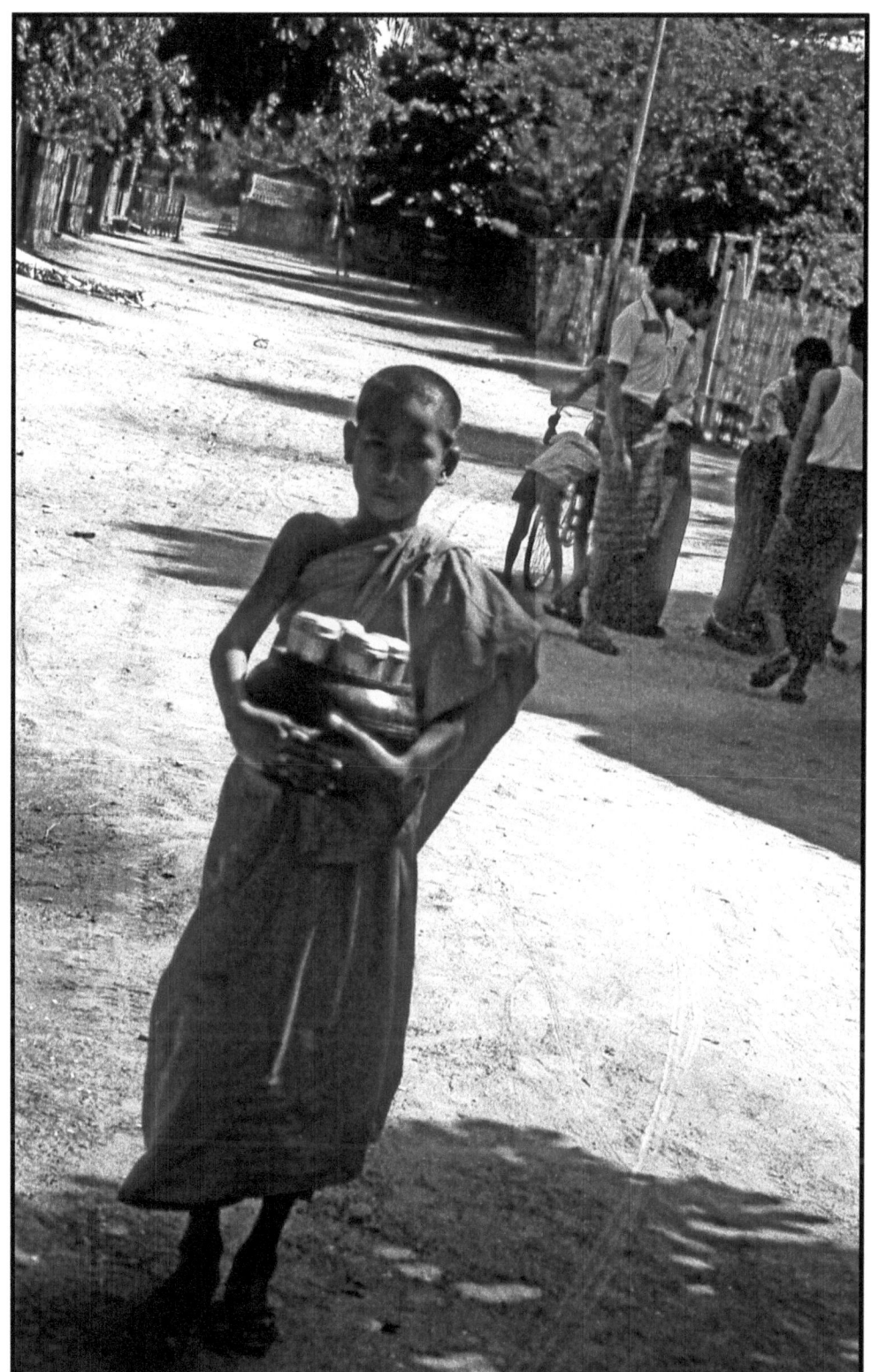

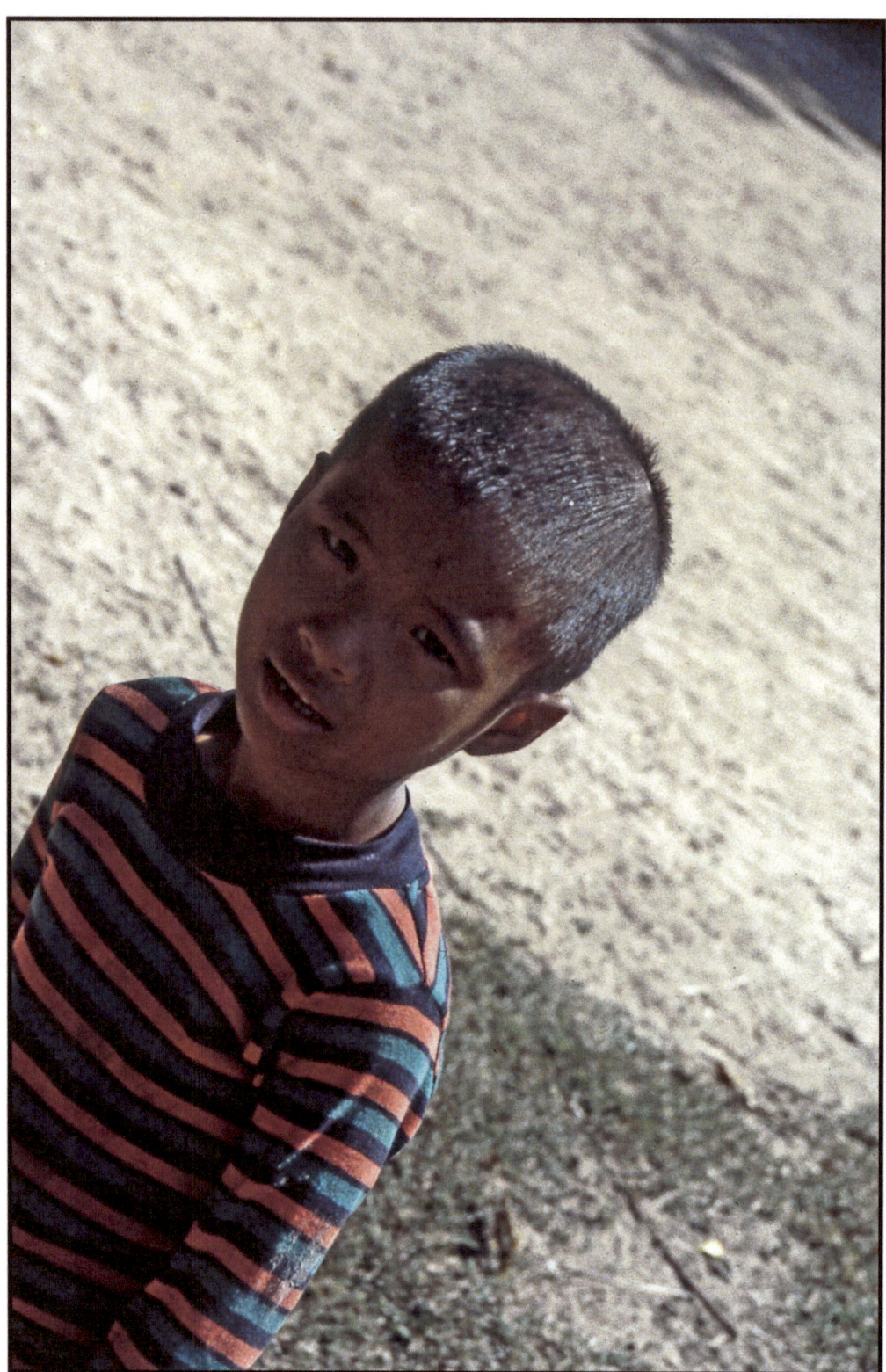

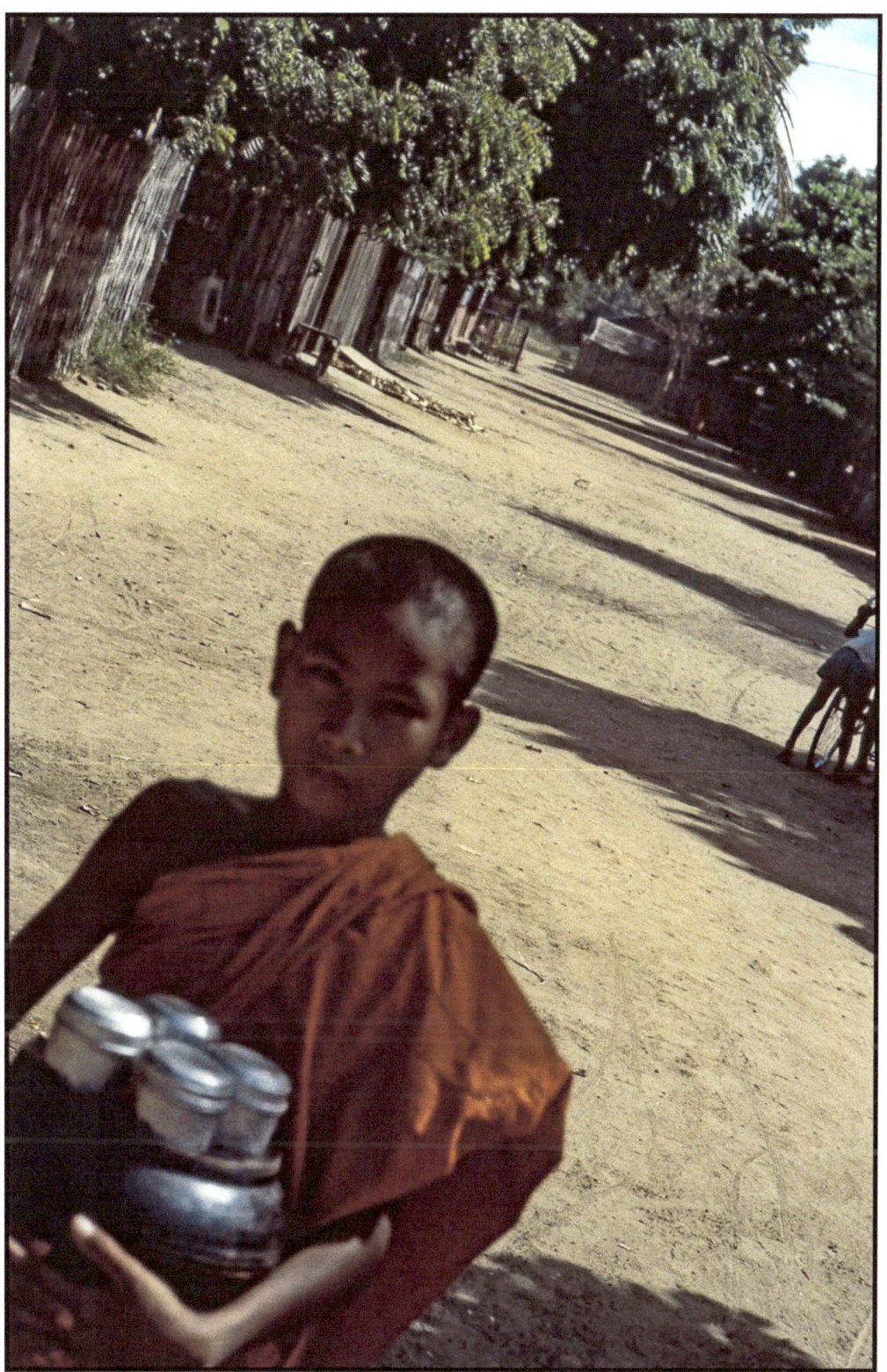

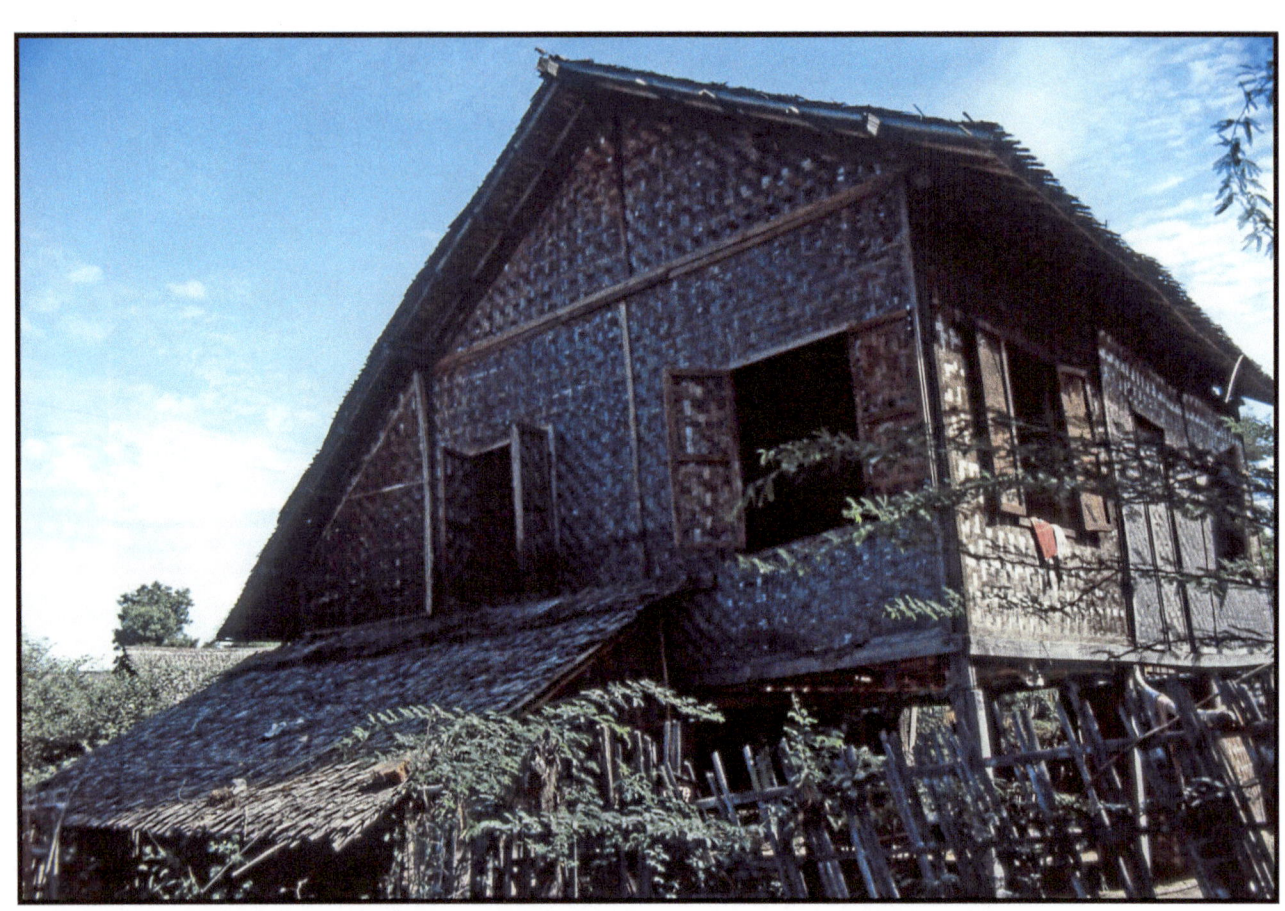

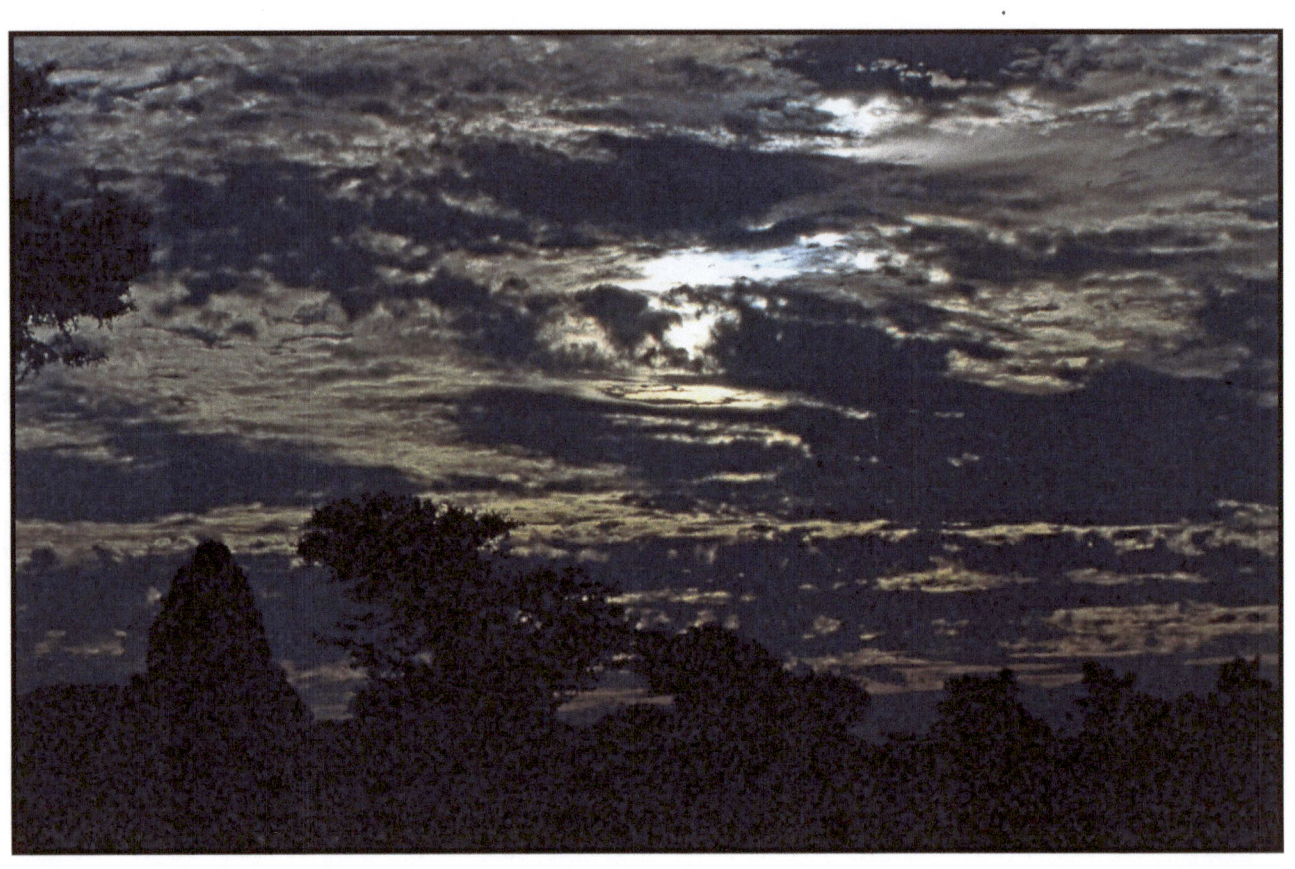

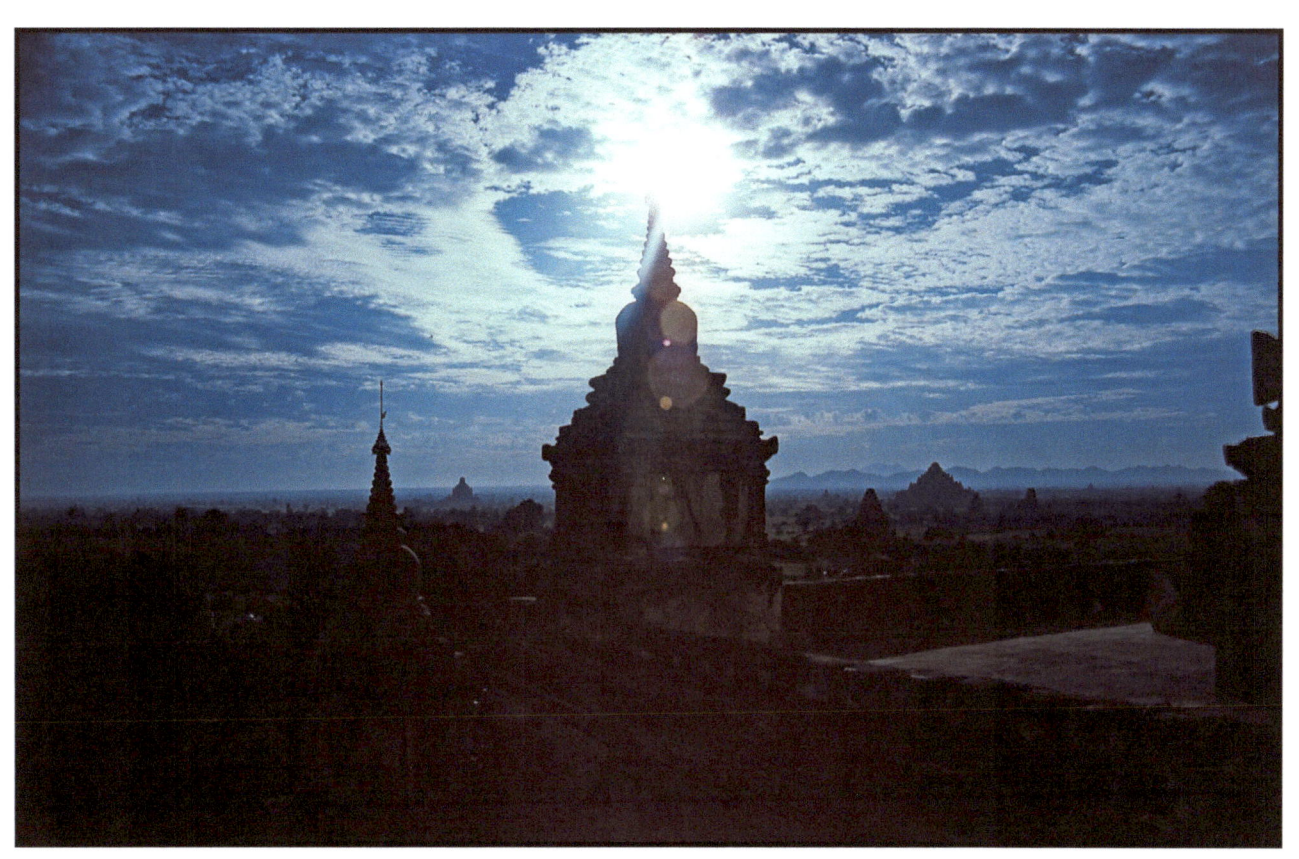

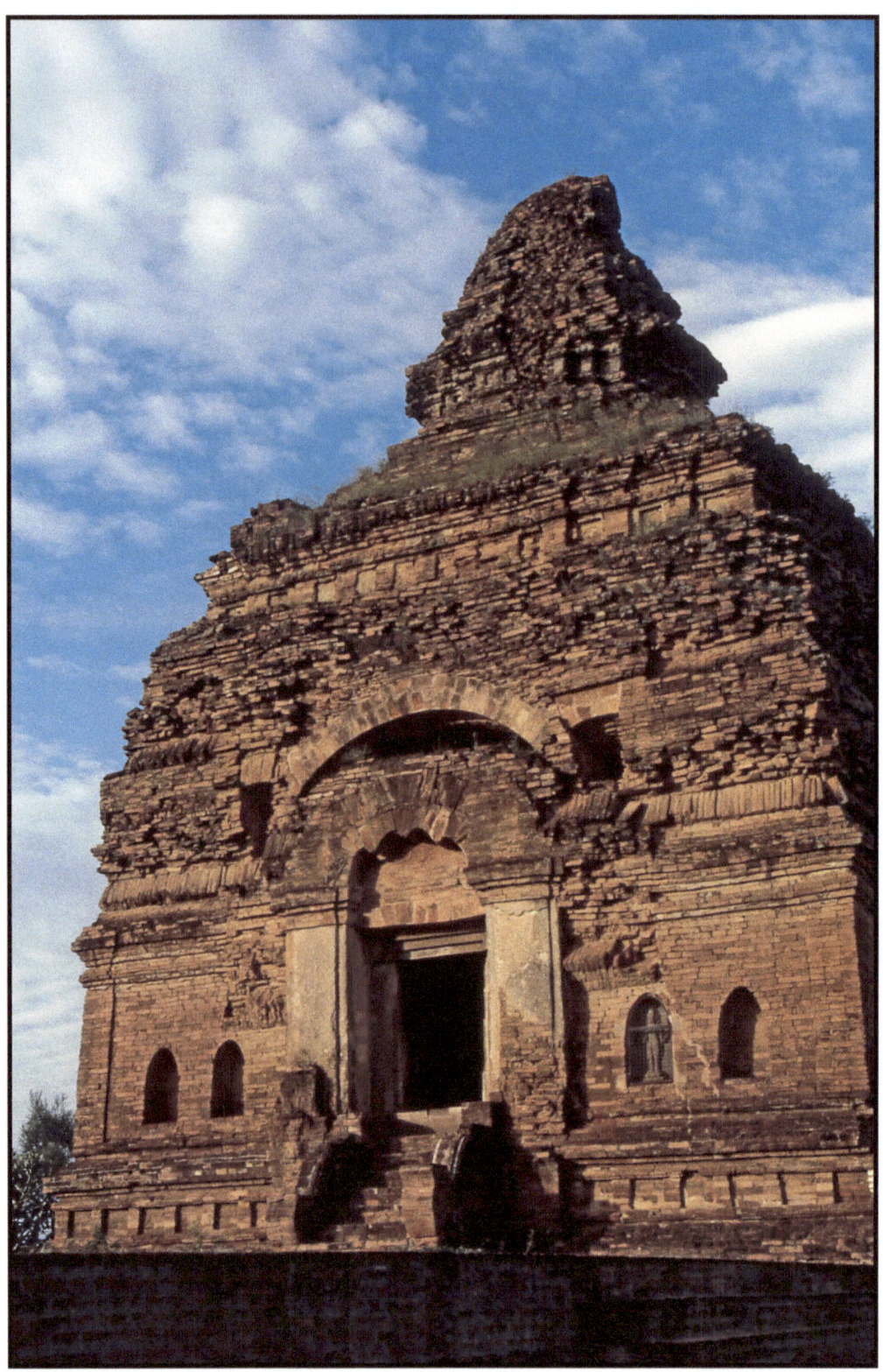

www.ingramcontent.com/pod-product-compliance
Lightning Source LLC
Chambersburg PA
CBHW051149220526
45473CB00003B/711